Jürgen Habermas was born in 1929, and grew up in
Gummersbach, West Germany. He was educated at the
Universities of Göttingen, Bonn, and Zurich, after which
he worked for a while as a freelance journalist. In 1956 he
became Adorno's assistant at the University of Frankfurt.
From 1961 to 1964 he taught philosophy in Heidelberg, and
from 1964 to 1971, philosophy and sociology in Frankfurt.
From 1971 to 1983 he was Director of the Max Planck
Institute for Research into the Life Conditions of the
Scientific-Technical World, in Starnberg. Since 1983 he
has once more been teaching at the Johann Wolfgang
Goethe University in Frankfurt. Among his influential
publications in English are: *Knowledge and Human
Interests* (1971), *Theory and Practice* (1973), *Legitimation
Crisis* (1975), *Communication and the Evolution of Society*
(1979), and *The Theory of Communicative Action* (1984).

Jürgen Habermas

Autonomy and Solidarity

Interviews

Edited and Introduced by
Peter Dews

VERSO

The Imprint of New Left Books

**British Library
Cataloguing in Publication Data**

Autonomy and Solidarity:
Interviews with Jürgen Habermas.
1. Philosophy
1. Dews, Peter
100 B72

First Published 1986
Interviews © Suhrkamp Verlag and *New Left Review* 1986
Introduction © Peter Dews 1986

Verso
15 Greek Street, London WIV 5LF

Typeset in Imprint by
Cover to Cover, Cambridge

Printed by The Thetford Press
Thetford, Norfolk

ISBN 0–86091–132–2
ISBN 0–86091–852–1 Pbk

Contents

Sources and Acknowledgements

'Ideologies and Society in the Post-War World': interview with Gad Freudenthal, Jerusalem 16 December 1977. First published in Hebrew in *Machschavot*, no. 48, 1979, pp. 68–79. Published in Habermas, *Kleine Politische Schriften I–IV*, Frankfurt 1981, pp. 467–90. Translated by Rodney Livingstone. Appears by kind permission of Suhrkamp Verlag. 'Conservatism and Capitalist Crisis': interview with Angelo Bolaffi, Starnberg 29 May 1978. First published in *Rinascita* 30/31, 28 July/4 August 1978. English translation, *New Left Review* 115, May–June 1979, pp. 73–84. Published in *Kleine Politische Schriften*, pp. 491–510. Appears by kind permission of Suhrkamp Verlag. 'Political Experience and the Renewal of Marxist Theory': interview with Detlef Horster and Willem van Reijen, Starnberg 23 March 1979. First published in Intermediair (Amsterdam), 29 June 1979. English translation by Ron Smith, *New German Critique*, no. 18, Fall 1979. Published in *Kleine Politische Schriften*, pp. 511–532. Appears by kind permission of Suhrkamp Verlag. 'Dialectics of Rationalization': interview with Axel Honneth, Eberhard Knödler-Bunte and Arno Widmann, Berlin 22 May 1981, and Starnberg 10 July 1981. First published in *Ästhetik und Kommunikation*, no. 45–46, 1981, pp. 126–55. English translation by Leslie Adelson, Philip Boehm, Barton Byg, Karen Jankowski, and Istvan Varkonyi, *Telos* 49, 1981, pp. 5–31. Published in Habermas, *Die Neue Unübersichtlichkeit: Kleine Politische Schriften v*, Frankfurt 1985, pp. 213–257. Appears by kind permission of Suhrkamp Verlag. 'Conservative Politics, Work, Socialism and Utopia Today': interview with Hans-Ulrich Reck, 2

April 1983. First published in *Basler Zeitung*, 7 January 1984. Published in *Die Neue Unübersichtlichkeit*, pp. 59–76. Translated by Peter Dews. Appears by kind permission of Suhrkamp Verlag. 'A Philosophico-Political Profile': written interview with Perry Anderson and Peter Dews, conducted November 1984. First published in *New Left Review* 151, May–June 1985, pp. 75–105. Translated by Peter Dews. Published in *Die Neue Unübersichtlichkeit*, pp. 213–257. 'Life-forms, Morality, and the Task of the Philosopher', interview with Perry Anderson and Peter Dews, Starnberg 6 December 1984. First publication. All translations from the German revised by Peter Dews.

Editor's Introduction

In an intellectual climate on the left strongly marked by a tendency to seek for truth in the fragmentary and the perspectival, to suspect comprehensive theoretical enterprises of authoritarian aspirations— even when such distrust is itself articulated on the grand scale— and in some cases even to reject the notion of theory itself as an imposture, the work of Jürgen Habermas stands out as a remarkable exception. For over twenty-five years Habermas has pursued and developed a project which is rooted in the traditions of Critical Theory, the form of interdisciplinary Marxist social analysis initiated by members of the Frankfurt Institute for Social Research, under the aegis of Max Horkheimer, during the 1930s. As the inheritor of this tradition, Habermas accepts that philosophy can no longer sustain its claims to reveal the fundamental nature of reality; but he also denies that contemporary thought is obliged to choose between trivialized technicality or a grandiose arbitrariness. Philosophy *can* continue to deal with substantive questions, but only by acknowledging that it can no longer do so alone, through a collaboration with empirical disciplines. In Habermas's work philosophy functions as the problem-sensitive medium which integrates the results of the individual social and human sciences into a multi-faceted, yet coherent, account of our history, our present dilemmas, and our prospects. In its most recent reformulation, the project which this conception informs has emerged as the attempt to produce a theory of modern society which will be neither complacent nor indiscriminately critical, which will be sensitive both to the failures of modernity and its achievements, to its distortions and its still-unrealized potential for a humane collective life.

But if Habermas's work is systematic, in a way which has no serious rival among contemporary philosophers and social theorists, it also confutes the facile equations which are often currently made between systematicity and dogmatism. Whereas his predecessors in the Frankfurt School—as he remarks in these interviews—tended to restrict themselves to a comparatively narrow range of canonical texts, Habermas has opened out Critical Theory towards the most important currents of contemporary thought, while retaining its fundamental insights into the reified structures and menacing dynamic of capitalist society. This broadening of the frame of reference of Critical Theory has in large part taken place through a series of debates—some of which have become milestones in recent intellectual history—in which Habermas, while defending his basic convictions, has also learned something of enduring value from his opponents. Thus, in the early sixties, Habermas sided with Theodor Adorno in the well-known 'positivist dispute'—the debate with Karl Popper and his adherents over the philosophical foundations of the social sciences. Yet, while firmly defending the need for social science to be reflexively conscious of its own social function, against the technocratic thrust of Popperian 'critical rationalism', Habermas did acquire from Popper a sense of the fallibility of all knowledge-claims which was to become an important point of distinction between his own version of Critical Theory and that of his predecessors.[1] Similarly, Hans-Georg Gadamer's powerful restatement of the tradition of hermeneutic thought in *Truth and Method* aided Habermas to formulate his own critique of Wittgenstein, and to render more precise his objections to a positivist conception of the social sciences. Yet Habermas has also been a leading critic of the claims which Gadamer has made for the universal priority of understanding, arguing that a purely hermeneutic approach is not adequate to those phenomena of 'systematically distorted communication' which are the concern of ideology-critique.[2] In the 1970s Habermas's reading of systems theory, in particular the work of Talcott Parsons and Niklas Luhmann, enabled him to abandon the notion of a

---

1. Habermas's contributions to this debate are 'The Analytical Theory of Science and Dialectics' and 'A Positivistically Bisected Rationalism', in Theodor W. Adorno et al., *The Positivist Dispute in German Sociology*, London 1976, pp. 131–162, and pp. 198–225.

2. See 'A Review of Gadamer's *Truth and Method*', in F. Dallmayr and T. McCarthy, eds., *Understanding and Social Enquiry*, Notre Dame 1977, pp. 335–363.

macro-subject of the historical process which he now believes to have encumbered much of the Western Marxist tradition. Nevertheless, he has continued to criticize systems theory for its reductionist account of social evolution as a process of increasing capacity for adaptation.[3] Finally, and most recently, Habermas has addressed himself to the antecedents and implications of post-structuralist thought in a book of lectures on the 'philosophical discourse of modernity'.[4]

In this last case, however, despite the genuine tributes which he has paid to Foucault,[5] Habermas leaves the impression of having far less to learn from his opponents — more than any other of his major writings, *Der Philosophische Diskurs der Moderne* is a combative work. The reasons for this difference of tone are readily apparent. For, whereas Habermas understands Critical Theory as the most self-reflexive outpost of the radical traditions of the Enlightenment, post-structuralist thought has launched an attack on the inheritance of the Enlightenment as a whole, severing the link between freedom and reason which has been central to modern political consciousness. Aware of the ambiguity of this move, Habermas, in a lecture first delivered in 1980, suggested that the radical credentials of post-structuralism should not be taken so readily for granted.[6] In doing so, he undoubtedly touched a raw point of contemporary intellectual life. For, since then, a widespread international debate has developed around these questions, including, most recently, Habermas's own book on the discourse of modernity, an exchange between Richard Rorty and Jean-François Lyotard, and contributions by other defenders of the Critical Theory position.[7] This discussion, in which the influential arguments of recent French philosophy have been

---

3. See, for example, 'Toward a Reconstruction of Historical Materialism', in *Communication and the Evolution of Society*, London 1979, pp. 174–5.

4. Jürgen Habermas, *Der Philosophische Diskurs der Moderne*, Frankfurt 1985.

5. See Habermas's obituary article, 'Mit dem Pfeil ins Herz der Gegenwart: Zu Foucaults Vorlesung über Kants *Was ist Aufklärung*', in Jürgen Habermas, *Die Neue Unübersichtlichkeit*, Frankfurt 1985, pp. 126–131.

6. Jürgen Habermas, 'Modernity versus Postmodernity', *New German Critique*, no. 22, Winter 1981. Reprinted in Hal Foster, ed., *Postmodern Culture*, London 1985, pp. 3–15.

7. See Jean-François Lyotard, 'Histoire Universelle et Différences Culturelles', and Richard Rorty, 'Le Cosmopolitisme sans Emancipation', followed by a discussion between Lyotard and Rorty, in *Critique*, no. 456, May 1985. For the Critical Theory position see Axel Honneth, 'Der Affekt gegen das Allgemeine: Zu Lyotards Konzept der Postmoderne', in *Merkur*, Dec. 1984, pp. 893–902; and, most notably, Albrecht Wellmer, *Zur Dialektik von Moderne und Postmoderne*, Frankfurt 1985. The title essay of this collection has been translated as 'On the Dialectic of Modernism and Postmodernism', *Praxis International*, vol. 4, no. 4, pp. 337–362.

directly pitted for the first time against the major surviving current of the Western Marxist tradition, can be seen as revolving around a single central preoccupation: the question of whether we are currently experiencing the final exhaustion of the resources of modernity, and the transition to a much-prophesied 'post-modernity', or whether our present discontent and disillusionment stem from the fact that—in its capitalist and state-socialist forms—the possibilities of modernity have only been onesidedly and inadequately realized.

There are a number of reasons, however, why this debate between Habermas and his sympathizers, on the one hand, and thinkers influenced by post-structuralism, on the other, is unlikely to gain the balanced reception which it merits in the English-speaking world. Firstly, because of the esoterically technical or specialized character of much Anglo-Saxon philosophy in the twentieth century, broader questions of culture and society, which on the Continent would be the natural province of philosophy, have tended to be debated on the terrain of literary theory and literary criticism. Accordingly, post-structuralist thought, whose central concern with problems of discourse, textuality and interpretation reinforces this initial affinity, has far more readily been assimilated by art and literature departments than by philosophy departments in the English-speaking world. From here the characteristic themes and tropes of post-structuralism have permeated the more general texture of cultural theory and criticism, and have become familiar to a wider public of broadly left-wing sympathies. By contrast, Habermas's work is centred on problems in social rather than literary theory, and has been taken up to a much more limited extent—and with very little wider resonance—by sociologists, political scientists and philosophers. Secondly, not only does Habermas frequently write forbiddingly dense philosophical prose—in sharp contrast to the allusive, rhetorical, 'polyphonic' style of much post-structuralist work, which conceals its often considerable scholarship beneath an immediately enticing surface—but his references to a range of contemporary specialist literatures, and the rootedness of his thought in the problems of German philosophy from Kant, through Hegel to Marx and beyond, make the evaluation of the overall structure and intent of his corpus a formidable undertaking. Lastly, and most obviously, the French language, and consequently the French cultural tradition, are far more familiar to the average educated person in Britain or North America than are those of Germany. As a result of this constellation of factors there is a serious risk that the central assumptions and implications of the debate between post-structuralism and Critical Theory will be inadequately grasped by a broader public. In the worst cases, the conflict between the prophets of postmodernity and the defenders of modernity is liable to be trivialized into a choice between the playful style of post-structuralism and a somewhat oppressive Teutonic earnestness, with their presumed political extensions—a liberating pluralism on the one hand, a constraining systematicity on the other.

It is to be hoped that the present collection of interviews, which includes all those which Habermas has reprinted in the two volumes of his shorter political writings, plus a further interview with *New Left Review* not previously published, will help to broaden and redress the reception of Habermas's work in the English-speaking world. It is arguable that, despite their complexity, the structures of Habermas's theory have developed from a core of insights into our current historical situation, its dilemmas and possibilities, which are at least as intuitively plausible as those of the renouncers of modernity, even if they do not so directly express the contemporary mood of disenchantment. And, in the medium of the spoken word, these central convictions, the fundamental modes of response which inform Habermas's work, as well as many incidental sidelights and emphases not available in his more formal writings, emerge with especial vivacity. In the course of these discussions Habermas recounts his own political biography, explains his relation to his theoretical predecessors, analyses present-day cultural and social movements in the advanced capitalist world, and offers some pointers towards future possibilities, in a way which should make the essentials of his thought familiar even to a reader who has no prior knowledge of his work. In consequence, I do not intend, in the remainder of this introduction, to attempt an outline of Habermas's project as a whole, a task which has in any case already been ably accomplished.[8] It will perhaps be more useful to highlight a small number of areas in which Habermas's thought has most frequently been subject to attack, not to say misrepresentation, and to indicate how it might be defended against some recurrent objections, which have most recently been reformulated in post-structuralist guise. In doing so I shall employ the work of Jean-François Lyotard as my major point of reference. For Lyotard must be accounted not only

---

8. For a fullscale account of Habermas's work, see Thomas McCarthy, *The Critical Theory of Jürgen Habermas*, London 1978. For a briefer survey, see Richard J. Bernstein's introduction to Bernstein, ed., *Habermas and Modernity*, Cambridge 1985, pp. 1–32.

the most politically alert of post-structuralist thinkers, but also the one who has spelled out most clearly the implications of recent French thought for our evaluation of modernity as a whole.

1. The Decline of 'Grand Narratives' and the Theory of History

In an influential book, Lyotard has defined postmodernity in terms of an increasing incredulity towards what he calls 'grand narratives', historical accounts of the past and correlative anticipations of the future of a people, nation, or other community, which perform functions of social integration and political legitimation. Members of contemporary societies, Lyotard argues, no longer find it possible to believe in their history as an epic of progress or emancipation. The promises of prosperity, freedom and justice associated with the Enlightenment project of scientific control over nature and a rational organization of society have signally failed to be realized, and we have no reason to suppose that they will be in the future, either in their bourgeois or their Marxist versions. Not only this, but even the regret for the absence of such metaphysical guarantees of shared meaning has largely disappeared from 'postmodern' society. 'Most people,' Lyotard suggests, 'have lost the nostalgia for the lost narrative.'[9]

There are some striking parallels between this account of post-modernity and the 'end of ideology' debate which preoccupied English-speaking political scientists in the late fifties and early sixties. Indeed, it is curious to observe how the conception of ideology developed by American political science during the first Cold War is reduplicated in many of the themes of the 'left' Nietzscheanism of Paris during the 1970s. Daniel Bell's definition of a 'total ideology' as an 'all-inclusive system of comprehensive reality', a 'set of beliefs infused with passion' which 'seeks to transform the whole of a way of life', captures the burden of this conception, which—independently of any direct Nietzschean influence—is congruent with Nietzsche's fundamental convictions.[10] Nietzsche insists that any comprehensive theoretical or philosophical system must inevitably distort and simplify reality (for Bell, 'Ideology makes it unnecessary for people to

---

9. Jean-François Lyotard, *The Postmodern Condition*, Manchester 1984, p. 41.
10. Daniel Bell, 'The End of Ideology in the West: an Epilogue', in *The End of Ideology*, New York 1962, p. 400.

confront individual issues on their individual merits.'), that the energy which enters into the construction of such systems always derives from pre-rational needs and drives (for Bell, 'the most important latent function of ideology is to tap emotion'), and that concepts have an ineliminable pragmatic dimension (for Bell, 'not only does ideology transform ideas, it transforms people as well')[11]. Furthermore, like Lyotard, the end-of-ideology theorists portrayed ideological thought as a compensation for the collapse of traditional religious worldviews, and attributed its decline to the political and social disasters of the twentieth century. Indeed, it is much the same litany of catastrophes, most notably fascism and Stalinism, which is recited in both cases.[12] Here, however, the parallels between the two positions cease. For Bell, Shils, Lipset and company the post-war boom made possible the complacent assumption that Western societies had 'weathered the storm of ideologies', that a final dissolution of the principled opposition of left and right was taking place, in favour of a middle-ground consensus on the virtues of the mixed economy and the welfare state. Liberalism parted company with Nietzsche at the point at which a non-ideological standpoint was implicitly attributed to this consensus. For the theorists of postmodernity, however, the informing political experience is precisely the collapse of the welfar- ist consensus, with the consequent proliferation of new forms of political opposition, themselves the inheritors of an earlier upsurge of lifestyle experimentation. Accordingly, Lyotard follows Nietzsche through to a drastic pluralism, suggesting that the 'grand narratives' have been irreparably fragmented into a multiplicity of 'language- games' whose truth-claims are localized, and which are played with an ironic consciousness of their own relativity.

Against this background, it is important to note that Habermas has never denied the metaphysical core of the classic philosophies of history—indeed, he would concur with Lyotard that what he terms the 'objectivistic philosophy of history' must be considered as the last embodiment of an 'illusion of order' which was first generated by myth, and later preserved by philosophical systems. What Habermas refuses to accept, however, is that—from Vico onwards—the philo- sophy of history has *simply* been a means of satisfying a craving for

---

11. Ibid., pp. 405, 400, 401.

12. Bell mentions 'such calamities as the Moscow Trials, the Nazi-Soviet pact, the concentration camps, the suppression of the Hungarian workers': ibid., p. 402. Lyotard cites 'Auschwitz and Stalinism' as the liquidators of the hopes of modernity. See 'Sprache, Zeit, Arbeit', in Jean-François Lyotard et al., *Immaterialität und Postmoderne*, Berlin 1985, p. 37.

coherence and order. Rather, he suggests, the philosophy of history emerged in response to novel historical experiences associated with the rise of capitalism. In an essay dating from 1972 Habermas lists four fundamental experiences which played a role in this process: an awareness of accelerated and directed social change, resulting from the growth of the forces of production, and from attempts to control the effects of this growth; a consciousness of the gap between the need for regulation of increasingly complex social processes, and a lagging capacity for control which generates unpredictable side-effects of its own as it advances; a sensitivity to the unresolved conflict between the universal scope of bourgeois moral principles and the continuing 'state of nature' which exists between national communities; and, lastly, the disintegration of traditional world-views as securers of social identity.[13] In Habermas's account, the historico-philosophical sketches of the eighteenth century, and the theories of social evolution of the nineteenth, were attempts to comprehend and propose solutions to these problems, through a construal of universal history with scientific intentions. Such theories address the contradictory fact that human beings continue to suffer the consequences of a historical process which is in some sense the outcome of their own actions. Habermas views Marx's critique of capitalist society as a materialist transformation of this tradition, like its predecessors connecting an awareness of the crisis of contemporary society with an interpretation of the pattern of human history as a whole.

Insofar as experiences of uncontrolled contingency and of the ambivalence of progress—rather than its absence—remain central to contemporary consciousness, Habermas appears justified in arguing that 'all counter-ideologies, which claim to have overcome the problems of the philosophy of history, come under suspicion of escapism'.[14] To suggest—as Lyotard does—that theories of history are necessarily metaphysical, either because of their narrative forms or because of their scale, is simply to reproduce the fundamental prejudices of positivism. Such a position excludes the course, which Habermas advocates, of radicalizing the philosophy of history by eliminating its dogmatic residues. In this respect there are two

13. See Jürgen Habermas, 'Über das Subjekt der Geschichte: Diskussionsbemerkungen zu falsch gestellten Alternativen', in *Kultur und Kritik: Verstreute Aufsätze*, Frankfurt 1973, pp. 390–393.

14. Jürgen Habermas, 'Between Philosophy and Science: Marxism as Critique', in *Theory and Practice*, London 1973, p. 251 (trs. altered).

fundamental difficulties to be resolved. The first concerns 'objectivism' — the belief in a 'meaning' of history which is logically independent of any practical orientation towards the transformation of society. In his early writings, Habermas contends that Marx had already overcome this problem, having understood that 'the meaning of history can be theoretically recognized to the extent that human beings set about making it practically true.'[15] The second difficulty concerns the empirical controls on such a philosophy of history, or — more broadly conceived — the problem of the relation between philosophy and science.

Habermas's early conception of such an 'empirically falsifiable philosophy of history with practical intent' emerges with particular clarity in a discussion of Merleau-Ponty which he wrote in 1957, as part of a report on recent philosophical debates around Marxism.[16] Habermas argues that — among Western Marxists — it is Merleau-Ponty who has come closest to grasping the distinctive epistemological status of Marx's theory, insofar as he seeks to undermine the notion of history as governed by an inexorable logic, without lapsing into Sartre's equation of revolutionary practice with an abrupt, meaning-bestowing act of transcendence. Merleau-Ponty's position is summarized in a manner which reveals more than a hint of Adorno's influence: 'Where the logic of history, the condition of any possible philosophy of history, remains without any metaphysical guarantee, the philosophy of history is itself no longer philosophical; it rather becomes the critical prologue to a practice, to which it delivers up its own logos along with the logic of history as a whole . . . The experimental philosophy of history no longer searches for a hidden meaning; it saves such a meaning by producing it. Strictly speaking there "is" no meaning, only a progressive elimination of unmeaning.'[17] However, although Habermas praises Merleau-Ponty for this elucidation, there is one crucial respect in which he disagrees with the French phenomenologist's position. Merleau-Ponty's acceptance of the contingency of political practice, of the fact that 'the revolutionary event is not inscribed anywhere, in

---

15. Ibid., p. 248 (trs. altered). More recently, Habermas has suggested that both Hegel and Marx, in the course of their careers, make the transition from a practically-oriented to an 'objectivist' interpretation of history: *Der Philosophische Diskurs der Moderne*, pp. 79–82.

16. Jürgen Habermas, 'Literaturbericht zur Philosophischen Diskussion um Marx und den Marxismus', in *Theorie und Praxis*, 2nd edn., Frankfurt 1971, pp. 387–456. The discussion of Merleau-Ponty appears on pp. 425–428.

17. Ibid., pp. 425–6.

any metaphysical heaven', does not lead to an appreciation of the need for an empirical investigation of the preconditions of social transformation. The qualification of the proletariat as the bearer of revolution, for example, is not seen as something to be empirically demonstrated. Ultimately, Habermas suggests, Merleau-Ponty cannot attribute any independent role to social-scientific analysis within his conception of philosophical critique because he is unable to break with the traditional assumption that philosophical insight must be self-validating, and consequently fails to appreciate that 'an analysis of the question of meaning will only enter the dimension of the meaning of history when it comprehends this question from the determinate, historically-constituted situation in which it appears or disappears.'[18] Thus, for Habermas, the metaphysical features of the philosophy of history can only be eliminated through a relation of philosophy *both* to practice and to the empirical social sciences. A practical theory, he suggests, must be 'dependent on the social sciences, so long as it does not believe that it can get by with a dialectic which—prior to and at the basis of all history—unfolds in accordance with the hourstrokes of metaphysical necessity. So long as it rather considers dialectic to be as contingent as history itself, it must allow everything which it wishes to know to be empirically given, and this means with the procedures of the objectifying sciences; of course, the results of these are treated by philosophy as the material for its interpretations.'[19]

This conception of a close collaboration, and reciprocal dependence, of philosophy and the social sciences is central to Habermas's work as it develops through the 1960s. By the early 1970s, however, Habermas will be forced to recognize that even such a collaboration is not sufficient to strip the philosophy of history of certain dogmatic residues, of a kind which we shall be considering in more detail in a moment. As a result, Habermas eventually drops the ambiguous notion of a 'philosophy of history' altogether, and, during the 1970s, embarks on the collaborative project of a reconstruction of historical materialism as a theory of social evolution. The most distinctive feature of this reconstruction is Habermas's argument that what Marxists have traditionally referred to as the 'forces of production' and the 'relations of production'—labour-power, technical knowledge transformable into instruments of production, and organizational skills on the one hand, and the manner in which labour-

---

18. Ibid., pp. 427.
19. Ibid., p. 443.

power is combined with the means of production and the social product distributed, on the other—must be considered as two separate dimensions in which progress can take place. Marxists have usually placed most emphasis on the forces of production in their explanations of historical development, arguing that it is the relations of production which must eventually come into line with an expansion of the productive forces. Habermas, however, developing a distinction between 'work' and 'interaction' which has been central to his thought ever since the beginning, discerns an autonomous logic in the moral-practical sphere of the relations of production. Furthermore, since it is ultimately only socialized *individuals* who can learn, even if their attainments may eventually become part of a culturally-transmitted collective fund of knowledge, psychological theories of cognitive and moral development—here Habermas takes Piaget and Kohlberg as his guides—can provide the basis for a theory of evolutionary stages in the domain of law and morality, of ego-demarcations and worldviews, and of individual and collective identity formations. Habermas is anxious to stress that such a 'twin-track' theory of social evolution neither abandons materialism nor revives a teleological conception of history as inevitable progress towards a pre-ordained goal. To identify a series of stages in the development of normative structures is not to reduce the dynamics of history to an internal history of mind, nor is it to deny the possibility of stagnation or regression by asserting the inevitability of the transition from one stage to another. The materialism of Habermas's theory consists in the view that such transitions only take place as a means of resolving crises in the domain of social production and reproduction, while the rejection of any 'logification' of history results from the fact that both such crises and their successful resolution are regarded as contingent events—there is no guarantee that learning-processes will be institutionalized.[20] By drawing a sharp line in this way between the 'logical space' of possibilities of development and the contingency of the historical process, Habermas is able finally to overcome the ambiguities of the philosophy of history. A general theory of social evolution, he suggests, can provide a promise of a 'meaning'—in the sense of an overcoming

---

20. Jürgen Habermas, 'Historical Materialism and the Development of Normative Structures', in *Communication and the Evolution of Society*, pp. 120–122. A helpful brief account of the development of Habermas's views on history is provided by Axel Honneth, 'Vorbemerkungen', in Urs Jaeggi and Axel Honneth, eds., *Theorien des Historischen Materialismus*, Frankfurt 1977, pp. 453–464.

of contingency—no longer available from collapsed metaphysical worldviews. But it does so not through the rationalization of hazard, but rather by making possible an analysis of the present on which a practical overcoming of uncontrolled contingencies can be based.

2. Subjectivity and Emancipation

Even if it is admitted that a general theory of history is not intrinsically 'metaphysical', and may even be indispensable for the analysis of contemporary social developments, there remains a further reason, which demands to be taken seriously, for the current distrust of notions of 'revolution' and 'emancipation'. To a certain extent in Marx himself, and in the Hegelian Marxist tradition—beginning with Lukács' *History and Class Consciousness*—the notion of a subject of the historical process, which is eventually able to comprehend itself as such, plays a major role. Even in the work of Adorno, who, in *Negative Dialectics*, develops a radical critique of many aspects of the Hegelian Marxist tradition, the view that society is a 'potentially self-determining subject' remains central. Thus, in his 'Introduction' to *The Positivist Dispute in German Sociology*, Adorno exposes the reification of social reality through the argument that 'society is objective because, on account of its underlying structure, it cannot perceive its own subjectivity, because it does not possess a total subject and through its own organization it thwarts the installation of such a subject.'[21]

The validity of this conception, however, according to which the impersonal objectivity of social structures can be theorized in terms of alienation, has long been open to question. As Habermas points out in *Der Philosophische Diskurs der Moderne*, the viability of the corresponding conception of revolution as a reappropriation of alienated powers was already one of the central issues between the first generation of Left and Right Hegelians. In opposition to the notion that political power could be dissolved into the self-organization of society, the Right Hegelians argued that the individualism and competitiveness of bourgeois society must rather be held in check by the state, and that any attempt to abolish this counterweight could lead only to chaos. 'How can one collectively administer', one liberal follower of Hegel enquires, echoing many more recent arguments, 'that which does not constitute a closed whole, and which is daily

---

21. Theodor Adorno, 'Introduction', in *The Positivist Dispute in German Sociology*, p. 33.

generated and formed anew through the infinite and infinitely mani-
fold production of individuals?'[22] This critique was radicalized by
Max Weber, who predicted—before the Russian Revolution—that
abolition of private ownership of the means of production would not
lead to a self-managed society, but only to an intensification of bureaucracy, and has also been a feature of post-structuralist thought. It is
implicit in Foucault's insistence on the ineliminability of relations of
power, and becomes more explicit and topical in Lyotard's recent discussions of 'immateriality'—a term which he associates with the
erosion of identity, the breaking-down of stable barriers between the
self and a manipulable world produced by our implication in opaquely
labyrinthine technological and social systems. A similar account of
late capitalism has been developed by Fredric Jameson, who is,
however, markedly more ambivalent about its implications.[24] In
general, the phenomenology of 'postmodernity' gives the lie to the
notion that society could ever become 'transparent' to itself, through
a process which could be conceptualized as the self-reflection of a
collective social subject.

In much of his earlier work, Habermas had relied on the concept
of a subject of the historical process, although he considered this
subject to be the human species, rather than a social class such as the
proletariat, and although he argued that the subject of history—in
the form of a global humanity unified by modern networks of
commerce and communication—was not to be hypostatized, but
was itself a product of the historical process. However, Habermas
has become increasingly aware of the basic problems generated by
the conceptual framework of the philosophy of consciousness. One
major turning point can be located in his debate with the systems
theorist Niklas Luhmann, which was published in 1971. Here, for
the first time, Habermas stresses the inappropriateness of theorizing
social collectivities in terms of a constitutive subject. He suggests
that even in Hegel—despite a shift towards intersubjectivity—a
monological absolute subject is ultimately restored, with significant
consequences for the Marxist tradition, including his own position in
Theory and Practice and *Knowledge and Human Interests*.[25] In this

22. Oppenheim, cited in *Der Philosophische Diskurs der Moderne*, p. 88n.

23. See Jean-François Lyotard, 'Immaterialien', and 'Philosophie in der Diaspora',
in *Immaterialität und Postmoderne*, pp. 9–26.

24. See Fredric Jameson, 'Postmodernism, or the Cultural Logic of Late Capitalism', in *New Left Review*, no. 146, pp. 53–92.

25. Jürgen Habermas, 'Theorie der Gesellschaft oder Sozialtechnologie?', in
Habermas and Niklas Luhmann, *Theorie der Gesellschaft oder Sozialtechnologie—
Was Leistet der Systemforschung?*, Frankfurt 1971, pp. 176–181.

context even French structuralism—an intellectual movement from which Habermas is in most respects distant—is sympathetically referred to as resulting from a justified dissatisfaction, with the application of concepts derived from the philosophy of reflexion to social processes. Habermas himself, however, prefers to turn towards systems theory for the conceptual tools with which to overcome this weakness in the tradition of Western Marxism. Thus, in his 1976 essay on the reconstruction of historical materialism, Habermas argues that 'Historical materialism does not need to assume a *species*-subject that undergoes evolution. The bearers of evolution are rather societies and the acting subjects integrated into them; social evolution can be discerned in those structures that are replaced by more comprehensive structures in accord with a pattern that is to be rationally reconstructed.'[26]

However, just as with other major conceptual borrowings, Habermas's assimilation of systems theory takes place through the medium of critique. Habermas rejects attempts to make systems theory alone the basis of a theory of social evolution, arguing that a self-sufficient functionalism cannot appreciate the fact that increases in complexity are in each case only possible at the learning level attained in the organizational principle of the society in question. In other words, in terms of the distinction between functional and normative structures which we have already noted, the modes of action embodied in social systems first have to be made possible through evolutionary learning processes in the moral-practical dimension. In his more recent work Habermas has explored the implications of this conception of evolutionary processes in terms of the relation between systems and the 'life-world'. In the domain of everyday life concerned with the transmission of culture, social integration, and the socialization of individuals, what Habermas terms 'communicative action', the co-ordination of action through implicit or argumentatively attained agreement, is indispensable. By contrast, the achievement of systems such as the capitalist economy and bureaucratic administrations, is to operate via 'steering media'—money and power—which enable us to dispense with the common orientation of actors. In one respect this dualism of system and life-world, which Habermas has placed at the centre of the most ambitious formulation of his social theory to date, *The Theory of Communicative Action*, is simply an attempt to solve one of the oldest conundrums of sociology—the problem of reconciling the apparently autonomous logic of social

---

26. 'Towards a Reconstruction of Historical Materialism', p. 140.

processes with the equally inescapable fact that society is the outcome of human interactions. However, this distinction also enables Habermas to develop a new account of the contradictions and characteristic forms of political struggle of advanced capitalism. In line with his general conception, Habermas argues that it is only on the basis of a 'modernization' of the life-world (the process whereby the concepts of truth, moral rightness, and truthfulness or authenticity, which are inseparably interwoven in traditional forms of life, become differentiated into three distinct spheres of value) that systems can separate out from the life-world—as they did fully for the first time under capitalism. For much of its historical existence capitalism has survived and expanded by consuming the substance of traditional forms of life. However, we have now reached a stage, Habermas contends, when the uncontrolled growth of autonomous systems has begun to undermine its own foundations, as it were, by commodifying and bureaucratizing life-world activities which are intrinsically bound to communicative action. The result is the generation of social pathologies, of the kind which have called forth the defensive and communitarian impulses manifest in the New Social Movements.

On the basis of this conception, in which it is not systems as such, but their 'colonization' of the life-world, which generates phenomena structurally analogous to those which Marx designated with the term 'alienation', Habermas is able to pinpoint the ambiguity in Marx's work which has led to the current distrust of traditional conceptions of revolution and social emancipation. 'Marx's error', Habermas suggests, 'can be traced back to that dialectical clamping together of system analysis and life-world analysis, which does not permit a sufficiently sharp separation between the level of system-differentiation achieved by modernity and the class-specific forms of its institutionalization . . . Otherwise he would not have been able to overlook the fact that any modern society, no matter what the nature of its class-structure, must demonstrate a high level of structural differentiation.'[27] Echoing a critique which has been developed from different angles, and in widely differing theoretical contexts, by authors such as André Gorz and Alec Nove,[28] Habermas argues that because

---

27. Jürgen Habermas, *Theorie des Kommunikativen Handelns*, Frankfurt 1981, vol. 2, p. 501.

28. See André Gorz, *Farewell to the Working Class*, London 1982, especially chapters 2–5; and Alec Nove, *The Economics of Feasible Socialism*, London 1983, especially chapters 1–2. Although formulated more intuitively than in Habermas, the suggestion that Marxism has traditionally underestimated the autonomy of systems is central to both these works.

Marx borrows a conceptual apparatus from Hegel which is neutral in relation to the distinction of system and life-world, he is misled into viewing the capitalist system as 'nothing more than the ghostly form of class-relations which have been inverted and fetishized into anonymity'.[29] This has the unfortunate consequence that Marx's theory of revolution awakens the illusory expectation that 'in principle of all social relations which have been objectified, rendered systematically autonomous, can be brought back within the horizons of the life-world.'[30] It is then a comparatively easy matter, as we have already seen, for opponents to unmask the 'unifying power of reason' as an illusion in the face of such 'stubborn complexities'.

The critique of Marx's social theory and of his theory of revolution clearly has important consequences for our conception of the goals and procedures of a contemporary socialist politics. Because Marx's explanatory model for the pathologies of capitalism remains Hegel's *entzweite Sittlichkeit* — a torn-apart traditional life-world — which he theorizes in terms of a self-divided macro-subject, he is able to group these disturbances around a single, central class antagonism. Once we abandon this model, however, by distinguishing between the modernization of the life-world, and the reification of an already modernized life-world, we must admit the more diverse and contingent character of the pathological traits of advanced capitalism, and reject the notion that the knowledge and organization of the social totality can be conceptualized as the self-reflection and self-transformation of a social subject. A no less important consequence is that the prospect of a thoroughgoing internal reorganization of administration and economy on the basis of workers' control is no longer plausible. For the efficiency of these subsystems, which is in fact their *raison d'être,* derives from their use of 'steering media' which can be considered as impoverished and standardized languages, abstracted from the more context-specific forms of agreement which are required for the co-ordination of action in the life-world. Habermas denies, however, that the recognition of these constraints must lead us to abandon the very ideal of a democratization of society. Rather, such democratization must take the form of a fostering of 'counter public-spheres', 'centres of concentrated communication which naturally arise out of the micro-domains of everyday practice',[31] and which can focus the impulses of the life-

---

29. *Theorie des Kommunikativen Handelns*, vol. 2, p. 499.
30. *Der Philosophische Diskurs der Moderne*, p. 83.
31. Ibid., p. 422.

world. In this way state and economy could be sensitized to the goals established by participatory decision-making processes. These counter public-spheres must, of course, maintain themselves below the level of complexity which would carry them over the threshold of the life-world, operating instead at the interface of life-world and system. Only in this way, Habermas suggests, can the ideals of solidarity and self-determination built into modernity be reconciled with the level of system-complexity on which modern societies rely for their material well-being.

3. Morality and Ethical Life

The criticisms of the Marxist tradition which we have considered in the previous section are based on the argument that the complexity and objectivity of social systems are not simply abstract, dependent moments of the self-relation and self-movement of a potentially revolutionary subject of society. As we have seen, Habermas both accommodates and counters this objection by suggesting that it is the immanent rationality of linguistic *inter*-subjectivity which resists submission to the functional imperatives of economy and administration. However, Habermas has also had to respond to objections from another, very different quarter—here the contention is not that subjectivity is impotent in the face of objective social processes, but rather that the notion of a 'rational' consensus, based purely on argumentation, which Habermas employs as the normative foundation of his critical social theory, is chimerical. Objections of this kind have frequently been brought by thinkers in the hermeneutic tradition, most notably Hans-Georg Gadamer, who, in his important debate with Habermas in the late sixties, accused Habermas of being unconsciously guided by the image of an 'anarchistic utopia', in so far as he believed it possible to submit all inherited authority to a demand for rational justification.[32] For Gadamer, 'It is not so much our judgments as it is our prejudices that constitute our being'[33]— 'tradition' reaches deeper than any possible explicitly attained consensus. More surprisingly, given the iconoclastic posture of much post-structuralist thought, a similar lesson can and has been drawn

---

32. See Hans-Georg Gadamer, 'On the Scope and Function of Hermeneutical Reflection', in, David E. Linge, ed., *Philosophical Hermeneutics*, London 1976, p. 42.

33. Hans-Georg Gadamer, 'The Universality of the Hermeneutic Problem', in ibid., p. 9.

from Jacques Derrida's portrayal of subjectivity as always caught up in the play of a 'general text' whose meaning it can never make fully perspicuous to itself. It has also informed Jean-François Lyotard's attempts to develop a 'postmodern' conception of justice. Unlike some of his contemporaries, Lyotard fully acknowledges the central role which the ideal of autonomy has played in modern politics, the principle that 'only that totality of prescriptions will be considered just which is produced by the social body to which these prescriptions apply.'[34] However, Lyotard also dismisses such self-determination as an impossible ideal, since, as participants in a life-world, our selves are shaped by forms of 'narrative knowledge', networks of belief and evaluation which are the implicit basis from which all argument begins. 'People begin by listening to a language', Lyotard affirms, 'not by speaking it, and what they hear as children are stories . . . That implies the contrary of autonomy, heteronomy. It also implies that, fundamentally, it is not true that a people can ever give itself its own institutions.'[35]

In this area, too, Habermas has modified his position, introducing further discriminations, over the last ten years or so. In some of his earlier statements Habermas had given the impression that the concept of what he terms an 'ideal speech situation'—a situation of dialogue characterized by full reciprocity, and by an absence of external coercions and internal distortions—could provide the lineaments of a possible future form of life. Now, however, Habermas acknowledges that the content of particular life-forms depends on traditions, no matter how reflexively appropriated, and that 'socialized individuals cannot relate hypothetically to the form of life or to the life-history through which their own identity has been formed.'[36] Recently Habermas has summarized, in terms of a series of arguments developed by Albrecht Wellmer, the limitations which such considerations place on a 'discourse ethics'—an ethics based on the principle that a norm can be considered objectively right if it would be consented to in free discussion by all concerned as consonant with their interests.[37] Firstly, practical disourse cannot generate the content of norms, but can only serve as a means of resolving disputes concerning norms and practices which have already become

---

34. Jean-François Lyotard and Jean-Loup Thebaud, *Au Juste*, Paris 1979, p. 52.
35. Ibid., pp. 68–9.
36. Jürgen Habermas, 'Diskursethik—Notizen zu einem Begründungsprogramm', in *Moralbewusstsein und Kommunikatives Handeln*, Frankfurt 1983, p. 114.
37. See ibid., p. 113–118.

problematic: 'Without the horizon of the life-world of a specific social group, and without conflicts of action in a specific situation . . . it would be senseless to want to conduct a practical discourse.'[38] Secondly, a discourse ethics cannot resolve questions of the 'good life', since 'ideas of the good life are not representations, which hover before us as an abstract ought; they stamp the identity of groups and individuals in such a way that they form an integrated component of the particular culture or personality.'[39] Thirdly, because of their degree of universality, moral insights acquired under conditions of practical discourse must be complemented by a non-formalizable hermeneutic sensitivity, in order to be applied to concrete situations. Lastly, moral discourses themselves, stand under a number of restrictions: since they are concerned with the interpretation of needs they are necessarily permeated by motifs of aesthetic and therapeutic critique which cannot themselves be conclusively validated; since the problems with which they deal result from a disturbance of intersubjective relations, an element of the 'struggle for recognition' is built into them; finally, the achievement of consensus is by no means the socially predominant form of conflict resolution, so that ethical principles are confronted with the difficulties of instatement through strategic political action. All these factors, Habermas suggests, bring into play the 'power of history over against the transcending claims and interests of reason.'[40]

Recently, Habermas has argued that these conflicts between history and reason can be summarized under the heading of the relation between morality and 'ethical life', in the Hegelian sense of *Sittlichkeit*—the concrete customs of a community.[41] For it was Hegel who first definitively exposed the formalism of Kantian ethics, showing that the mere principle of universalizability cannot generate determinate moral norms, and is dependent for its content on the actual practices of a society. In this respect Habermas admits that his discourse ethics, which radicalizes Kant by proposing that universal norms should be the outcome of a discussion in which individual needs and interests are expressed, pays for its enhancement of the rationality or moral norms with a number of drawbacks—most

---

37. See ibid., p. 113–118.
38. Ibid., p. 113.
39. Ibid., p. 118.
40. Ibid., p. 116.
41. See Jürgen Habermas, 'Über Moralität und Sittlichkeit—Was macht ein Lebensform "Rational"?', in Herbert Schnädelbach, ed., *Rationalität*, Frankfurt 1984, pp. 218–235.

importantly, an abstraction from concrete situations of application, and a loss of the force of empirically effective motives.[42] On the other hand, Habermas also contends that it is no longer possible for the critics of formalism—without the guarantee of Hegel's absolute spirit—simply to appeal to *Sittlichkeit*, to what happens to be done, unless they are willing to countenance an unqualified moral relativism. Habermas's current solution to these difficulties is to suggest that questions of justice in the narrow sense, normative questions, must first be separated from evaluative questions of the good life—the former being amenable to procedures of rational argumentation, while the latter are not—and then reintegrated at a later stage. The resulting problem of the historical mediation of morality and ethical life is made considerably easier for us, Habermas contends, by the fact that modern life-worlds 'come to meet us halfway'. This is true both in relation to the problem of application and of motivation. Firstly, hermeneutic tact does not entirely dissolve the transcending force of principles into the relativity of particular situations. In some cases we can interpret the history of the application of a principle as a learning-process, in which partial and interest-distorted attempts at installation retrospectively appear as such in the light of the universal content of the principle in question. Habermas gives the example of the establishment of fundamental norms such as freedom of speech and the adult franchise in modern parliamentary democracies to illustrate such a learning-process. He points out, in addition, that the more the institutions of a society are organized in accordance with such principles, the more their further extension is facilitated. Secondly, while it must be admitted that a universalistic morality which is not 'to hang in the thin air of good intentions' must be anchored in personality structures, it can be argued that modernized life-worlds, which push processes of individuation beyond the limits of an identity tied to specific social roles, towards the flexibility of what Habermas terms 'ego-identity', tend to provide such an

---

42. See ibid., p. 228. Kant, of course, was well aware of both the problem of application and the problem of motivation posed by his moral philosophy. In *Groundwork of the Metaphysic of Morals* he admits that the a priori laws of morality 'require in addition a power of judgement sharpened by experience, partly in order to distinguish the cases to which they apply, partly in order to secure for them admittance to the will of man and influence over practice; for man, affected as he is by so many inclinations, is capable of the Idea of pure practical reason, but he has not so easily the power to realise the Idea *in concreto* in his conduct of life.' *The Moral Law* (Kant's Groundwork of the Metaphysic of Morals), translated and analysed by H. J. Paton, London 1948, p. 55.

anchorage. In this respect too, modern societies can be said to compensate for the abstraction of modern morality.

One further problem which arises in this context, and to which Habermas has devoted considerable attention in recent years, is how to accommodate the concept of 'progress' within an approach which accepts the duality of morality and ethical life. For, if we admit that conflicting ideas of the good life cannot be arbitrated through discourse in the same way as questions of justice, we must also admit that there can be no formal criterion which would allow us to pronounce one form of life superior to another. Here again Habermas has considerably modified traditional Marxist conceptions of historical progress. Marx himself, as the *Communist Manifesto* shows, often downplayed the costs of the shattering of traditional ways of life, in favour of what he considered to be the emancipatory dynamic of the capitalist mode of production. Although he is not entirely immune to the poignancy of the destruction of ancient cultures—particularly in a colonial context—Marx's historical optimism leads him to assume that rationalization and happiness, secured through the full realization of human capacities, must eventually coincide.[43] In Habermas's view, however, we can no longer claim Marx's confidence. While firmly opposing any politically-motivated romanticization of the past, which conveniently neglects the levels of material misery prevalent in premodern societies, Habermas nevertheless insists that our assessment of a form of life as successful or unsuccessful, good or bad, ultimately depends on unformalizable 'clinical' intuitions: a mediaeval society—even with higher levels of oppression—might be considered less alienated than a modern capitalist metropolis. The abandonment of the philosophy of history, which we have already examined, in favour of a theory of social evolution, which filters out universal structures from concrete forms of life, and strictly separates the logic from the dynamics of development, requires us to 'give up critically judging and normatively classifying totalities, world-views, epochs, forms of life and cultures, complexes of life as a whole.'[44] It is important to add, however, that this line of argument does *not* plunge us into relativism as far as our own society is

---

43. A fine illustration of the balance of Marx's sensibilities on this subject is provided by his article on 'The British Rule in India', in *Surveys from Exile*, Penguin/NLR edn., Harmondsworth 1973, pp. 301–307.

44. Jürgen Habermas, 'A Reply to my Critics', in John B. Thompson and David Held, eds., *Habermas: Critical Debates*, London 1982, p. 254.

concerned. For if it is true that the substance of a way of life cannot be justified from a universalist standpoint, it is equally true that moral demands which run counter to the degree of rationalization which a society has already achieved will generate social pathologies—as the extreme case of fascism in the twentieth century graphically shows. To this extent we can say that, for us, as members of a modern society, there is no turning back—if we are to move towards a less commodified and bureaucratized form of life, it cannot be through a return to an undifferentiated life-world, but only on the basis of the forms of communicative action which modernity has already released.

4. Truth, Consensus and Conformity

There remains one final charge against Habermas which merits discussion in this context, and which—again—has been perhaps most clearly and forcefully stated in *The Postmodern Condition*. In the work of influential contemporary thinkers such as Lyotard and Feyerabend—behind whom, of course, stands the figure of Nietzsche—the very notions of 'truth', 'objectivity', 'consensus', are seen as possessing a coercive moment, as implying the enforced unification of plurality. In his more recent writings Lyotard has sought to break out of this coercion by adopting the Wittgensteinian notion of language-games, which are inherently multiple and irreducible to any universal model of language. Habermas's error can then be portrayed as the belief that 'humanity as a collective (universal) subject seeks its common emancipation through the regularization of the "moves" permitted in all the language-games'. The Critical Theorist's 'narrative of emancipation' unfortunately relies on a *telos* of collective agreement which 'does violence to the heterogeneity of language-games'.[45]

There are three distinct levels at which this critique of Habermas must be criticized in its turn. Firstly, at the philosophical level, Lyotard's arguments depend on a chronic confusion between *language-games* and *validity-claims*. He fails to distinguish between the differentiation of the life-world into three distinct spheres of value, concerned respectively with cognitive, moral and aesthetic

---

45. *The Postmodern Condition*, pp. 66, xxv. For a useful commentary on this argument, which fails, however, to question its basic assumption, see Manfred Frank, *Was ist Neostrukturalismus?*, Frankfurt 1983, pp. 102–115.

questions, and what Habermas terms a 'pluralization of diverging universes of discourse [which] belongs to specifically modern experience'.[46] This confusion is particularly apparent in Lyotard's repeated twinning of Kant and Wittgenstein, exemplified by his recent statement that 'it is basically through Kant and Wittgenstein that I understood that there is no metalanguage in general'.[47] For to say that there is no metalanguage in general is ambiguous, interpretable either in a 'horizontal' or a 'vertical' sense. On the former— more Wittgensteinian—construal, what is meant is that there are no specifiable universal features of language at all: universality is fragmented into a variety of linguistic practices. On a Kantian interpretation, however, what is meant is that there are *several* metalanguages, governing different spheres of value. Far from defending a cognitive or moral pluralism, Kant's concern is precisely to uphold the possibility of claims to universality in different spheres, by clarifying the distinct epistemological statuses of different kinds of judgement. Thus, while admitting the plurality of language-games in contemporary culture, it is possible to argue that validity-claims (which are not themselves a specific kind of linguistic activity, but arise within different linguistic activities) *cut across* this multiplicity. In other words, there will be clashes of viewpoint concerning cognitive, moral and aesthetic questions, but we cannot claim that these conflicts are *in principle* unamenable to discussion, and to possible resolution. Habermas makes a similar point in the course of his critique of Max Weber, who, like Lyotard, tends to run together value-contents and aspects of validity. 'Weber goes too far', Habermas suggests, 'when he infers from the loss of the substantial unity of reason a polytheism of gods and demons struggling with one another, with their irreducibility rooted in a pluralism of incompatible validity-claims. The unity of rationality, in the multiplicity of value-spheres, rationalized according to their inner logics, is secured precisely at the formal level of the argumentative redemption of validity claims.'[48]

---

46. Jürgen Habermas, 'Questions and Counterquestions', in *Habermas and Modernity*, p. 192.

47. 'Sprache, Zeit, Arbeit', p. 41. This confusion appears particularly clearly when Lyotard almost inadvertently lists Habermas's three aspects of validity, but describes them rather as 'régimes de phrases' ('regimes of sentences'): 'Appendice Svelte à la Question Postmoderne', in *Tombeau de l'Intellectuel et Autres Papiers*, Paris 1984, p. 84.

48. *The Theory of Communicative Action*, vol. 1, trans. Thomas McCarthy, Boston 1984, p. 249.

Secondly, on the political level, Lyotard's position is unsatisfactory insofar as it does not even address the issue of social conflict. One of the principal reasons for this is the anodyne connotations of the term 'language-game', which Lyotard employs with excessive laxity. Had he employed an alternative term such as 'social practices', and had he considered that this category would include activities such as pumping pollutants into the environment, closing down industries in depressed areas, and driving under the influence of alcohol, he would have found it less plausible to portray conflict merely as a kind of verbal jousting ('agonistics') internal to each language-game. A further important reason is that, as soon as Lyotard attempts to address the problem of the reciprocal relations of 'language-games' he is confronted with the nemesis of all relativism. For to argue that 'the recognition of the heteromorphous nature of language-games' implies 'the renunciation of terror, which assumes that they are isomorphic and tries to make them so',[49] is again to rely on an equivocation, between 'recognition' as the registering of a state of affairs, or as an acknowledgement of validity. Unless such recognition, in the second sense, is more than simply one language-game among others, it is difficult to comprehend how Lyotard can claim priority for it. Had Lyotard reflected a little further on this, he would have appreciated that Habermas's theory of consensus has nothing to do with the homogenization of language-games, or with the establishment of the supremacy of one language-game, but rather with the condition of possibility of plurality: the regulation of the effects of social practices on each other in the light of the freely expressed interests of all those concerned.

But not only is Lyotard's position philosophically and politically dubious, it is also historically inaccurate, in so far as it fails to perceive that the universalization of principles and the individualization of lifestyles are two sides of the same process. In modern societies, Habermas suggests, the co-ordination of action becomes increasingly dependent on explicit, argumentatively attained agreement, rather than on the background consensus of the life-world. But, to the extent that this is the case, concrete life-forms and general life-world structures increasingly separate out from each other. It is possible for a proliferation of subcultures to take place precisely because the need for agreement on basic rules of social interaction is satisfied at ever higher levels of abstraction. Because he

49. *The Postmodern Condition*, p. 66.
50. Ibid., p. 72.

entirely neglects this universalistic component of modern consciousness, Lyotard equates an emancipatory pluralism with a retreat into
fragmented and particularistic forms of consciousness, which has to
some extent replaced the function of ideologies, with their 'danger-
ously' promissory and utopian content. The basic philosophical
confusion behind this position emerges clearly in Lyotard's recent
suggestion that 'the decline, perhaps the ruin of the universal idea
can liberate thought and life from totalizing obsessions.'[51] Strangely
enough, for a thinker who has recently made so much of Kantian
motifs, Lyotard assumes that the universalism of Enlightenment
moral consciousness must collapse along with the ambitions of
traditional metaphysics. In consequence, he misinterprets Habermas as believing that 'the aim of the project of modernity [is] the
constitution of sociocultural unity within which all the elements of
daily life and of thought would take their places as in an organic
whole.'[52] Lyotard is unable to distinguish between a concern with
the re-establishing of connections between split-off specialist cultures and an irreversibly modernized life-world, and a longing for
the lost totality of pre-modern culture.

In fact, one of the major distinctions between Habermas's work
and the traditions of Hegelian Marxism from which it emerged, is
Habermas's Kantian insistence on the irreducible distinctions between value-spheres. Thus, at the risk of attack from more ecologically-
minded radicals, Habermas has argued that the differentiation of
modern life-forms must be preserved, 'in order that the reflexivity of
traditions, the individuation of the social subject, and the universalistic foundations of justice and morality do not all go to hell.'[53] Far
from advocating an organically integrated society, his vision is rather
of a transformation from a society dominated by instrumental rationality to one in which the currently isolated spheres of the cognitive,
the moral and the aesthetic can be brought into a new equilibrium
and interaction, a task which he compares not to a melt-down into a
new totality, but rather to the setting-in-motion of a mobile which
has become obstinately entangled. This vision is encapsulated in
Habermas's statement, from one of these interviews, that the 'motivating thought' which lies at the heart of his work concerns 'the

51. Jean-François Lyotard, 'Tombeau de l'Intellectuel', in *Tombeau de l'Intellectuel
et Autres Papiers*, p. 21.

52. Jean-François Lyotard, 'Answering the Question: What is Postmodernism?', in
The Postmodern Condition, p. 72.

53. 'The Dialectics of Rationalization', p. 107 below.

reconciliation of a modernity which has fallen apart, the idea that, without surrendering the differentiation which modernity has made possible in the social and economic spheres, one can find forms of living together in which autonomy and dependency can truly enter into a non-antagonistic relation, that one can walk tall in a collectivity which does not have the dubious quality of backward-looking substantial forms of community.'[54]

Conclusion

The incoherences and omissions of Lyotard's thought, considered as the paradigm for a self-proclaimed postmodern philosophy, point towards some of the general, underlying problems with post-structuralist-inspired accounts of postmodernity. As we have already noted, in considering Lyotard's attitude to the philosophy of history, the Nietzschean influence on post-structuralism ensures that the metaphysical character of theories is equated with their systematicity. For Habermas, however, it is not systematicity as such which poses the problem, but the fact that philosophical systems—interpretations of the world as a whole—were based upon a fundamental principal immunized against critical probing, that philosophy traditionally conceived itself as a discourse operating at a level entirely distinct from that of empirical confirmation or disconfirmation. Habermas shares with the post-structuralists a sense of the crisis of philosophy after Hegel, of its struggle to step over into another medium. But he continues the materialist argument of the original Frankfurt School in suggesting that this medium must consist of a practically-oriented collaboration between philosophy and empirical social science. Through such a co-operation philosophy preserves the social and human sciences from empiricist and elementarist myopia, while the sciences lend philosophy a substantive, but non-dogmatic, content. For Habermas, in other words, it is not the *universality* of philosophical truth-claims which is to be abandoned, but rather their non-fallibilist aspect. Post-structuralism, however, through its critique of the universal, is driven into an abandonment of systematic cognitive claims, indeed frequently into a quasi-aesthetic suspension of truth-claims as such. The result of this manoeuvre, however, is that genuine attempts at social and cultural analysis become vulnerable to anecdotal and inadequately theorized evidence, a fact which explains

---

54. Ibid., p. 125 below.

the constitutive vagueness and portentousness of general accounts of postmodernity. Indeed, this vulnerability can be seen in the diffusion of the term postmodernism itself. In the domains of architecture and the visual arts, the word possesses a determinate meaning, referring to a renunciation and critique of distinct traditions, of a levelling technocratic functionalism in architecture, and of a programme of negation in modern art which lead from abstract expressionism, through minimalism, to conceptual art (the last modernist movement which could be meaningfully described as avant-garde). It is certainly the case that these localized crises are symptomatic of more fundamental problems of modernity, problems of technology, of aesthetic experience and commodification, of environmentalism and democratic control. But this in itself does not justify the inflation of the term 'postmodernity' into a term of epochal diagnosis, an announcement of the collapse of the 'Enlightenment project' as a whole.

One cannot, in other words, provide a coherent account of post-modernity without a determinate concept of modernity; and such a concept cannot be developed a priori, but is necessarily dependent on the theorization of long-term historical processes, of the kind which Habermas attempts in his reconstruction of historical materialism. Lyotard and other contemporary thinkers often seem to ignore this basic requirement, assuming that it is sufficient to recite the disasters of the twentieth century in order to blacken the entire Enlightenment heritage. At the crudest level this position appears to imply a denial of the meaningfulness of any counterfactual history, the belief that no epoch can contain possibilities other than those which have been actually realized. Thus Lyotard affirms—in explicit opposition to Habermas—'Modernity is not "incomplete", rather it has been liquidated. After Auschwitz and Stalinism it is certain that no-one can maintain that the hopes, which were bound up with modernity, have been fulfilled. To be sure, they have not been forgotten, but rather destroyed.'[55] The implausibility of this argument is intensified by the fact that it is only in the light of the democratic and humanitarian aspirations of the Enlightenment that fascism and Stalinism appear in their full horror. In general, the discourse of postmodernity, in its constant oscillations between depression and exhilaration, its bitter-sweet ambivalence, provides evidence in favour of Habermas's contention that modern conscious is essentially constituted by an intersection of historical and utopian

---

55. 'Sprache, Zeit, Arbeit', pp. 37–38.

perspectives, the one—for example, in the form of the memory of the political disasters which Lyotard evokes—providing a necessary ballast for the other. For Habermas, what has been exhausted is not utopian energies as such, but a particular model of utopia based on the notion of self-realization through labour, which is dubious both in its philosophico-anthropological origins, and in its lack of purchase on modern industrial processes. Whether the decline of this particular model of self-realizing subjectivity signals a collapse of belief in the possibility of progress as such, depends upon one's theoretical conception of the potentials of modernity.

In the case of post-structuralist thought, the rational principle of modernity is equated—although more often implicitly than explicitly—with cognitive-instrumental thought. This then permits post-structuralist theories to invoke the characteristic experiences of aesthetic modernism—of a subjectivity freed from the demands of utility and morality—as the radical other of Enlightenment reason and societal modernization. In viewing cultural modernity as a disruptive intruder, post-structuralism and neo-conservatism coincide, although the polarity of values is reversed from one position to the other. For the neo-conservatives, the spread of lifestyles and attitudes inspired by aesthetic modernism poses a threat to the ideology of achievement and obedience which is essential to the continuing process of capitalist modernization. For post-structuralism, by contrast, the celebration of the untamed energies of mind and body—of madness, intensity, desire—is the only means of opposing a modernity conceptualized exclusively in terms of economic and administrative rationalization. It is important to note that Habermas by no means underestimates the emancipatory potential of modern culture, although he would argue—against the onesidedness of post-structuralism—that a concern for human and civil rights, and for democratic self-determination is no less central to cultural modernity than the values of expressive subjectivity. He even accepts the contemporary 'cult of immediacy, the deflation of noble forms, anarchism of the soul, the celebration of the concrete all along the line, relativism even in the theory of science'—developments which go against the grain of many of Habermas's basic convictions—as expressions of 'the need for concretion, the wish for engagement, the attempt to test the critical content of ideas here and now, to take ideas seriously in the way one live's one's life.'[56] In their post-structuralist form, however, these attitudes have

---

56. Jürgen Habermas, 'Introduction', in Habermas, ed., *Observations on the Spiritual Situation of the Age*, Boston 1984, pp. 21–22 (trs. altered).

implications which cannot be exempted from criticism. Perhaps the most significant of these concern the rejection of an anticipatory relation to practice in philosophical thought, and a reliance on the normative content of aesthetic experience itself.

In one sense, Lyotard is perfectly correct in suggesting that Adorno's thought can be seen as teetering on the brink of post-modernity, if we understand by this the collapse of any rationally-justified belief in the possibility of a better future. Indeed, the classical Frankfurt School as a whole, once it had come to doubt the revolutionary role of the proletariat, emphasized the fragility of its own critical perspective—and devoted a great deal of energy to the problem which this fragility posed. In his 1937 essay on 'Traditional and Critical Theory', Horkheimer remarks that—from the conventional standpoint—a critical theory of society could only appear as 'an aimless intellectual game, half conceptual poetry, half impotent expression of states of mind'.[57] And in his complementary essay of the same year, Marcuse, too, admits that 'strong emphasis on the role of phantasy seems to contradict the rigorously scientific character that critical theory has always made a criterion of its concepts', but nevertheless insists—more defiantly than Horkheimer—that 'without phantasy, all philosophical knowledge remains in the grip of the present or the past and severed from the future, which is the only link between philosophy and the real history of mankind.'[58] It is in the work of Adorno, however, that the shift of emphasis from historical process to the subjective resources of the individual, the view that 'reason has retreated behind a windowless wall of idiosyncrasies, which the holders of power arbitrarily reproach with arbitrariness',[59] takes its most extreme form. While it is true that in Adorno the possibility of reconciliation is not arbitrarily posited, but is rather the logical outcome of an immanent critique of identity-thinking, nevertheless, in Adorno's later works—particularly *Negative Dialectics*—an almost unbearable tension is generated, an absurd disproportion, between the utopian glimmerings, on the one hand, and the total system of delusion, on the other. It is revealing that, in the early seventies, Lyotard finds his own experience as a former militant of the far Left reflected in this tension; and that it is

57. Max Horkheimer, 'Traditional and Critical Theory', in *Critical Theory*, New York 1972, p. 209.
58. Herbert Marcuse, 'Philosophy and Critical Theory', in *Negations*, Harmondsworth 1968, p. 155.
59. Theodor Adorno, *Minima Moralia*, London 1974, p. 70.

precisely by means of a contrast with Adorno—who was, at that time, little known in France—that Lyotard articulates the break from the tormented negativity of a prospectless critique, to an affirmative Nietzschean stance, a break which he describes in *Économie Libidinale* as 'la résolution d'une longue douleur'.

From one point of view, this shift can be seen as motivated by sound political intuition, which is also embodied in the Hegelian inheritance of Marxism—an awareness that, as Albrecht Wellmer has recently recalled—'theory must have an appropriate concept of the already *existing* forms of freedom, if it is to anticipate emancipation not as the mere negation, but as the *"Aufhebung"* of this freedom'.[60] In the philosophy of postmodernity, however, the conservation and supersession of existing freedoms no longer comes into question at all, any more than it does in the facade of playfulness and individuality which postmodern architecture superimposes on anonymous concentrations of wealth and power, or in the reconciliation with the art market of neo-expressionist painting. Rather than abandoning the utopian perspective and retreating into stoicism, Lyotard tends to consider it as already realized in the present, thereby collapsing the relation of philosophy to a transformative practice no longer considered necessary. The problem with this position, however, is that it is no less based on wish-fulfillment than the position which it replaces: Lyotard's suggestion, for example, that 'the extension of the technical criterion, even in its capitalist usage, to the majority of activities does not only have the effect of subjugating them to the interests of the system', but also 'favours the discovery that every activity is also an art *(technè)*',[61] is far from convincing. The perpetuation of illusion implicit in this attempt to escape the tension between the real and the ideal was well perceived by Adorno in his critique of Nietzschean *amor fati* in *Minima Moralia* : 'Love of stone walls and barred windows is the last resort of someone who sees and has nothing else to love. Both are cases of the same ignominious adaptation which, in order to endure the world's horror attributes reality to wishes and meaning to senseless compulsion.'[62] Furthermore, the accusation which Lyotard levels against Habermas, of a refusal to draw the necessary distinctions

---

60. Albrecht Wellmer, 'Terrorism and the Critique of Society', in *Observations on the Spiritual Situation of the Age*, p. 304 (trs. altered).

61. Jean-François Lyotard, 'Introduction' to *Des Dispositifs Pulsionnels*, 2nd edn., Paris 1980, p. 11.

62. *Minima Moralia*, p. 98.

between language-games, of a longing for the 'unity of experience', appears bizarre in the light of what can be seen as the fundamental project of *The Postmodern Condition:* an attempt to portray the cognitive and the aesthetic as *already* reconciled, under the headings of 'paralogism' and 'experimentation', and then to employ this con-flation as basis for an account of justice. In general, post-structuralist thought, with its strong resistance to categorial distinctions, and its inflation of concepts such as 'desire', 'power', or even 'language-game', seems in a poor position to accuse other theoretical traditions of totalizing aspirations.

The second enduring difficulty of post-structuralist thought con-cerns the discrepancy between a philosophical anti-humanism and a continued commitment to political principles whose content cannot be derived from aesthetic experience alone. Habermas pays tribute to the sensitivity of post-structuralism to the 'complex injuries and subliminal violences' of contemporary societies, but goes on to suggest that this sensitivity is implicitly dependent on 'the image of an undamaged intersubjectivity which first appeared to Hegel in the form of an ethical totality'.[63] The values of grace and illumination, ecstatic delight, corporeal integrity, wish-fulfillment and protective intimacy, which post-structuralist thinkers espouse, do not cover the moral bill which they implicitly draw on an intact everyday life-practice. There is a disparity between declared and disguised norm-ative foundations which can only be explained in terms of an undialectical rejection of subjectivity: the failure to recognize that the concept of the subject in modern thought does not merely imply a damagingly objectified relation to self, but also contains the promise of a self-conscious practice in which solidarity and auto-nomy can be reconciled. Habermas's argument appears confirmed by the fact that hints of this unacknowledged foundation occasionally intrude—almost like a lapsus—into the texts of post-structuralism. In *Discipline and Punish*, for example, Foucault remarks that the prisoner caught within the Panoptic system 'is seen, but he does not see; he is the object of information, never a subject in communi-cation.'[64] More generally, the development of French thought in the 1970s reveals—and Lyotard's well-meaning, but theoretically incoherent, interdictions of coercion and 'terror' clearly illustrate this point—that a liberal-universalist safety net was always tacitly spread beneath the highwire of the new Nietzscheanism. Nietzsche

---

63. *Der Philosophische Diskurs der Moderne*, p. 391.
64. Michel Foucault, *Discipline and Punish*, Harmondsworth 1979, p. 200.

well appreciated, and accepted, the consequences of a full-blown perspectivism. He understood that, if claims to universality can never be more than the mask of particular forces and interests, then 'life' cannot take the form of a harmonious plurality of standpoints, but is '*essentially* appropriation, injury, overpowering of the strange and weaker, suppression, severity, imposition of one's own forms, incorporation and, at the least and mildest, exploitation.'[65] It is from this implication of 'left' Nietzscheanism, almost as much as from Marxism, that the 'New Philosophers' recoiled in horror in the later nineteen seventies, ushering in the current French preoccupation with phenomenological ethics, liberal political theory, and the philosophy of human rights.

These theoretical gyrations, in their contrast with the steady development of Habermas's project, must ultimately be understood against the background of national history and politics. In a country where a revolutionary tradition—reinforced by the experience of the Resistance—spans the distinction between Left and Right, outright attacks on the 'totalitarianism' of Enlightenment inevitably take on something of the appearance of self-indulgent play: the political reaction to Marxism in France has taken the form of an oversimplified espousal of democratic and human rights. In Germany however, the country which, in Marx's phrase, has shared in the restorations of modern peoples, without sharing in their revolutions, the heritage of the bourgeois emancipation movements cannot be taken so readily for granted. The general contours of Habermas's work spring far more sharply into relief if one bears in mind the fragility of progressive bourgeois traditions in Germany, and indeed the origins of the Federal Republic itself: not the achievement of a capitalist class in pursuit of its own freedoms, or of a popular upheaval, but an imposition of victorious foreign armies. Habermas's critique of capitalism has never relied on an undervaluation of the historical achievement of the constitutional state: rather it is based on the inability of bourgeois society to fulfill its own initial democratic promise. In view of Habermas's repeated engagement, over the last ten years, in a defence of liberties, of the rights of dissent and civil disobedience, against an encroaching neo-conservatism, Lyotard's hints that the stress on 'communicational consensus' implies a 'call for order, a desire for unity, for identity, for security, or popularity', sound rather hollow.[66] It is tempting to reply that such consequences

---

65. Friedrich Nietzsche, *Beyond Good and Evil*, para. 259.
66. 'Answering the Question: What is Postmodernism', p. 73.

are far more likely to flow from a badly-thought-through assault on Enlightenment universalism.

Particularities of historical location and political culture need not simply result in a distortion or biasing of thought. Anomalous situations may also make possible a more acute insight into what is in fact a more general problem or condition. Habermas's shift from a production to a communications paradigm within Marxism can be seen in this light. By theorizing the moral-practical as an autonomous dimension of historical development, Habermas is able to resolve the problem to which accounts of postmodernity also propose a solution—the problem of linking up with existing forms of freedom and overcoming the sterility of total critique—without lapsing into a self-deluding transfiguration of the status quo. Participatory democracy, implying the restraint of the currently uncontrolled imperatives of economy and bureaucracy, is not simply a groundless utopian ideal, but an impulse and an aspiration which is actively embedded in modern societies. Furthermore, once the blinkers of an analysis based exclusively on the dialectic of instrumental reason—and which is shared by earlier Critical Theory and poststructuralism—are shed, this aspiration appears unmistakably as central to the Enlightenment project. It is true that Habermas's work does not hold up a mirror to contemporary experiences of fragmentation, loss of identity, and libidinal release, in the manner which has enabled post-structuralist writing to provide the 'natural' descriptive vocabulary for the culture of advanced consumer capitalism. But neither does it pay for its expressive adequacy and immediacy with a lack of theoretical and historical perspective.

The importance of such perspective is, of course, most clearly underlined by the contrast between postmodern theory's melodramatic portrayal of the grand finale of modernity, and Habermas's contention that modernity is necessarily subject to recurrent crisis, insofar as it is the first form of society which cannot draw uncritically on the resources of tradition, but is obliged to unfold its fundamental norms from within itself. From this standpoint, the post-structuralist thinkers appear simply as the most recent of a long line of critics who—under the pressure of social crisis—have doubted the capacity of modernity to generate such norms. Admittedly, there are difficulties and ambiguities in Habermas's present position, as there would be in any project of comparable scope. For some, the stress on the irreducibility of system to life-world sets up too sharp a distinction between domains of action, and represents an unjustified a priori containment of democratic aspirations. For others, Habermas's account of the rational structures of communication fails to link up adequately with the necessarily concrete forms of political association and struggle. Furthermore, it could be contended that Habermas's central concern with the reification of the life-world tends to obscure the continued importance of traditional forms of gender- and class-based domination—although, in the latter case, Habermas appears to believe that the future quiescence of major class conflict will depend on the retention of at least the basic fabric of the welfare state.[67] However, the most cogent objections to Habermas have usually come from within the left, and this means from amongst those committed to the achievements of modernity, and aware of the difficulties and dangers of their casual dismissal. No postmodern thinker has yet succeeded in demonstrating that the vision of an 'undamaged intersubjectivity' has lost its hold over the modern political imagination; or that the autonomous logic of communicative action which modernity has laid bare is *inherently* incapable of sustaining a social order beyond the constraints and oppressions of both authoritarian socialism, and an increasingly troubled late capitalism.

Peter Dews

67. For critical essays raising some of these issues, see the special number of *New German Critique* on Habermas, no. 35, Spring/Summer 1985.

1.

Ideologies and Society in the Post-War World

I should like to begin with the general theme of our Special Issue, 'Thirty Years After'. For us these thirty years refer to the founding of the State of Israel. What does this date mean to you? What hopes did you have in 1948, what expectations have been fulfilled after thirty years and what disappointments have there been?

If any expectations have been fulfilled, they are not the ones we had as schoolboys at the time. Following a brief interregnum lasting a few years, the Currency Reform ushered in the reconstruction of the capitalist economy and a social restoration whose dynamism exceeded my wildest imaginings at the end of the war. My expectations and those of my friends were in fact somewhat idealistic. We were living in a state of shock at the Nazi atrocities, which were first revealed at the Nuremberg Tribunal, and a little later in a series of documentary films. We believed that a spiritual and moral renewal was indispensable and inevitable. Nothing much came of it. And it did not take thirty years to perceive this. I remember an election-campaign meeting of the chairman of the national-conservative German Party in 1949, all decorated with the black-white-and-red flag. I ran out on the spur of the moment when they sang the first stanza of *Deutschland über Alles*.[1] Some months later the same man, Herr Seebohm, became a minister in the first Federal Government under Adenauer. In short, the hopes I had at that time were so unrealistic that I cannot begin to relate them to the present day.

---

1. Since 1945 only the third stanza is officially acknowledged. Black, white and red were the colours of Prussia and the Reich.

Then let me give the question a personal slant. How did the world appear to you as a 15/16 year old who had experienced five years of war and spent his entire youth under the Hitler regime? What influence did this have on your intellectual development? And did these factors have a general significance?

Although the town in which I returned to school in the autumn of 1945 was not very badly damaged, we experienced our world as it was reflected in the spare prose of Andersch, Richter and, later, Böll, in the so-called *Trümmerliteratur* [literature of the rubble] and in anti-fascist memoirs. Books that come to mind are Ernst Kogon's *SS State*, Günter Weisenborn's *Memorial*, and then Sartre's *The Flies* and *In Camera*. Material deprivation (hunger and cold to begin with), the reduction of the economy to basics, the purely local nature of the authorities, the duplication of the administration into civil and military spheres, then the predominance of small groups and primary relations after the collapse of the central institutions and organizations—at the time all this constituted the horizon which delimited our unsociological view of the world. Our problems were moral and existential in the first instance. The grand anthropological concepts we brought to bear were grotesquely irrelevant to the social and economic problems of a reconstruction which, as soon became apparent, had been set up irreversibly along capitalist lines. And for me personally all this took place against the background of a mood of War Socialism and a programme of the 'Third Way' which would cut across all party differences.

We younger people were mainly absorbed in a step-by-step recuperation of the modern movement which had been suppressed in Germany. This meant in the first instance the years following the First World War: the Haubrich Collection opened our eyes to expressionist painting; we read expressionist poems from Trakl to Benn, and were introduced to functionalism and the Bauhaus. Sartre's novels and O. F. Bollnow's account of existentialism led us back to Kafka and Rilke. The contemporary cultural scene was dominated by novels like Thomas Mann's *Dr Faustus* and Hesse's *The Glass Bead Game*. Films like *The Third Man* stamped the experience of an entire generation.

Looking back now I realize with some astonishment just how German and how provincial these perspectives were, even though for us they opened up a whole new world. While I was still studying in Bonn, that is to say up to 1954, I found myself in a university environment where, in the arts and social sciences, the thirties and forties had not implied any break, and the traditions of the 1920s were simply resumed without debate. Admittedly, in philosophical anthropology we now read Plessner as well as Gehlen, and in phenomenology we learned about Eugen Fink and Ludwig Landgrebe as well as Oskar Becker. We also made use of the books Löwith had written in emigration. But we were told nothing about Marx, any more than about analytical philosophy, Freud, sociology or social theory. While I was still at school I had read the pamphlets of Marx and Engels, which were published in East Berlin and distributed by the Communist bookshop in Gummersbach, at a time when there was not much else to read apart from Rowohlt magazines.[2] By chance I also came across Lukács's early writings while I was still a student. Of course the scene changed dramatically during the fifties. With the return of René König to Cologne, Plessner to Göttingen, Francis to Munich and Horkheimer to Frankfurt, sociology was re-established as an academic discipline. Sociological ideas even entered public consciousness. Thanks to the writings of Bloch and Adorno we discovered, to our astonishment, that Marx was not over and done with, that the Marxist tradition was of more than historical and philological interest, and could be of relevance to systematic inquiry. The same was true of psychoanalysis. I had, in fact, studied psychology and had even heard of 'depth psychology'. But it was not until 1956, when I heard the Freud lectures which were organized on the initiative of Max Horkheimer and Alexander Mitscherlich, that I grasped the fact that Freud had created a scientific theory which had to be taken seriously, and a school of psychoanalysis of far-reaching importance. Finally, we became familiar with the dominant philosophical school in the Anglo-Saxon countries through the writings of Carnap, Wittgenstein and Popper. We realized that the theory of science and liguistic analysis had set standards of rigour which continental philosophy could no longer satisfy. In literature, music and art, in art-criticism and art-theory too, the reception of that genuine modernism which is sustained by a radical avant-garde consciousness became more widespread, but not, if I remember rightly, until the second half of the fifties. As the chief interpreters of this modernism, Adorno, and through him Benjamin, played a vital role.

---

2. Before Rowohlt started to print their paperback books, following the occupation of Germany, they published books in newspaper format.

You ask about the influence of Hitlerism on my intellectual development and also what possible general significance it had. Well, all biographical facts have an idiosyncratic element. Perhaps I could say in general that the intellectual and cultural provincialism we were plunged into by the Nazis was not overcome at a stroke, but relatively slowly. The traditions of the Enlightenment and of radical modernism did not become generally accepted before the end of the fifties. However, when they did achieve a breakthrough, it was with fewer reservations than at any previous time in German history. Incidentally, this breakthrough would have been scarcely conceivable without the outstanding intellectual impact of the last generation of German-Jewish scholars, philosophers and artists who returned to Germany after everything was over, either in person or through their works and writings. Their productivity had been dammed up during the emigration, but it now flowed all the more vigorously. I myself did not become aware of the part played by intellectuals of Jewish origin in the cultural development of the Federal Republic until 1959, when I prepared a study of the role of Jewish philosophers in German Idealism as part of a series of broadcasts portraying aspects of German-Jewish intellectual history.

Why do you emphasize that? In what sense did Jews have an influence as Jews *in German intellectual life, particularly after 1945?*

Gershom Scholem has said what there is to say about the price the Jews had to pay for their assimilation into German culture throughout the nineteenth and twentieth centuries. On the other hand, not even Scholem denies that German culture enjoyed one of its happiest moments at the very period when the ghettoes opened and the assimilation of the Jews began. This explains the enthusiasm of Jewish intellectuals for the epoch of German Classicism, and it provides one reason for the incomparable creative benefits brought to German culture by the Jews from that time on. Despite the rich fruits that fell to German culture as a result of this process, not even the Jewish intellectuals, the 'cultured Jews' [*Bildungsjuden*] as the contemptuous phrase went, were permitted to achieve a complete assimilation. And of course this applied with even greater force to other Jews. Hence the condition of exile persisted in the midst of the most creative assimilation. The Zionists then drew their own consequences from this situation.

When we contemplate the ambivalence of German-Jewish intellectual history, we can perceive the unique opportunity which a crass

irony of history had given to the last generation of Jewish intellectuals, once the Nazis and their intellectual retinue had succeeded in
poisoning or obscuring even our best traditions. We young people,
who were privileged not by our merit, but simply by our age, were
able to acquire a distinctive perspective from the teachers who now
returned from emigration. H. Plessner once defined this perspective
in the words: without estrangement, no understanding. What it
amounts to is that those who had long been part of German culture,
without ever really belonging to it, taught us how to identify with
our own, with German traditions, and yet while standing within
them, to keep a certain distance from them, which enabled us to
continue them in a self-critical spirit, with the scepticism and the
clairvoyance of the man who has already once been fooled.

*I would like to go back to my initial question. You described the hopes
you had immediately after the war as unrealistic, and ruled them out
as a standard by which to judge the present. What about the hopes
and disappointments of the last thirty years? Which events had the
most powerful influence on you?*

Whatever view is taken today of the political significance of Stalin's
Note of March 1952,[3] this was a date that played a major role in my
own life because, in rejecting this offer, the Federal Government
ensured the military integration of the Federal Republic into the
Western hemisphere. This meant that we had to abandon all hope of
a neutralist solution which might have prevented the two social
systems on German soil from becoming sealed off from each other.
The change in *Ostpolitik* introduced a decade and a half later by
Willy Brandt was no more than the logical extension of this first (and
only) basic *foreign policy* decision taken by the Federal Republic.

As far as international relations in general are concerned, I am not
unaware of the significance of the strategic balance between the
superpowers. But I cannot claim to have ever been passionately
interested in East-West relations. The conflicts with an inbuilt
developmental dynamic are to be found on the North-South axis.
That could be seen very early on, at least as far back as the Bandung

---

3. Stalin's Note of March 1952 to the three Western powers proposed a peace treaty
with Germany and the creation of a united, neutral Germany on the basis of the
frontiers agreed at Potsdam in 1945. The Allies, with Adenauer's approval, refused to
discuss a peace treaty until after general elections had taken place throughout the
whole of Germany. It is widely believed in Germany, particularly on the Left, that
the last opportunity for a real settlement was thus missed.

Conference. But it was not until later that the problematic nature of this relationship became dramatically clear, and was first taken seriously, on the domestic front. In this context the American intervention in the civil war in Vietnam, the Chinese Cultural Revolution and the oil crisis have highlighted the underlying tensions more effectively than the national liberation movements themselves.

In Germany the Adenauer-Erhard regime established itself for the long term, following its return to power with an absolute majority in 1953, even though there was to be sharp conflict on the question of equipping the *Bundeswehr* with nuclear weapons. Against this back-cloth of a long period of political stagnation, the election of Heinemann as Federal President and the formation of the first Brandt government in 1969 were events that made a deep impression on me.

I was also relieved to see that the student movement did not immediately trigger off the much-feared backlash but led instead to a loosening of the political fronts, a liberalization of the intellectual climate and even to the spread of radical democratic ideas. But the profound shifts of attitude that marked this phase did not last long. From around 1972 the reactions set in. In addition economic crises made their appearance. They are still with us today and are cleverly manipulated by a crisis management that uses them as a means of maintaining a feeling of anxiety and inducing a sense of 'realism', behind which are hidden the economistic values of the postwar reconstruction generation (as embodied in Helmut Schmidt). Today, stimulated by these newly aroused economic fears, neo-conservative attitudes are gaining ground. They involve the abandonment of the abstract universalism of the Enlightenment, the discrediting of notions of progress, the revaluation of traditional ways of life, historicist modes of thought, the development of subcultures based on oriental traditions, and so on.

In this context I find the vulnerability of our political culture disturbing. This vulnerability becomes more apparent the more tightly acts of terrorism—themselves hard to explain—intermesh with a bureaucratic control of ideas which flourishes in the shadow of terrorism. I mention terrorist outrages in the same breath as the practice of vetting applicants for the public service (and recently this has included their relatives as well) because both the terrorists and those who derive advantage from terrorism promote a form of consciousness that is very typical of the way in which Germans tend to fetishize security under the rule of law. This fetishizing of the rule of law did not succeed in defending us against Hitler's legalistic rise to power, but time and again it has dulled our capacity to distinguish between an authoritarian and a democratic form of state.

If you were to compare the social systems in East and West—what you would call 'late-capitalist' and 'state-socialist' societies—how would you judge the achievements of the past thirty years? Which hopes have been fulfilled and which haven't?

A large and rather difficult question. Anyone who grew up as I did in West Germany after the war, in other words, face to face with the DDR, had no chance of being under any illusions about the repressive conditions prevailing in the Soviet sphere of influence. Those of us who became socialists under the intellectual influence of an unorthodox Western Marxism did so despite, and not because of, conditions in the Eastern bloc. I am unable to persuade myself that, from the standpoint of social evolution, state socialism is any more 'mature' or 'progressive' than late capitalism. It is probable that both forms of society represent variants of the same stage of development in which, as we can see from the growing dependence of the countries with state-controlled trade on the capitalist world market, the USA, the EEC and Japan are still the pacesetters. If you really want to analyse trends in social development you probably have to look at the internal conflicts in the advanced capitalist societies, and at the conflicts generated by the international division of labour, in other words the North-South antagonisms.

I can understand neither those students in our universities who, after the collapse of the protest movement, went over to a party on the Soviet model, nor the so-called 'New Philosophers' in Paris who remained unaware of the true nature of bureaucratic socialism until they had read Solzhenitsyn—and who now throw out the baby with the bathwater. These things are two sides of the same coin. I welcome the move towards Eurocommunism in the Western parties —although it has been far too long in coming. But I only say this by way of explaining why for me Soviet Marxism could never be the privileged object of vast hopes or profound disappointments, and why I was never able to get excited about it.

How would you characterize the two social systems today? How far do they share common problems, similar crises? What direction are they moving in? What analogies or distinctions would you draw?

If one has to address such huge issues in the framework of an interview, in other words, casually, I suppose one has to be willing to simplify. In both East and West we have modern class societies, that is to say societies in which the state and the economy assume distinct forms. I am using the word 'class' in its Marxist sense. Class structures persist as long as the means of production and socially useful labour-power are deployed according to preferences which reflect sectional interests in society. At any rate they do not express the universal interests of the population as a whole, or the compromises the population might be prepared to make. In state-socialist societies the bureaucratic elites which control the means of production form an opaque, complex system. This system is essentially authoritarian and has shown itself to be impervious to democratic decision-making processes with regard to the priorities of society as a whole. In late capitalist societies the power structures are even less transparent. To the extent to which the priorities of society take shape in an unplanned way, as the secondary consequences of the strategies of private enterprise, class structures survive here too. Control over the means of production by political elites, on the one hand, and by private privilege, on the other, are variant forms of class relations at the stage of development reached by modern societies. It is noteworthy that Western societies are the more successful in *both* dimensions, in the development of the forces of production and in what Max Weber called 'legal domination'. Carter's 'human rights' policy has obvious ideological components, but it can base itself on the fact that it is only in Western nations that the precarious and continually threatened achievements of bcurgeois emancipation and the workers' movement are guaranteed to any extent worth mentioning. This applies, incidentally, to the Federal Republic too, despite the disturbing weaknesses and the shallow historical roots of our political culture. And we know just how important bourgeois freedoms are. For when things go wrong it is those on the Left who become the first victims.

Where do you see the main crisis tendencies on both sides?

That can't be answered in a few words. Both systems find themselves confronting similar problems in their own way. Putting on one side the question of the strategic relations of the super-powers, the first set of problems arises in the wake of bureaucratization, of the development of overcomplex forms of organization, in relation to the running of the state administration and the economy. These developments ensure that crisis-management becomes a permanent problem on every level, a problem of which the public becomes increasingly conscious and one which, as I have already suggested, gives rise to diffuse anxieties and possibilities of intimidation. The fear of crisis favours forces that can present themselves as the guardians of order. On occasion it can be a party like the PCI which assumes this role; but the Bonapartist, or perhaps rather Francoist danger stems from the fact that such power vacuums can arise in the first place.

I have already discussed the second set of problems, those arising from the power relations which structure the world economy, and from the international division of labour. Thirdly, ecological problems will intensify but probably on a longer time-scale than suggested by the dramatic prognoses of the early seventies. But I do not feel especially competent to judge these matters.

As to the specific trends in Western societies, I must admit that I do not have much confidence in the predictive power of the various economic crisis theories. But I do believe that the continuing vitality of the capitalist global economy is giving rise to a succession of problems which could impede the further advance of the accumulation process. And in that event I do not see how capitalist societies could adjust, if not to zero growth, then at least to a greatly reduced and qualitatively regulated process of growth, without its affecting the very foundations of capitalism.

It may be an idiosyncrasy of mine, or perhaps rather a legacy of the Frankfurt School, that, of all these side-effects, I find myself most fascinated by those which jeopardize social and cultural integration—that is to say, the potential crises that initially assume socio-psychological form. Referring to these new problems of motivation and legitimation Dan Bell talks of 'the cultural contradictions of capitalism'. Such matters may not be of burning importance in Israel, given present circumstances. But this situation could easily change. If the present genuine prospects for peace were realized, and a settlement reached with her Arab neighbours, an economic development could result in which Israel would emerge as a sort of German Federal Republic of the Middle East.

Let us stay with a comparison of the two systems, for a moment. Which strata are responsible for change in each case? What is the role played in this context by movements such as the student movement on the one side, and the dissidents on the other?

You cannot draw a direct parallel between the two movements; they are not functional equivalents. In countries where social integration has to be secured by means of a state-licensed world view, any criticism emanating from the intellectuals represents a direct political threat. Dissidents who are willing to put themselves at risk can put the state's power of veto to good use. Furthermore they can lay claim to rights that are in part guaranteed by existing law, in part integral components of the official ideology. In either case they can appeal to the humanist content of socialism. The more they take their stand on socialist principles and develop a radical, yet fundamentally immanent critique, the greater the threat they pose to the party bureaucracy. By the same token, the more they tend to criticize socialism from outside and forge alliances with conservative forces in the West, the weaker their influence is likely to be. Of course their chances of success are also related to the speed with which structural pressures of modernization are making the outmoded ideological mechanisms of integration ineffective. They depend too on an effective feedback between the internal socialist opposition and the Eurocommunist parties in the West. I can see trends here that justify a cautious optimism. However that may be, these opposition movements are in the tradition of the European Enlightenment, the bourgeois liberation movements and the classical workers' movement.

The youth rebellion of the sixties is a complex phenomenon with a *different* historical significance. Here I can only venture hypotheses. Regarded as a social movement, the students had at best a nuisance value which, under certain circumstances, sufficed to achieve a malfunctioning of various aspects of society, but not to bring about a rational transformation of fundamental social structures—something which the dissident movement might conceivably achieve in the future. Looking back now on the protest movement that sprang up in the universities in the West, I see it as arising from certain favoured social strata, and as marked by the circumstances of the economic boom. As such I regard it as a special case of those neo-populist currents which cannot be properly absorbed by the political parties. Such movements react to the forms of economic and administrative rationality which permeate every aspect of life in the wake of the process of capitalist growth. Such forms penetrate deeper and deeper into the self-regenerating processes of nature, and consume the historical substance of traditional, pre-bourgeois ways of life, but without creating any new forms of solidarity or any new possibilities of a non-instrumental relation with nature, whether with outer nature or with the human body. The student movement was a transitory phenomenon, but it resembles other grassroots movements of a similarly ambivalent character, partly progressive, partly backward-looking. Comparable needs are articulated in the women's movement, in the ecological protest groups, in citizen's initiatives, in the resistance of the anti-nuclear lobby, in regionalist movements, unofficial strikes and factory occupations. The student movement directed people's attention in a spectacular way to these new areas of potential conflict.

Could you say something more about these movements from the standpoint of alienation? To what extent can people become conscious of an objectively existing alienation? Are the anarchist Left, the ecological movement, the anti-psychiatry movement also the expression of what we might call a falsely objectified alienation? Do these movements tend to miss the point because they only address the symptoms, since their members have in fact internalized the normative structures of capitalism all too thoroughly? Is there such a thing as an unconscious class struggle? And are there ways of raising it to consciousness?

I don't much care for the term 'alienation'; it is too woolly. In bourgeois cultural criticism it signifies a sort of anthropological or even metaphysical disaster. In American social psychology 'alienation' covers almost every form of deviant, or even simply non-conformist behaviour. In the young Marx the concept was clearly linked to the structure of alienated labour, of the labour process under conditions of commodity production. It is precisely when one wishes to retain such a concept of alienation in social theory that one is forced to concede that a definition based exclusively on the production process has become too narrow. We have to take the arguments of the systems theorists seriously. All modern economies are so complex that a complete shift to participatory decision-making processes, that is to say, a democratic restructuring at *every* level, would inevitably do damage to some of the sensitive requirements of contemporary organizations. If we wish to maintain such organizations at their present level of complexity, then it is probable that the idea of socialism can no longer (and need no longer) be realized by means of the emancipation from alienated labour. It may be that initiatives to democratize global economic priorities and to create humane working conditions can only come from outside in future, by which I mean that a *thoroughgoing internal* reorganization of the economy in accordance with the principles of self-administration is neither possible nor necessary. Such an *external* linking of the economy—to overstate the case a little—to democratic decision-making processes is a necessary condition, though not a sufficient one, for communal forms of collective life, for forms of life which are no longer regulated by the uncontrolled process of accumulation, or moulded by forms of economic and administrative rationality. Conversely, without a reorganization of living conditions, the basis for an effective democratic will-formation will be missing. I have put this very crudely and misleadingly in order to establish a particular, not undangerous thesis: a concept of alienation in contemporary social theory would have to be reformulated in a more abstract way. It would lead away from the analysis of the commodity form towards a critique of instrumental and functional rationality.

What would that mean when applied to the movements we were speaking of?

You mentioned the revival of anarchist thinking on the Left. You might also have included the rediscovery of Surrealism in the sixties, or the intellectual spin-offs of the student movement—for example, Foucault's critique of the forms and norms of bourgeois rationality in medicine, law and sexuality (already anticipated in the *Dialectic of Enlightenment*), or such practical consequences of the protest movement as anti-psychiatry, the critical law movement, criticism of the media (along the lines of Enzensberger's theory of the media), as well as the experiments in anti-authoritarian education, the 'democratization of art', and the emergence of a professional radicalism among doctors, architects, lawyers, scientists, the clergy, and so forth. These are all phenomena which resist decoding in terms of the classical concept of alienated labour because, without exception, they are the outcome of experiences outside the sphere of production. You are absolutely right that they contain a potential whose ambivalent nature needs much closer scrutiny before we can arrive at a theoretical explanation. It seems that we are faced neither with organized resistance of a clearly political nature, nor, as your question would seem to suggest, with a new kind of false consciousness. What we have is rather a highly selective set of sensitivities and rebellions, confined to certain strata, directed against reifying tendencies in predominantly cultural sectors which have suffered the encroachment of economic and administrative rationality. They are also in my view reactions against the displacement of social conflicts into realms which hitherto have come into the category of the private sphere, the merely psychological. That is to say they are reactions against the off-loading of social costs onto the isolated individual.

Such mechanisms for resolving conflict are gaining in importance in countries like the Federal Republic where social integration still functions smoothly at the level of institutions, the trade unions, political parties, law courts, the mass media, and so on. We will discover in the coming decades whether the potential for deviant behaviour, the substance of conflict, which today is being transferred to the private and cultural spheres, will be absorbed by rapidly growing social bureaucracies. We will see whether this substance, which is currently revealed in criminal activities, schooling problems, psychosomatic illness, alcoholism, the proliferation of group therapies, the retreat to rural communes, the fascination with gurus, the revival of meditational techniques (even in the Churches) and also in a new religiosity, and is fragmented into various subcultural domains, can be processed administratively, that is within the permitted forms of rationality. If so, this would give rise to a huge administrative apparatus dedicated to the control of motivation and, basically, to social therapy. This apparatus would stretch from the security services and the authorities concerned with controlling opinion, through a psychologized penal system, socio-psychiatric institutions, psychotherapeutic guidance systems for parents, young people and the old, and through to the public education system. In my view one of the great achievements of the student movement and its offshoots is that a start has been made on deprivatizing such sources of conflict and on opening them up to forms of practical rationality. I would not speak in terms of an unconscious class struggle. But a theory which could analyse these new areas of conflict would have to start from the premise that structurally-based class conflict is in a state of suspension in politically sensitive key areas and has instead been shifted into the margins of society.

Could you say something more specifically about the role of the intellectual in contemporary society? To start with: what were the most important ideologies in Europe between 1948 and 1978? What is your view of existentialism in particular?

If by 'ideology' you mean the most important intellectual movements, the most influential, philosophically-inspired styles of thought, I would in fact nominate existentialism for the post-war period, particularly in its Sartrean variant; after that I would mention positivism, which brought technocratic conceptions in its wake; and lastly, Western Marxism, which assumed phenomenological and later structuralist features in France, while in Germany it developed along Hegelian lines, in a tradition leading from Lukács and Korsch to Critical Theory. Like my friend K. O. Apel, I have always regarded existentialism and positivism in the wider sense as complementary phenomena. Between them they implement a division of labour. Positivism, and in this context I would include Popper's philosophy under this heading, sees its task as being to establish the objective status of the sciences, to privilege them as the sole legitimate form of knowledge and the only way to achieve systematic cognitive progress. The theoretico-political impulse underlying the Vienna Circle was to draw a demarcation line between science and 'metaphysics', in other words, all other kinds of knowledge, which were thereby downgraded to mere forms of expression. The aim was to expel the charlatans once and for all from the temple of an Enlightenment which was now to be made watertight at the cost of a general levelling down. The search for demarcation criteria has long since been abandoned, but this impulse continued for a long time to animate the main currents of analytical philosophy. For its part, existentialism engaged in a complementary politics of demarcation. From the early Jaspers right through to the late Kolakowski the protagonists of this tendency have been agreed that an objectivist concept of science guarantees an autonomous sphere *beyond the reach of binding argument* to philosophical faith, intuitive thought, myth and, in general, all the non-objectifiable experiences of historical existence. Both schools reject as 'gnostic' everything which resists the dichotomy between an empiricist interpretation of science and an appeal to the powers of faith. Most characteristically, they reject the Marxist theory of society and psychoanalysis, since both attempt to introduce the element of self-reflexion into the construction of scientific theories. Critical Theory, for example, retains a concept of reason which asserts itself simultaneously against both scientistic mutilation and existentialist downgrading, and which is furthermore also critically applied to itself. In consequence a complacent faith in rationalism is ruled out, and neither does the philosophy of history degenerate into mystification. The *Dialectic of Enlightenment* attempts to salvage the normative substance of concepts such as ego-autonomy and the emancipation of society, by criticizing the ideological misuse of such concepts just as relentlessly as it does the positivist campaign to cleanse our consciousness of transcendental perspectives entirely.

You refer to the Dialectic of Enlightenment. *It is a book that appeared thirty years ago. Is it still representative of the Critical*

Theory you defend today?

It was not until the late sixties that the Frankfurt thinkers began to be considered as a school in the eyes of the politicized students and the general public. The fact is that a coherence of views powerful enough to form a school only existed in emigration in New York, when the old members of the Institute for Social Research, Pollock, Marcuse, Löwenthal, Adorno, Kirchheimer and Neumann, were working together closely and productively, with Horkheimer as the moving spirit. This phase lasted until 1940. After the War, Horkheimer and Adorno were influential in the Federal Republic, as was Marcuse somewhat later. It was only at this late stage that Critical Theory gained a wide audience; and this was not primarily through philosophical works such as Adorno's *Negative Dialectics* or *Aesthetic Theory*, but rather as a sort of pessimistically tinted cultural criticism. This fact actually exposes some real weaknesses. Adorno took the aphoristic mode of philosophizing to extremes. He made the idea of thinking in fragments into a programme, keeping his distance, an excessive distance in my view, from the general scientific enterprise. This led to three principal weaknesses. In the first place, Critical Theory never really took the theoretical contributions of the social sciences and analytical philosophy seriously. It never engaged with them systematically, as it should have done, given its own intentions. Hence, secondly, it took refuge in an abstract critique of instrumental reason and made only a limited contribution to the empirical analysis of the over-complex reality of our society. And finally, it failed to give an unambiguous account of its own normative foundations, its own status. Adorno denied that it was possible to provide a systematic grounding of the concept of reason to which he always implicitly appealed. This aporia, incidentally, is one reason why I have attempted to elaborate a theory of communicative action, of action orientated towards validity claims.

The demise of the Frankfurt School has often been announced.

I mention these three defects because they are a negative pointer to the direction in which my colleagues and I are trying to advance our theoretical work today. But there is no longer any question of a school, and that is undoubtedly a good thing. Furthermore, there have been trends in the Federal Republic during the seventies which react pretty sharply to what many people consider to be the 'cultural hegemony' of the Left. The forms taken by this change in climate [*Tendenzwende*] differ from country to country. To the critique of the 'New Philosophers' in Paris, and of the conservative sociological theorists grouped around East Coast journals like *Commentary* and *Social Policy* in the USA, there corresponds in the Federal Republic only a motley coalition which revives anti-Enlightenment ideological positions, and endows them with an emphasis which manages to be both liberal-conservative and scientistic at the same time. It draws on a broad heritage stretching from Carl Schmitt to certain variants of neo-Aristotelianism, taking up Gehlen and Heidegger *en route*. These diffuse trends only acquire a certain political and ideological coherence by virtue of their resolute assault on the common enemy.

And what role do intellectuals play in society? I am less interested in the sociological aspects of this question than in those concerning the philosophy of science. In this context how would you define the difference between your conception of science and that of Karl Popper? Could you say something about the accusation of decisionism that you levelled against Popper?

Popper's model of empirical-analytical science fails to do justice to the most fruitful theoretical developments in the social sciences, from Durkheim, Freud, Mead and Piaget down to Chomsky, Luhmann, Kohlberg and others. I do not need to emphasize that I have learned an enormous amount from Popper. He is one of the great figures in that admirable process of self-criticism through which the analytical theory of science has matured and cast off its dogmatism, culminating in the insight, which emerged from the controversy with Kuhn, that the rational reconstruction of the history of science is itself a hermeneutical enterprise *par excellence*. Of course, my view is that, in his legitimate criticism of the practice of reducing the theory of science to the investigation of the syntax and semantics of scientific language, Popper—to put it crudely—has not gone far enough. Even Ch. S. Peirce took a more radical view than Popper of the pragmatic dimension of scientific logic and of the systematic importance of the 'context of discovery' (and the 'context of application'). To my way of thinking Popper draws far too rigid a distinction between the logic of scientific discovery on the one hand, and its psychology and sociology on the other. The difference of opinion you have in mind is connected with this.

In his reconstructive analyses Popper does away with both the context of discovery and the context of application, from which the theories of the social sciences emerge and in which they become effective. Hence in his view only those sociological approaches have a legitimate status which yield information usable in social technologies, and which find their practical point of reference in piecemeal social engineering. As opposed to this, I would defend the traditions of research in social theory and psychoanalysis, as well as in cognitive developmental psychology, which have a different practical point of reference; they aim to enlighten people and groups who are in need of orientation about themselves and about their social situation, the network of interests and the formative processes which make their activities possible, control them, and—in certain cases— subject them to pathological constraints.

The reproach of decisionism is connected with something else, namely the problem of rational foundations. Popper over-extends the methodological power of the negative with his theory of falsification, and makes the critical method of refutation autonomous. In this he is not unlike Adorno (and for that matter he finds himself in agreement with the radical Jewish traditions whose roots have been uncovered by Scholem). In consequence he denies himself the possibility of validating criticism itself as a rational activity. For Popper criticism is ultimately just *one* option among others. He is forced to rely on a *decision* for rationality, on a critical attitude, a readiness to engage in criticism, and on the traditions that produce such a disposition. I believe I can show that a species that depends for its survival on the structures of linguistic communication and cooperative, purposive-rational action, must *of necessity* rely on reason. In the validity claims, however implicit, by means of which we are obliged to orientate ourselves in our communicative actions, a persistent, albeit repeatedly suppressed, claim of reason lies concealed.

Of course there are no metaphysical guarantees of any sort that this claim of reason will prove historically efficacious or assume an institutional form. But I believe that a partiality for reason has a different status from any other commitment.

How do you interpret the fact that in the Anglo-Saxon world the roles of the sociologist and the philosopher are rigorously separated, whereas your work is sociological and philosophical at the same time?

There is a trivial answer to that question. In the German educational system subjects like psychology and sociology only became distinct disciplines relatively late on. The process of professionalization started later in Germany that in the USA. Right up to the fifties we had philosophers who could still be taken seriously as psychologists (Rothacker), anthropologists (Gehlen) or sociologists (Plessner), maintaining combinations of a kind which Max Scheler represented in the 1920s. In the case of the old Frankfurt Institute members there is the additional factor that, in the Marxist tradition, a division of labour between philosophy on the one hand, and economics, psychology and the social sciences in general on the other, was only held to be meaningful if they were integrated within the context of a general programme of theoretical enquiry. The programmatic statements of the old Institute for Social Research, Horkheimer's Inaugural Lecture as Director in particular, all give expression to the conviction that only if philosophy establishes links with the social sciences can it survive as a significant discipline concerned with substantial questions, and thus escape the fate of withering away into a merely formalistic discipline. And by the same token, the social sciences can only be preserved from declining into a sterile positivism by functioning within the framework of a philosophically-based theory of society. Furthermore, Horkheimer—and this relates directly to your question—had actually distinguished Critical Theory from 'traditional' theory by the claim that Critical Theory remains conscious of its connection with practical life. How can the philosopher hope, if not to eliminate, then at least to undermine reflexively the role divisions of academic enquiry, if he allows himself to be cut off from all substantive questions and hence from a theoretically-informed stance towards contemporary political issues? As for myself, I am like one of the Last of the Mohicans. I studied mainly philosophy and psychology with Rothacker, learned sociology as Adorno's assistant, took my second doctorate in political science under Abendroth, and subsequently occupied Horkheimer's chair in Philosophy and Sociology. In 1971, after I had left Frankfurt, the chair ceased to cover the two disciplines. At the institutional level, then, the neat division of labour I referred to earlier was established in the Federal Republic—doubtless to the great satisfaction of our strictly sociological sociologists.

But your original question was less concerned with the institutional side. Can there and should there be philosophers who, without lowering their theoretical standards, and indeed by virtue of their theoretical expertise, can conceive of their profession as entailing a public, politically effective role? I think the answer is yes; and as the example of Charles Taylor proves, such people can also exist in the Anglo-Saxon world, and even in Oxford.

Furthermore, can and should a philosophy exist which communicates with the individual sciences, not just on a metatheoretical level, but in terms of substantive issues? If you defend the concept of distinct unitary sciences, however you interpret the term, both questions have to be answered in the negative. By contrast, I believe that to the extent that the human sciences convert philosophical questions into problems capable of scientific analysis, they will diverge increasingly from this empiricist model, and that in this context philosophy has a duty to promote strong theoretical strategies which are opposed to inductionism and elementarism. I regard philosophy as the hitherto irreplaceable representative of a claim to unity and universality, which of course can be satisfied seriously either in the human sciences or not at all.

One last question: to whom is your philosophy addressed—to the person who wishes to learn about an object by approaching it from the outside, or to the individual who desires to find his bearings in his own lived world, the individual caught up in the problems of life?

If we set aside the problems of life for the moment, I do not think we have to choose between a sociological knowledge which lays claim to objectivity, and a practical knowledge-interest that aims at the transformation of information into what we may call understandings of particular situations, and life-orientations. But that is only true where sociological theory is not objectivist to start with, where, unlike behaviourist learning theory, it does not by its choice of basic concepts rule out every reference to, and every possibility of translation into, the traditional concepts which structure our daily lives.

But what relevance has a social theory to the life of the individual?

Do you mean to imply that theories in the tradition of Marx and Hegel are unable to fill the gap left by existentialism? A theory of society can perhaps provide a perspective, can offer—to put it cautiously—hopes and starting-points for the conquest of unhappiness and misery which are generated by the structure of social life. But it can do nothing to overcome the fundamental perils of human existence—such as guilt, loneliness, sickness and death. You could say that social theory offers no consolation, has no bearing on the individual's need for salvation. Marxist hopes are of course directed towards a collective project, and hold out to the inividual only the vague prospect that forms of life with greater solidarity will be able to eradicate, or at least diminish, that element of guilt, loneliness, fear of sickness and death, for which social repressions bear the responsibility. But that is a poor substitute for consolation. It could even be said that a consciousness of the radical absence of consolation is fostered in the first place by theories which inform us about the stages of social development, more mature forms of organization, and the practice through which new social formations can be brought into existence, and in so doing repudiate religious notions of salvation. How can there be universal solidarity with the victims of merciless historical progress, when past crimes, when the sufferings, the humiliations and the misery of past generations, appear irreversible to the secular gaze, and beyond redress? Benjamin, groping for response to the horror of all this, developed the idea of an anamnetic solidarity, which could bring about atonement solely through the power of remembrance. Perhaps we can discern in Benjamin's sometimes crypto-theological reflections the outlines of a way of thinking which would attempt a serious answer to your question. I believe you will be more likely to find it there than in the early existentialist philosophy of Sartre. The problem is one which faces all modern societies once the religious traditions that point beyond the purely human realm have largely lost their former authority. I observe palpable regressions into new forms of paganism which undercut the ego-identity that was achieved by means of the major religions. If that is the case, then how can, if not the substance, then at any rate the humanizing power of traditions that protect us against such regressions, how can the legacy of religion be salvaged for the secular world? For the moment we can only say: not *as* a religious legacy.

Very well then, we should not ask too much of social theory. But how far can it exert a practical influence on the individual? And if you do aim at such an influence, what sort of commitment would you envisage?

Any practical, action-orientated influence on individuals and groups cannot be any better than the interpretations and explanations which the theoretical premises make possible in their application to specific situations. Beyond that, I can only give a strictly procedural reply: if a commitment is to be voluntarily entered into, then there must be sound reasons for it. Theories too can provide solid grounds. But reasons mediated by theory can only acquire will-forming force in political and moral-practical discourse. And since every commitment is concrete and specific, you cannot have any standard form of discourse, any discourse once and for all. In other words, not even a theory with practical intent can provide any more or anything other than, in the optimum case, a set of plausible hypotheses. It will depend on *continuities*, not only in the system of knowledge itself, but also in the discursive will-formation and in the self-reflexion of those who orientate themselves in action. For that there can be no substitute.

2.

Conservatism and Capitalist Crisis

There is much discussion today of the nature and causes of the crisis racking the advanced capitalist countries. How should we define its structural characteristics and draw up an initial balance sheet?

In general we can say that the economic crisis has got steadily worse. By now everyone knows that we are not dealing with a short recession, and that unemployment will be a problem well into the 1980s. This is an obvious fact. What we should explore is the impact of the slump on the consciousness of the working class. In Germany the crisis is having a disciplinary effect. That is, within the frame-work—or more accurately on the basis—of legally guaranteed social security, it has proved possible to nip protest movements in the bud. Although not entirely unexpected, this process demands some explanation. The constraining pressure of the crisis has not only prevented any electoral turbulence, it has evoked deep conservative sentiments amongst the population, which have found a cultural echo amongst intellectuals and in the rhetoric of political parties. This neo-conservative current, which first emerged in the early 1970s, has been enormously strengthened in the new economic environment.

In 1973 you gave a talk at the Goethe Institute in Rome whose title was Was Heisst Heute Krise? *Five years later, how would you reply to the same question: what is the meaning of 'crisis' today?*

I would say that in the last few years it has become clear that the origins of the crisis still lie in the economic system of capitalism, but that the Welfare State no longer allows the crisis to explode in an *immediately* economic form. Instead, when there is a recession and large-scale unemployment, the symptoms of the crisis are displaced into strains within the cultural and social order. Recent years have rather confirmed me in the conviction that today the onset of an economic crisis does not generally lead to a political response, either by organized workers or trade unions—or in our own case in Germany, by the Social Democratic Party—of a rationally calibrated type. Instead, reactions to the crisis take the very mediated form of an overloading of the mechanisms of social and cultural intergration. The result is a much bigger 'ideological discharge' than in periods of capitalist development characterized by high employment. The direction of this discharge is two-fold. On one hand the work ethic is incredibly re-inforced: there is a rehabilitation of competitive behaviour, pursuit of gain, and exaltation of virtues conducive to a high mobility of labour. For it is necessary to induce people to accept work they would not otherwise perform of their own free will, or for which they have not had the necessary preparation. The accent is thus placed on an acquisitive ethic and instrumental virtues. This orientation penetrates deeply into the first years of schooling, to the point of dominating the whole educational system.

The other direction taken by this 'ideological discharge' is a revitalization of traditional virtues and values: in the first instance those of an anti- or a-political private life, whose literary reflection is a new subjectivism, and a revival (in its own way a pleasing one) of poems and novels in lieu of critical or analytic works on the present historical epoch, or sociological and political treatises. The result is an essentially rhetorical response to the bureaucratization and other negative consequences of capitalist growth. But I think that we have to take seriously that aspect of the propaganda of the Right which deals with real needs and offers a conservative solution to real problems. For in the criticisms of bureaucratism, as in the revaluation of traditional ways of life, in the spontaneous reactions not only against the destruction of the environment but against the dangers of atomic energy, and even in the resistance to administratively imposed educational reforms, there is a basic problem at stake which was a very important one for both Marx and Weber. In the course of capitalist development and of a politically uncontrolled process of accumulation, the partial administrative and economic rationality that is functional to such an economic system gradually penetrates and restructures ever broader spheres of life, which should on their own be evolving completely different forms of rationality—that is, practical and moral agencies, democratic and participatory processes of forming a collective will. In other words, there is thus actually a greater need today for types of relations within which more sub-jectivity and more sentiment can find expression, in which affective conduct is taken more into account.

To conclude, one could say that the increased 'ideological discharge' that I have been discussing operates to diffuse conservative inter-pretations of problems which are properly speaking secondary dysfunctional effects of politically uncontrolled capitalist growth.

Should one include under this heading the outbreaks of apparently non-political protest, which seem typical of many Western countries today?

These represent the new element in what I call the 'potentials for protest'. The novelty of the situation in West Germany—it is probably different in Italy—is that the type of protest which domi-nated the national scene at the end of the sixties and the beginning of the seventies, emerging from the universities and spreading to strata of young workers and apprentices, has died down. This must also be numbered amongst the disciplinary effects of the crisis. In its place we have on the one hand the emergence of forms of revolt taking the direction of terrorism, and on the other hand less dramatic but emotionally powerful currents of neo-populist protest. The latter are a reflection of the inability of the traditional parties and trade union bureaucracies to canalize or specify key themes and conflicts ade-quately. I see in these protests the sign of a dissatisfaction which leads to an estrangement from parties as such. We have other indications of this: for example, public opinion polls now show that at any rate a significant percentage of the population is discontented, not merely with this or that party, this or that policy, but with the party system as such. This is the first time that this has happened in the Bundesrepublik since the war. Of course in other countries, this potential for protest has been canalized in petty-bourgeois directions: we need only think of Poujadism in France or the emergence of parties against taxes in Denmark. But in West Germany no canaliz-ation of this kind has so far occurred; we are still at the first stage of attempts to form parties on such economic issues. However, I am convinced that as soon as these currents organize themselves into parties, it will become clear that their real potential for protest cannot be encapsulated in this form. By nature they cannot let themselves be institutionally interpreted by parties and routed through parliaments, without the base of these movements feeling itself cheated.

You think that it is impossible or impracticable to organize or 'parliamentarize' these protests?

The present potentials for protest are heterogeneous and hard to analyse: anti-nuclear movements, civic initiatives which develop in response to very diverse circumstances—for instance, at the neighbourhood level, to stop a motorway destroying or dividing a residential area. If we ask ourselves what are the causes behind such protests, I would say that in the first instance they represent a reaction against administrative procedures and methods. Let us take, for example, the resistance to educational reforms in Germany: in this case parents react against their loss of a field which they have always considered *naturally belongs to them*, and which they now see stolen from them by an extension of the sphere of competence of the public authorities. For this reason I am sure that they would resist 'right wing' reforms no less: for what provokes their protests is not so much the educational content as the administrative form of the intervention concerned.

If we ask ourselves what these various movements of protest have in common, I would say that they reveal an increasing sensitivity towards, and readiness to rebel against, secondary dysfunctions of capitalist growth. There is a rising awareness of the 'infiltration' of capital into areas of life which until now were shielded from it by tradition, and within which the values of capitalist society (competition for status, pursuit of gain, instrumentalization of existence) were not hitherto dominant. Such currents do not represent the classical potential for protest delineated by Marxism, although workers are naturally also involved in them. Their social composition is heterogeneous. For example, the mobilization against nuclear plants in West Germany swept up conservative peasants as well as parts of the rural establishment like apothecaries, teachers, doctors or lawyers. Alongside them were detachments of students and young workers on the left, the heirs of 1968.

But surely such campaigns are of less importance than the emergence of the women's movement, which is by now a world phenomenon?

The women's movement is in many respects structurally distinct from this process. In the first place, of course, it represents a much greater potential. It does not spring from transient causes, but from a fundamental problem: unequal rights. In the second place, it is as much a part of the traditional bourgeois as the socialist movement for emancipation. From the ideological point of view it must be counted amongt those great mass movements which take up universal principles of equality. This does not apply to other contemporary movements of protest.

But women have gone beyond the demand for equality, converging with critics of Marxism as a mere theory of social equality to call for liberation?

Very true. But here there are some striking similarities with the processes I have just described. The social conflict which lies behind the women's movement is linked to the fact that capitalist economic development is now violating the hitherto relatively protected preserve of the bourgeois family in Western society, in particular amongst the middle classes. Women are beginning to form part of the reserve army of labour; moreover this change, until recently largely confined to the working class, is now affecting more and more bourgeois strata. The result is a conflict in parallel with the other protest movements, but which unlike them cannot be canalized in a traditionalist direction. In this lies the radical difference of the women's movement. Other protests can be keyed to attempts to conserve or recapture what has already been. For women there is no such possibility. There is no viable return, there is no *status quo ante* which is desirable or is worth restoring. For this reason there exists *a priori* a critical potential in the women's movement.

But if it is true that these conflicts do not immediately reproduce the classical Marxist picture of class conflict, they are nevertheless still structurally determined by the process of capitalist development. Is not the political need to reconnect cause and effect, in a conscious practice, all the greater?

As Marxists, our task is to interpret the experiences that find expression in these movements in such a way that our reading of them is ratified by the strata so mobilized: that is, we must be able to render our hypothesis that these phenomena are caused by the politically uncontrolled development of capitalism credible to them. If we fail, then this potential for protest can very easily be captured by parties of a conservative type: in West Germany, for example, the CDU and even the Bavarian CSU have adopted the catchword 'human administration' to confiscate the critical potential of anti-bureaucratic reactions for their own ends. For the moment such a prospect is not imminent, but it could happen—all the more so because by their very nature these potentials for protest cannot generate their own organizational forms, capable of action appropriate to their aims. The most they can do on their own is to precipitate a *rupture*—that is, depending on the circumstances, a rupture in the system of organized parties. If such tendencies were to prevail, their outcome would be decided by the responses to the rupture when it occurred. In principle there could be two possible reactions. One would be a move towards a major decentralization of the process of formation of the collective will, with the involvement in it of spheres of life which until now have been deemed private and non-political. The other would prepare the way for a conservative party of order bent on resolving all these problems by administrative means, using the potential for protest they arouse simply as a legitimation for a suspension of democratic rights, or in certain conditions even of the constitutional norms of a legal state.

Is there not a further possibility: the emergence of a new 'extremism' oscillating between autonomy and corporativism—in other words between a defence of its own radical alterity as itself the form and content of a political strategy, and a utilization and manipulation of welfare provisions; between a rejection of politics as a mere form of mediation and integration, and a corporatist use of certain political conquests and rights?

The unravelling of the controls of central leaderships and central bureaucracies in the party system is a very ambivalent process. It can develop towards a neo-fascist corporativism, or it can re-inforce anarchic tendencies to a point where they provoke reactions which no one could seek or want. It is necessary to insist that this is not a process without dangers, that can be supported blindly. But there can be no doubt that there is a real problem here, to which the parties of the Left must address themselves rationally. *How* they should do so is not a simple thing to say. To start with, they must elucidate and explain these processes, so that the potential for protest does not move in a corporatist direction. Secondly, to the extent that competition with other parties and an ever more centralized state apparatus allows, they will have to decentralize their own forms of organization, rendering them more supple and capable of absorbing and capturing the autonomous critical potentials within society, which if left to their own devices risk becoming destructive. This is only a hypothesis of mine: I have no ready-made answer. If I can speak of matters that I know only from a distance, I think that even the PCI could find itself in a dangerous situation where it could become the functional equivalent of an authoritarian party of order. Such historical-political constellations can take shape rapidly and unexpectedly. They will be the less likely, the more the PCI can decentralize the intimate structure of its organization, even if it is clear that in the first instance such a change would limit its freedom of decision and movement. I am well aware, in effect, that every bureaucracy has its rational attributes. There are no easy solutions: I can only hope that the PCI will be capable of giving a positive example of how to react to the new potentials for protest. Of course, we have not yet spoken of terrorism, which unfortunately makes all these questions much more difficult.

But are we not also witnessing today the emergence of a neo-liberal ideology which formally proposes to put back the clock of history before Keynes, but factually seeks to exploit the crisis of the Welfare State to impose a certain brand of economic policy?

On the Right, the real lines of battle are moving away from Keynesianism and towards the new monetarism of Friedmanesque orientation. Naturally, this trend has its political counterpart in demands for the destruction of the Welfare State and the limitation of bureaucracy. If there is a real attempt to impose these policies, the trade unions will have no alternative but to develop an offensive strategy, in West Germany as well. We would see the reappearance of the classical type of class struggle which has long lain hidden behind the veil of neo-Keynesianism. It is really impossible to imagine the Welfare State being dismantled without a massive reaction from the traditional workers' organizations. For that very reason I do not regard such an attempt as either probable or imminent. It is more likely that efforts will be made to muddle through, for worse rather than better, with forms of modified Keynesianism. A government that sought to proceed otherwise would have to be able to mobilize very powerful conservative reserves, and we would than find ourselves in a situation very different from the present one—much nearer to a mobilization of the fascistoid potential in contemporary society.

Finally I would venture the opinion that in the medium term the economic system can succeed in living with these difficulties very well. The truth is that it should be able to 'normalize' what seemed explosive only a few years ago. But on one condition: that the social security system continues to hold good. This system is now under stress and it is certainly not easy to maintain it at its present level. Yet it is precisely its deficits that allow it to maintain social peace, by displacing social conflict forward in time. Capitalism's capacity to adapt is very great: it is an incredibly flexible order, which still possesses significant cultural and motivational reserves. It is surprising how it has been able to combine different forms of social integration. This is an old idea of the Frankfurt School in the 1930s: when its theorists arrived in America they realized that what needed explanation was not so much the phenomena of capitalist economic crisis as the mechanisms of capitalist cultural integration. Today I would still say that this set of problems is of the greatest importance. Conflicts are provoked by economic mechanisms which are in themselves well known and sufficiently analysed. The real question is: how are they subdued and controlled, or displaced into marginal sectors of the system? What price must be paid for these outcomes? What other conflicts are brought into play in lieu of this central one? Finally, and most crucially, will contemporary economic difficulties increase to such a magnitude that the present model, which lives on 'small crises', will be unable to function any longer, and will usher in a crisis of classical dimensions? It would then remain to be seen how such a crisis would end. I think, given the strong possibility of a fatal outcome, that we could not invoke or await such a 'grand crisis' with a light heart.

We probably need to develop another sort of analysis for Italy and perhaps for other Mediterranean countries, where on the one hand the role, weight and strategy of the labour movement, and on the other hand the economic room for manoeuvre of capital, differ from those in Germany. However, your arguments essentially confirm the view, adumbrated by Gramsci, that there has been an enormous expansion of the sphere of politics since the 1920s and with it the capacity of the bourgeoisie to utilize economic crises politically — to the discomfort of economistic readings of Marx's works, which seem to be re-emerging in 'orthodox' positions against which you have explicitly polemicized.

The real position which differentiates me from traditional Marxist analyses is my conviction that even with the methods of the classical critique of political economy, we cannot make precise economic predictions today: for these presuppose an autonomous, self-reproducing economic system. This I do not believe in. In fact, the laws governing the contemporary economy are no longer identical with those analysed by Marx. This does not mean that his analysis of its mechanisms is inaccurate, but rather that this analysis only remains valid so long as the intervention of the political system is ignored, and in turn the guiding of the political system itself by economic mechanisms. For this reason I cannot agree with Altvater's analyses, for example. In contrast to him, I consider the problem of economic prediction to be an empirical question to which answers can in principle be given, but for which in practice we do not yet possess sufficiently developed explanations. We are dealing with a very complex system which operates an interaction of economy and *Kulturstaat*: it must be analysed in detail. A purely economic analysis is not a basis for accurate prognoses. It could be argued that what we need is a functional equivalent to the theory of Marx. But we do not possess one: each of us works and labours to understand systems which have become much more complex than in his time. So far as the mechanisms of the economic system proper are concerned, on the other hand, one might even say that they are relatively transparent today, to a point where there is little need for an extensive political economy, or critique of ideology, to understand how they work. Anyone who watches the television news in West Germany, for example, can see that an economic policy is being pursued which flouts any overall planning in favour of attempts to stimulate investment by indirect inducements alone. To ignite the 'motor of accumulation', options are being imposed which are manifestly unfavourable to working people. By now it is patent to everyone that business is trying to exploit the present economic difficulties for its own advantage.

Is it really so patent? Even in Italy, where the consciousness and combativity of the working class is certainly higher than in West Germany, there is no self-evident untruth—at least in a narrowly economic sense—in the claim of certain industrialists that if only workers would accept lower wages, there would be higher investments and therewith more jobs.

Of course, there is a whole series of economic mystifications and slogans which do need criticism. I only wanted to say that it is obvious to everyone that you cannot influence the behaviour of investors by indirect methods. In this respect the system is now more transparent. On the other hand, if we are speaking of the interaction of economic mechanisms with political-cultural institutions, we would have to insist that they have actually become more complex and impenetrable, to specialists as well.

There is a parallel between the economic crisis and the symptoms of a crisis of rational investigation. But the real problem is surely why these processes have not yet given rise to a true crisis of legitimation?

I would rather speak of *tendencies* towards such a crisis. We can all see the difficulties of attempts to solve the tendencies to economic crisis by administrative means. But these have not in practice had major delegitimizing effects so far. At least in West Germany, the management of economic policy has been staged for the public in a very effective way. The immediate results of this staging have been on the one hand the processes of intimidation and discipline that I have mentioned and on the other hand a possibly reinforced cynicism towards the way the system redistributes its costs. Hence the incipient estrangement from the political system, whose indicators I have already touched on. However, we certainly cannot speak of a real crisis of legitimation: people continue to vote, and in their vast majority vote for the traditional parties. Whereas, setting aside the phenomenon of terrorism and its stabilizing effect on conservative reaction, a real crisis of legitimation would signify a collapse of the traditional party system and the formation of a new party whose aims would at least transcend the existent economic system. This will not happen so long as the neo-populist currents do not grow to a point where they acquire a much greater strength and pose a real challenge to the established order; or—alternatively—so long as the government parties do not introduce economic policies that are an outright challenge to the trade unions.

Speaking of the 'crisis of legitimation', you have argued that the extension of citizens' possibilities for democratic action would help to prevent a putative disintegration of contemporary society. But is a democratic response to the crisis of a complex society really possible? Might not this complexity impose a society dominated by specialists, in which decisions are made apart from its citizens? Can the 'ungovernability' of Western democracies today favour a real democratization —let us call it a socialization of politics—or is a victory of technocrats and experts inevitable, a victory of complexity over democracy?

I am of the opinion that a greater democratization of our societies, in the sense of a decentralization of current decision making, and joint involvement in decisions previously taken either privately or administratively, through more discursive processes of formation of the collective will, would have two consequences. On one side, it could certainly lead to a loss of efficiency. It would not *have* to be so, but it *might* be. This is the objection advanced today by the theoreticians of the existing system. They hold that complex systems can only change their modes of operation and base themselves on participatory decision making at the cost of their functionality and rationality. There is enough truth in these objections for Marxists to have to ask themselves whether socialism today, under present conditions, can still really mean a *total* democratic restructuration from top to bottom, and vice versa, of the economic system: that is, a transformation of the capitalist economy according to models of self-management and council-based administration. I myself do not believe so. I think it would be sufficient to introduce *above* the decisions of the base into the productive structures of the economy, as their political premises; and *below* to democratize decision making within production as such to a point where all those imperatives which even under capitalism are expressed in such notions as the humanization of the world of work are satisfied. In other words, I wonder—this is an empirical question which cannot be answered abstractly, but only through experimental practice—if we should not preserve part of today's complexity within the economic system, limiting the discursive formation of the collective will precisely to the decisive and central structures of political power: that is, apart from the labour process as such, to the few but continuously made fundamental decisions which will determine the overall structure of social production and, naturally, of distribution.

On the other hand I am convinced that we want democratization not so much in order to improve the efficiency of the economy as to change the *structures* of power: and in the second place to set in motion ways of defining collective goals that merely administrative or power-oriented decisions would lead astray or cripple. It can be shown that there are collective needs which cannot be satisfied so long as the decision-making process remains administrative or power-oriented. This is the real reason for demanding their democratization; it is also the reason why those needs which are today expressed in the form of autonomous movements are articulated in an unorganized way, for until now the traditional mechanisms for taking decisions have excluded them. Thus, leaving aside the fact that a way of life that is in general worthy of men and women can only be realized if fundamental decisions are taken by the people who are affected by them—in other words the intrinsic value of democracy as such—the present system generates ample evidence that democratization, greater popular participation and decentralization of the processes of formation of the collective will are essential because the *market + administration* cannot satisfy a whole series of collective needs.

The crisis of the 1930s was overcome by the emergence of governments and administrations with greatly increased powers over democratic political bodies of opinion formation. This happened both in the East and the West—in the latter in many different forms, ranging from the New Deal to Nazism and Fascism. Can we emerge from the present crisis in the opposite direction, by a growth of democracy? Eurocommunism represents at once a critical reflection on the historical errors of the workers' movement which produced Stalinism, and a search for a democratic road to socialism—that is, for the form of a transition understood not as a sudden and absolute rupture but as a gradual process which will guarantee greater popular participation and a more democratic structure of power.

We must start from the fact that social systems as complex as highly developed capitalist societies would founder in chaos under any attempt to transform their fundamental structures overnight. In this respect you are absolutely right. I can only imagine a revolution as a long-term process which makes possible: (a) an experimental transformation, guided at every step by its successes and failures, of central decision-making structures; (b) simultaneously, if not indeed as an actual premise of this change, an 'acclimatization' to new democratic forms of life, through a gradual enlargement of democratic, participatory and discursive action. Such a path would, above all, prevent that mobilization of affective forces in a crisis which has always been a weapon of fascism. In fact, it is precisely in the throes of a transformation of complex societies that there is a particular danger of the emergence of parties appealing to fear, insecurity, and the latent disposition to prejudice hidden in all of us. In such circumstances the slogans of a fascist, or at any rate authoritarian-administrative, alternative gain assent and support. Hence the need to respect these two minimum conditions if we are to accomplish a prudent and long-term process of transformation. The task is a very difficult one, for which an extraordinarily intelligent party is necessary.

A flexible and non-bureaucratic one too.

Such a party must expose itself to the process of democratization, accepting all the possible consequences: in other words the risk of harming and even losing its capacity for bureaucratic action. These are, of course, empirical processes, in which the role of theory can at most be to set out the alternatives before us.

Can it not also indicate possible solutions, by studying the relations between knowledge and power? This would seem to be the explanation for the interest in Foucault's 'micro-physics of power' in Italy and elsewhere today.

Foucault imagines that a bourgeois rationality was somehow imposed on all spheres of life in the eighteenth century, which must now be generically done away with. I am not convinced by his undialectical negation. It is rather necessary to show that what Weber called 'rationalization' and which Foucault has well explored in a very different way—in the field of culture, sexual relations, criminality and insanity—is dangerous because it is partial. For it is characterized by its universalization of a single fundamental form of rationality—instrumental, economic and administrative reason. But we must be careful not to throw the baby out with the bath water and take flight in a new irrationalism. Foucault visibly falls into that danger.

But has he not also developed an important argument, to the effect that traditional Marxism has paid too little attention to the forms of 'power' in daily life, assuming that power and state coincide—even though Engels in his own way was concerned with the family?

Foucault has made an important contribution to the analysis of the forms of bourgeois domination. This is a subject that is directly related to my own research interests. I too think that relations of power are incorporated in the least ostensive forms of communication, and that analysis of systematically distorted communication yields results analogous to Foucault's analysis of discourses. Themes of this type have already been taken up by the reform movement and the student movement in West Germany, and are now furnishing ammunition for the neo-populist movements. The real problem is to understand what is hidden behind intuitions like those, for example, of the ecologists. I think what is involved is a sense that areas which were still more or less the sites of free interaction are now being infringed. Similarly, in spheres of traditional life not yet completely penetrated by capitalism, comparable forms of interaction probably also existed. We must not limit our critique of relationships of power to those institutions in which power is overtly declared, hence to political and social power only; we must extend it to those areas of life in which power is hidden behind the amiable countenance of cultural familiarity. These questions were long ago intuitively understood and anlaysed by the Frankfurt School, above all in *Dialectic of Enlightenment* or in Marcuse's theses on the women's movement.

In effect, you are arguing for a widening of critical horizons, an enlargement of the terrain to be explored, to some extent beyond that traditional to Marxism. But this does not mean either abandoning Marx or reducing him to a foe of the open society, or a theoretician of totalitarianism.

Such an idea is pure idiocy. The generation of 'New Philosophers' who propound it thought ahistorically in 1968, and think ahistorically today, believing they are correcting an old error while merely committing it anew. They cannot see that the theoretical tradition of Marx and the practical-political tradition of the labour movement demand our affiliation in full historical consciousness. What they present as a great novelty—that there cannot be any socialism without a radical and coherent appropriation of the gains of the movements of bourgeois emancipation, of in effect the potential of bourgeois civic rights—is something that Western Marxism has always known, if we set aside the actions of Stalinist parties (including the PCI for a certain period). Instead of constructing an anti-Marxism, they should have learnt from Lukács, Korsch, Gramsci and the Frankfurt School that socialism and liberty are identical.

Hasn't the history of Marxism—its better variety—always been that of its revision and critique?

I consider the so-called New Philosophers to be a generational salon phenomenon. The least one could expect is that they realize criticisms of Stalinism did not begin with them.

Can we conclude with your views on a question which has remained suspended throughout our discussion, yet which presses most urgently on us today—the phenomenon of terrorism? A precipitate of all the elements of the structural, spiritual and institutional crisis that we have discussed, in some respects it also lends the problem of intellecuals and of new generations a frighteningly new cast.

Terrorism should be seen together with neo-populism as a reaction against the contraction of politics to administration on the one hand, and pure acclamation on the other. Reactions to this process of reduction can go in two directions. One of these directions is an attempt to introduce aesthetically expressive elements into politics, and the other to introduce more intransigently moral elements. Both have an authoritarian and an anti-authoritarian variant. The classical example of authoritarian attempts at the aestheticization of politics was fascism. An example of anti-authoritarian aestheticization can be found in certain forms of anarchism. The phenomenon of moralization is not dissimilar. The authoritarian version of an attempt to moralize politics leads to despotic-authoritarian forms of political revolt against the Welfare State. The anti-authoritarian response, which demands a *remoralization* of politics, points rather towards democratization, decentralization and socialist positions. If we accept the general schema, where do terrorist actions fit in? Here in Germany it is very fashionable to assert that the terrorists are the children of a misguided moralism. I don't believe this. Obviously, I am only speaking of Germany, where terrorist actions have had an extraordinary resemblance to a show, a performance of representation and self-gratification. That is to say, these actions do not really correspond functionally to their aims. If this is right, and if we take into account the remarkable degree of militarization, discipline and obedience within the terrorist organizations, then I would rather tend to interpret the 'terrorist game' under way in the Bundesrepublik as a counter-pole to fascism. In other words, I view it as an authoritarian version of the attempt to introduce aesthetically expressive elements into politics, like a small-scale underground. Terrorism does not fall from the sky. It is a structural phenomenon, and the fact that its most serious manifestations have occurred in nations like Germany, Italy and Japan can obviously be explained through the fact that in these countries political culture is less stable than elsewhere, historically less well anchored, and therefore more prone to extreme reactions to the same cultural phenomena than other countries. Although this may be a very unpopular view, I think we must say that terrorism is not an irrational phenomenon but should be categorized with other attempts to react against the same structural processes: in its own way, it is an attempt to reaffirm politics in the face of pure administration.

3.

Political Experience and the Renewal of Marxist Theory

Herr Habermas, when the war ended you were sixteen years old; when the Nazis first seized power you were barely four. Your socialization took place for the most part under fascist domination. What influence did that have on your political development?

I'd rather not say terribly much about my youth. A true retrospective can only be made at seventy, not fifty. I grew up in Gummersbach, in a small town environment. My father was head of the Bureau of Trade and Industry there. My grandfather was a minister and director of the local seminary. The political climate in our family home was probably not unusual for the time. It was marked by a bourgeois adaptation to a political situation with which one did not fully identify, but which one didn't seriously criticize either. What really determined my political views was the year 1945. At that point the rhythm of my personal development intersected with the great historical events of the time. I was fifteen years old. The radio was reporting the Nuremberg trials, movie theatres were showing the first documentary films, the concentration camp films that we're seeing again today. These experiences undoubtedly helped develop motifs which then further determined my thinking.

Weren't your parents shocked back then? Today a film such as Holocaust *affects both young people and older ones as well. How can we explain the fact that the earlier films you spoke of had no effect at all, since it is obvious today that most people haven't assimilated their experiences from that time?*

The reactions to the early films and the reactions to *Holocaust* are two different things. I can only presume that the tremendous effect of *Holocaust* rests in part on the fact that here, in the circle of the family, where the television is, young people have been questioning their parents about those events. We didn't do that. I think we were too inhibited at the time to convert our own personal shock into a direct family confrontation. I was in the Hitler Youth; at fifteen I was sent to man the western defences. Our situation was completely different from that of today's youth. Our own history was suddenly cast in a light that made all its essential aspects appear radically different. All at once we saw that we had been living in a politically criminal system. I had never imagined that before.

Does that mean that you weren't aware of what was happening to the Jews, that you didn't take the propaganda literally?

In 1939 I was ten years old, so I had no chance to get a particularly clear picture. But of course at that time we had the impression of a normality which afterwards proved to be an illusion. For us to see suddenly that those people were criminals—that had quite a different quality.

Given the background of these moral jolts, did you from the very beginning have a positive picture of the society which was then established, and which developed into the Federal Republic?

At first 1945 was a liberation, historically and personally. We had, as I recall, very fine weather then. I experienced all of this naively and intuitively as beautiful. At that time I was simply overwhelmed by a number of impressions. I devoured the first books from the Rororo newspaper series[1] and the ones from the Marxist-Leninist Library which were available in the communist bookstores. The first great political disappointments came with the formation of the government in 1949.

Why were you disappointed?

I'd started my studies in Göttingen. My first political disappoint-

---

1. See note 2, in 'Ideologies and Society in the Post-War World', p. 37 above.

ment came with the electoral meetings in Göttingen for the first Federal Parliament. I heard all sorts of people, among them Herr Seebohm, who belonged to the DVP. The party meeting was decorated with black-white-red banners and closed with the national anthem. I stormed out in an emotional furor—I just couldn't stand it. And this man became Minister of Transport. I thought to myself, it's just not possible that someone who embodies this historical continuity could be in the first cabinet. But the real political problem was rearmament. Heinemann (also a minister in the first cabinet) was against it. I myself had a very neutralist attitude at that period. The experience·of the war had made me a pacifist. Heinemann's resignation made a deep impression on me at the time.

Was the situation ambiguous for you then—on the one hand the Nazi element, on the other a hope for the realization of bourgeois freedoms? For many (Abendroth, for example), it was very clear—the restoration of capitalism.

No, nothing was clear then. I was nineteen, and one is still very immature at that age. During my time at the university, from 1949 to 1954, the politically dominant factors for me were first of all a strong moral reaction to the Nazi era, and secondly the fear that a real break with the past had not been made. I thought then what one cannot say today without criticism: if only there had been some spontaneous sweeping away, some explosive act, which then could have served to begin the formation of a political identity. After such an eruption we would have at least known what we couldn't go back to. There simply was no struggle. I think it makes a difference whether one says that looking forward or looking back.

Why did the German people have no possibility of creating a political identity?

What I mean, in concrete terms, is this: there was no spontaneous uprising either before or during the Allied invasion; no battles were fought; no one took a risk in order to put an end to the whole mess.

I myself am a product of 're-education', and not, I hope, an all too negative one. By this I mean that it was at that time that we learned that the bourgeois constitutional state in its French or American or English form is a historical achievement. This is an important biographical difference between those who experienced what a half-hearted bourgeois republic like the Weimar Republic can lead to, and those whose political consciousness was formed at a later date.

And the Republic after 1949 seemed more stable to you?

Of course. To me this state represented a real opportunity.

But in many ways you were in a negative frame of mind, didn't you just say?

I had no direct link to any particular party. Certainly not to the CDU. This party was founded right after 1945 by anti-fascists. But then you could see who went into it. In a small town you know right away what's going on. And social democracy—that's a difficult concept for the son of a bourgeois family. It's hard to imagine today, but the middle classes saw it as the re-emergence of the Social Democracy of the Weimar period. And what is more, it was then following the Schumacher line. He came out of the concentration camp obsessed with the idea that we had abandoned the national question to the Nazis in 1933. With that he ran directly into conflict with the mood of the general public. The idea that one should be 'national' seemed absurd to us. It made absolutely no difference to me whether the Saar was German or not.

You have to take into consideration the limited perspective which one had, being educated at a university that had remained essentially unbroken in its continuity since the 1920s. All the professors who had any importance for me were already professors before 1933 and, with one exception, namely Litt, remained in their positions. In a number of departments (philosophy, history, German, and psychology) it was an apolitical and almost ethnocentrically German university, with a consciousness that would have been justified in 1910, when great scientific achievements took place at German universities. In philosophy in Bonn, for example, the Anglo-Saxon currents were non-existent, as was the analytical philosophy which had been created by German emigrants, not to mention Critical Theory.

But in 1954 you too wrote a dissertation in this traditional sense. Were you able to free yourself very quickly from this tradition?

Until the appearance of Heidegger's *Introduction to Metaphysics* in 1953 my political and my philosophical 'confessions', if you will, were two completely different things. They were two universes which hardly touched one another. Then I saw that Heidegger, in whose philosophy I had been living, had given this lecture in 1935 and published it without a word of explanation—that's what really disturbed me. I then wrote one of my first articles about it for the *Frankfurter Allgemeine Zeitung*. I was terribly naive and thought, how can one of our greatest philosophers do such a thing? Of course one could have found out about that a lot earlier, but I hadn't been brought up that way. Around the same time, by the way, I read Lukács's *History and Class Consciousness*, which excited me a great deal.

How did you get hold of History and Class Consciousness *at that time?*

It was in the seminar library, which was relatively small. We were at home there; we practically lived there. We knew every book.

It was through Löwith that I first came into contact with the young Marx. That was why I later wrote an essay on the Young Hegelians as an introduction to my dissertation. I suppose I came across Lukács in that way, too. I thought, it's too bad one can't systematically revive these motifs. On the one hand, I was fascinated; on the other hand, I knew that nowadays it can't be done that way.

I was certainly politically moved by it at the time. And then memories began to return. I knew Marx of course from the bookstore in Gummersbach, but I had forgotten him in the meantime. I had the feeling that it would be good if all this could be taken up in such a way that a systematic argument could be developed from it. But I realized with a certain sadness that it wouldn't work with Lukács. And then—if I may leap ahead here—in 1955 I read Horkheimer and Adorno's *Dialectic of Enlightenment*. What fascinated me right away wih those two was that they weren't engaged in a reception of Marx, that was not what they were up to at all—they were utilizing him. It was a great experience for me to see that one could relate systematically to the 'Marxist tradition'. Here were people who weren't writing a historical work on Aristotle, Kant, or Hegel; they were working out a theory of the dialectical development of present-day society, and in doing so they were proceeding from a tradition of Marxist thought. That was a tremendous thing for me. Of course I had been prepared for it on the basis of my reading of Lukács. At that point philosophical and political things began to come together for the first time.

Then you wrote Strukturwandel der Öffentlichkeit?

I first learned empirical social research, then came *Student und Politik* and finally *Strukturwandel der Öffentlichkeit*.

That book had a disillusioning effect on the younger generation's faith in democracy. It turned my political orientation, at least, completely upside down. The only alternative I could see after that was the sds. Did you intend that kind of an impact?

I always had a strong academic interest in the question. And of course I wrote *Strukturwandel* first and foremost as an attempt to clarify for myself the darker aspects and the flaws in our political system, whose merits I never doubted. A climate of social and political restoration dominated the time. This climate was so ingrained that I was startled when my friend Apel publicly called me a Neo-Marxist for the first time. Then I thought it over and decided he was right. Today I value being considered a Marxist.

That was the background to my work on the 'structural transformation of the public sphere' as well. The question that interested me was: how can we get to the bottom of what is somehow wrong with this political system with regard to its political intentions, in spite of the Constitution. When the sds was excluded from the spd I was one of the three or four professors who, together with Abendroth, founded the Socialist League [*Sozialistischer Bund*]. We were sort of an 'old folks' section' of the sds. I can't say that I wrote the book to guide people toward the sds. I wrote the book to make it clear to myself and others that the political system of the Federal Republic has inherent weaknesses which can become dangerous.

As a question I'd like to quote Marx, who says that the limits of this system lie within the system itself. Do you see something similar here, that perhaps something is wrong with the basic liberal values? That this self-destruction is unavoidable? Or to put it differently: where do you get your optimism?

Optimism? We need to distinguish a number of things here. It is true that I do not share the basic premise of Critical Theory, as it took shape during the early 1940s, the premise that instrumental reason has gained such dominance that there is really no way out of a total system of delusion [*Verblendungszusammenhang*], in which insight is achieved only in flashes by isolated individuals. There is a contradiction here which irritates me even today. On the one hand, our social system is relatively stable (that applies to capitalist society in general, but perhaps to the Federal Republic in particular) and not just economically. It not only guarantees a relatively conflict-free mode of collective life, it has institutionalized political freedoms which must in the first instance be assessed and approved from a historical perspective. On the other hand, this society displays many symptoms which frighten me. On an intuitive level I'm quite convinced that something in this system is deeply amiss. That irritates me; it also motivates my theoretical efforts and is perhaps a reason for a certain oscillation. I'm not a Marxist in the sense of believing in Marxism as a sure-fire explanation. Still, Marxism did give me both the impetus and the analytical means to investigate the development of the relationship between democracy and capitalism.

But does that mean that you really are convinced that existing power structures can be broken by means of a theoretical analysis?

Yes, I'm firmly convinced that the Left in general, and the Marxist Left in particular, can claim one advantage over all other political forces. This is the belief in the possibility of introducing theoretical analyses with a middle- or long-range perspective into day-to-day politics. This is one tradition that should not be sacrificed. On the other hand, I also believe that now, more than ever before, we lack convincing analyses. That is perhaps one reason why for a time I clashed harder with the students than was perhaps politically necessary. At bottom, what I couldn't understand were the dogmas that prevailed even among the anarchist students. No doubt they were less dogmatic in their life styles and social relations . . .

But your criticism at that time centred on another point, namely that the SDS *was putting theoretical ideas into practice in such a direct and unreflective way. Certain charges against the* SDS—*and in this I certainly agree with the people who were critical at the time—have proved to have been justified. For example, it's a delusion to believe one can take over a society simply by hoisting a red flag in a seminar. But was it correct to make your criticism in that way at that time? Oskar Negt has accused you of a lack of solidarity in your actions, in the sense that on the one hand you helped inspire the student revolt, but on the other hand you distanced yourself from it and criticized it from the outside. Shouldn't there have been a discussion of social problems rather than a criticism using clinical concepts? Didn't you realize that by acting that way you would create an unbridgeable gap between yourself and the students?*

I'd like to challenge one premise—that I placed myself outside the framework of the student movement. I never saw it that way; I never intended it so.

Weren't you trying to put a stop to discussion with your statements?

No, the discussion hadn't even begun when I made that rather out-of-place statement about left fascism. No, there can be no question of finality.

I made two public criticisms. The first was after the Benno Ohnesorg demonstration in Hannover.[2] What I meant there I later published in 1969, in *Protestbewegung und Hochschulreform*. I still consider the substance of this statement to be correct. But I should have said it differently. The other time was at Pentecost, right after the withdrawal of the emergency regulations. The SDS had planned a conference for school and university students. Students came from all over the Federal Republic. A march was planned from the opera house to the university, which was occupied by the police. I considered it irresponsible and said so to the participants themselves. This can all be looked up. That was the time of May 1968 in France, and the students really thought the revolution was breaking out. That was the context of the situation.

As far as content is concerned, yes, but the manner . . .

I know, I adopted a psychologizing standpoint, but for every sentence I could tell you a story behind it, explaining what led me to put it like that. You simply have to see how immediate and concrete everything was. Everyone was aware of it at the time. Today people read it in a different way. And at the time it was an *internal* critique of the methods of the protest movement. You ask me about my lack of solidarity. It's true that I didn't grow up in any organization—which one would it have been? So I did perhaps react a shade too

---

2. Benno Ohnesorg, a West German student, was shot dead by a policeman during a demonstration against the Shah of Iran outside the Opera House in West Berlin, on 2 June 1967. A congress of the student Left held in Hannover on 9 June 1967, on the occasion of Ohnesorg's funeral, marked the moment at which the Berlin protest movement spilled over into the Federal Republic. Habermas's interventions at the congress can be found in his *Kleine Politische Schriften i-iv*, Frankfurt 1981, pp. 213–215.

much like a bourgeois intellectual. On the other hand, the impression the students had, that they were a living continuation of the tradition of the workers' movement, was equally false. So I don't think, even in retrospect, that I would have had a chance if I had stayed closer to the group.

Didn't that shake your faith in such political discussions, since you didn't have any influence on the events?

But I tried, I wanted to have an influence. The days when the SDS leadership spoke completely openly with me were gone by the middle of 1967. My attempt to have an influence had to take the form it did. Then people got the impression that Habermas really was setting himself apart from the protest movement. But even the introduction to *Protestbewegung und Hochschulreform* was a clear identification with the goals of the protest movement.

A representative of the other faction, Klaus Meschkat, has accused you of having a strange relationship to current events, because one could not tell from your speech in Frankfurt that May 1968 in France and the Easter demonstrations all over Germany had even taken place. Looking back, wouldn't you concede that there was more going on than you perceived at the time? Didn't much more happen then, in terms of people's consciousness, than anyone could have perceived? The student movement marked, in a way, a point of no return.

But that's contained in my essays. Take a look at the last essay. It really does express optimism in regard to the protest movement.

Is that still your view today, that the protest movement was of tremendous importance for the development of the Federal Republic?

It brought about a certain rupture in the normative area, in attitudes, in the cultural value system.

Today people would probably assert the opposite, that students today are more willing than ever to submit to all sorts of restrictions.

No, there are studies which show through international comparisons that the value system of the population as a whole has changed. What Frau Noelle-Neuman characterized as a proletarianization of middle-class values can be described a bit more aptly.[3] What is reflected in this change is a distancing from the value orientations which shaped the culture of the 1950s in such an extreme way. Value syndromes that were instrumental, privatist, and competition-, career-, or family-oriented have become less fixed in parts of the population, as the shift from the 'old' to the 'new' politics shows.

But isn't it the case that where such attitudes are changed, no political change results? We can ascertain changes in attitudes, but people who change their attitudes drop out of the political system and become systematically under-privileged. So we don't have the values of the 1950s any more—but what do we have instead?

We are only beginning to see the effects of the protest movement. Changes in family structure and child rearing had started earlier. In part, the protest movement was already a product of altered forms of socialization. One has to see that in a longer term perspective. But we're all agreed that the protest movement was effective in terms of cultural reorientations.

You're asking me what political results such changes have. Don't we have to be somewhat sceptical in that regard? You're pushing me more and more into the false role of an optimist. Here's how I see it at the moment: new political potentials are being created which can have dysfunctional results and which can exercise a power of veto. This power could in the long run introduce a reorganization of the party system—and not necessarily of the kind which Strauss would like. But I don't want to make specific predictions. We're dealing here with historical trends that are hard to diagnose. I think there's a relatively large range of alternatives within which the party system can react to such challenges. If we had a rightist government that pursued, logically and thoroughly, a new economic policy in the manner of Milton Friedmann—well, that would mean a dismantling of the welfare state. That in turn could lead to a revival of traditional class struggles. But I presume such a government also would be smart enough to weigh such risks.

I agree with you that the dismantling of the welfare state won't take place so quickly. On the other hand, what did trouble me (though I don't want to overestimate an isolated phenomenon) was this discus-

---

3. Elizabeth Noelle-Neumann is the head of the Allensbach Institute, a conservatively-oriented opinion poll organization in West Germany linked to the CDU.

sion with Kohl in Holland. There was tremendous uproar. Apparently the Germans, including Kohl, were more shocked by a certain framework of discussion being transgressed than by having to discuss sensitive topics. The fact that in a television interview the moderator and Kohl were not able to maintain control—that was extraordinary. The Dutch audience said, we'll decide what's an answer and what isn't. That shocked German viewers. I wonder whether there isn't a greater tendency in Germany than in Holland to regulate the shaping of the public sphere, whether what was revealed by such a program isn't perhaps typical.

I didn't see the program. But I assume it's symptomatic of corporatistic restrictions of a functioning bourgeous pluralism. And such symptoms are, in my experience, more pronounced in Germany than in America or England. It isn't as though I only see clear skies ahead; quite the contrary. After the Schleyer kidnapping the politicians and the media (including nearly all of the press, not just the papers downmarket and to the right of the *Frankfurter Allgemeine Zeitung*) tore down the barriers of the political culture which had been so arduously built up during the first two decades after the war. In those years an official attitude was created which was far more liberal than the general attitude of the public. That healthy system of restrictions has been broken down. Suddenly it was OK to call for Böll's emigration, to consider shooting hostages, and so on. Those feelings exist, of course, but up to now it wasn't permissible to express them. In addition to that we saw public outrage that was bureaucratically orchestrated, along with attempts to turn the entire public into police assistants, and so on. I remember a press conference where the League for Academic Freedom [*Bund Freiheit der Wissenschaft*] read a list of names of professors and colleagues who were alleged to be terrorist sympathizers. I believe that the high degree of social integration in the Federal Republic is a deceptive phenomenon and has another side to it: strongly repressed emotions and attitudes which in extreme situations rise to the surface. They do, at any rate, when one of the major parties takes the lead. If the CDU hadn't joined in, we'd never have had a German Autumn.[4]

4. The phrase 'German Autumn' refers to the right-wing backlash in autumn 1977 which followed the emergence of political terrorism in West Germany, and in particular the kidnap and murder of the president of the West German employers' federation, Hans-Martin Schleyer, in September–October of that year. In the course of this backlash left-wing intellectuals were accused of complicity with terrorism and threatened with legal sanctions.

You created quite a stir at the time in your Spiegel *essay.[5] Many people were happy to see you publicly join in political discussion again. But nevertheless you didn't take part in the Russell Tribunal.[6]*

I'm afraid I miscalculated the effect of the first Russell Tribunal. I was afraid that afterwards the entire discussion of professional proscription would be driven into illegality. I thought that the institutional framework of the Russell Tribunal (which was in fact inappropriate for the Federal Republic) would discredit the whole affair so badly that the entire cause would be lost. Then I had the idea—you might say, a typical liberal intellectual idea—that we could get ten or twenty people together in Harheim to counteract the expected effect—we could say we didn't support the Russell Tribunal, but that what it brought to light was the real scandal. But I never got the group together. Anyway, they should have stopped after the first tribunal, because the second one had only a single issue, the *Kontaktsperre* law.[7] The cases in question were examples of real censorship, but censorship is no worse in the FRG than in any other Western country.

Take the Buback affair,[8] Paragraph 88a,[9] and students who avoid dealing with Marx in their examinations because they want to be teachers—aren't those things somehow typical for the situation in the Federal Republic?

Of course!

---

5. 'Probe für Volksjustiz', *Der Spiegel*, 10 October 1977. Reprinted in *Kleine Politische Schriften*, pp. 364–7.

6. The Third International Russell Tribunal, concerned with aspects of human rights in the German Federal Republic, was held in Harheim, near Frankfurt, 28 March to 4 April 1978 and in Cologne, 3 to 8 January 1979.

7. The *Kontaktsperregesetz*, passed by the West German parliament on 30 September 1977, was intended to restrict the contact of terrorist detainees with each other, and with the outside world.

8. *Generalbundesanwalt* (general state prosecutor) Siegfried Buback, West Germany's leading terrorist-hunter, was shot dead in an ambush on 7 April 1977. An article published under the pseudonym 'Mescalero' in a Göttingen student newspaper, which expressed 'scarcely concealed joy' at the killing, resulted in police raids and legal action against the student union. In protest, it was republished in a dossier by a group of university teachers, generating a further political furore.

9. Paragraph 88a of the West German criminal code, introduced on 22 April 1976, made the advocacy, encouragement or approval of acts of violence illegal. It was revoked on 12 June 1980, against the votes of the opposition.

This suppression of the formation of public opinion . . .

Well, any liberal would answer you (and, I hope, with some justification) that we have the worst behind us. Mr Nixon, too, had to be deposed first of course. A democracy doesn't endure because of the things that pass through it, but because of the way it purges itself of them.

But there's something that needs to mentioned in this context — the accusation of lack of loyalty that was lodged against the university teachers in Lower Saxony . . .

What Pestel did there is a scandal, a resurgence of the McCarthy era. By the way, the fact that most of the professors signed the papers when it was demanded of them is also a scandal.[10]

That's an issue which concerns not just the Federal Republic, but also the smaller countries around it. The FRG has such a mighty economic power that it affects the political structure of its neighbours.

I've never been a fan of the idea of a 'unified Europe', even when it was fashionable, and I'm still not one today. But one does have to be glad to see a certain growing integration of the European nations.

About the confrontation with systems which place more value on political education and the formation of political opinion?

But also in a framework containing France, England and especially the Romance language countries with strong Communist parties. In the FRG, too, a stronger Eurocommunist party could be in many ways a liberalizing factor. Many things would be normalized. For instance, in this country you can't be a professor or a director of the Max Planck Institute and at the same time a Marxist. As long as that's the case the basis of political culture is not liberal.

One last question about politics — where do you see your own future political effectiveness?

---

10. Eduard Pestel, CDU Minister for Culture in Lower Saxony in this period, forced eleven university teachers connected with the 'Mescalero' affair to sign a humiliatingly-worded 'oath of loyalty', declaring their abhorrence of violence and their active allegiance to the state.

I'm not sure whether I can still have any effect on the political consciousness of the Left in the FRG. That doesn't mean, of course, that one can't have the usual academic effect, on students, for example.

And your theoretical influence? Does your target group consist of young academics?

You could put it like that. But what does 'young academic' mean? There is something to the conservative outcry over the 'mediators of meaning' [*Sinnvermittler*], insofar as the normative horizon of our society has become more sensitive. It's no antiquated eighteenth-century Enlightenment illusion to contend that one can effectively alter the state of an argument by means of books. One can, if necessary, play a part in a change of attitude through articles in the daily press, a change which is not brought about intentionally, but for which interpretations are nevertheless important. Now I'll say something very old-fashioned: if one can illuminate somewhat a situation which nobody can really understand, then that has to touch the understanding, even the self-understanding, of broad social groups. That has to do with our extraordinarily effective media system. But at the moment I don't see any 'target group'. We have already spoken a bit about these new political potentials. My idea was to contribute something to the interpretation of conflicts which arise on the edges of over-legalized and bureaucratized areas of life. When someone correctly interprets an unclear situation, he or she not only has the success of advancing just a bit towards the truth, but may also influence a self-understanding which in the long run helps determine political orientations. On the other hand, heaven knows, I don't share the instrumentalist idea which is so widespread among our literary exponents of the new right-wing mood: that one can move the objective spirit to the left or right by means of ideological planning and a politics of language.

I have just one practical problem—getting across to students the problems contained in Communication and the Evolution of Society. *The massive synthesis of various theories causes students gradually to despair and say, well, if we first have to begin fulfilling the sociological conditions and then those related to the theory of evolution, and so on . . .*

But we have to be allowed to write theory . . .

Right, of course, but I see the problem differently. I would also concede that there are practical difficulties in conveying your theory. But the difficulties are rooted in the material. Bloch always said he couldn't write more simply about the material because the material itself was not simple. For dogmatic Marxism this doesn't present a problem—they shake an analysis of society right out of their sleeves. However, one cannot cogently explain the present crisis with the crude instruments of Marxist theory—for example, with the tendency of the rate of profit to fall. For the object 'society', which is being analyzed, is itself hard to grasp. That is shown by other sociological theories which look around for possibilities of combination with still further sociological theories in the hope of getting a better grip on the object they're trying to analyze. I grant you that it's a problem for students, trying to learn all those theories. But if one pays due regard to the subject one can't get around it, or else I'm getting my analysis of society on the cheap. That's precisely what I see in your theoretical writings.

I'm very sympathetic to what you're saying. But Herr van Reijen is correct in one respect—what is mirrored in the difficulties of my texts is of course my own lack of clarity on certain points. There's no question about that.

You just said you found what I was saying was sympathetic. Are you merely sympathetic, or do you share that understanding of your own enterprise?

Yes, I do.

If you agree with that, then I have another question. Your theory is the synthesis of various theories with differing paradigms, for example theory of action, philosophy of language, Marxist theory, theory of evolution. The discussions at the most recent sociology convention revolved around the possibility of theory comparison and theory synthesis. Which criteria do you use in your own syntheses? Can theories with such different paradigms even be synthesized?

I see things somewhat differently. If you were to ask me about the possibility of a 'marriage' between behaviorist theory (for example small-group research into the theory of learning, as developed in America in the 1950s) and a sociology based on a theory of action (whether derived from Parsons or Marx), then I would have to say no, I don't think it's possible. Their basic concepts are mutually exclusive. In the first case one conceptualizes the object by eliminating the concept of 'sense'; in the other, one deals with intentional action, communicative action, or value-oriented action as a fundamental concept. Those are clear alternatives. I would never try to integrate such theoretical premises. On the other hand, I don't agree at all that there is such a wide variety of paradigms. That's more likely the artificial product of a scientific rhetoric that was unintentionally inspired by Kuhn. Throughout the history of sociological theory, insofar as it laid claim to being a theory of society (through Marx, Durkheim, Weber, up to Parsons, or whomever), the same problem has always existed in regard to fundamental concepts: how do we reconcile the systems paradigm with the action paradigm, or the systems paradigm with that of the life-world? Marx avoided the problem completely by accepting Hegel's fundamental concepts, because Hegel's conceptual apparatus is neutral, so to speak, with regard to such differentiation. This allowed Marx to develop a labour theory of value which served to translate the functionalist analysis of the process of realization of capital (systems analysis) into analyses based on class conflicts, on active subjects and groups. However, I don't consider the retention of the labour theory of value to be feasible. That's one of the reasons, by the way, why many people don't consider me a Marxist. Granted, there must be some systematic equivalent. In the course of his development, Parsons transformed his action theory into a systems theory, although there was something left over. That can be seen in the status of the so-called 'general frame of action', which was promoted to a general action system. I contend that the problem lies in relating the two paradigms to one another not merely rhetorically, but in a genuinely satisfactory manner. Only then can one deal systematically with the fundamental question posed by Marx. Loosely speaking, that is the question of how capitalist expansion (which must be systematically analyzed) affects the structures of the life-world (first of the classes directly involved, today of more and more of the total population). The dialectic of objectified and living labour was supposed to explain how the destruction of traditional forms of life took place in the social strata from which the proletariat emerged. It was concerned with explaining the proletarianization of forms of life. That was Marx's practical impetus, and in that regard one can relate his thesis to our present circumstances. Our problem still consists in explaining how this capitalist economic system (whose growth rate isn't bad at all) destroys conditions of life which are so structured that they must be described in categories of action theory. As soon as one erases the infrastructure of life-worlds, through the use of systems theory, as soon as one admits on the analytical level only domains of social life which are systematically regulated—at that point we can no longer speak of socialized individuals; at most we can speak of Martians, of creatures that are so defined that one can no longer recognize under these descriptions socialized individuals and their problems.

Well, I can see from structuralist interpretations of Marx that there's no very great difference between systems theory and those interpretations. But can action theory and Marxist theory be synthesized so easily? As far as human actions are concerned, action theory cannot encompass all that goes on behind people's backs, and penetrate their consciousness. The silent compulsion of social relations falls right through the analytical net.

I think what interested Marx—the ability of objective life-circumstances to penetrate through the consciousness and action-orientations of the subjects involved—can be best reconstructed if one remembers that there is an idealism built into the basic tenets of action theory. In the most consistent theoretical versions of action theory, such as the linguistic (Winch), the phenomenological (Schülz) or the ethnomethodological (Garfinkel), society is basically defined as a life-world which is completely transparent. I would prefer instead to see it as consisting in systematically stabilized patterns of action of socially integrated groups. If we could succeed in conceptually linking paradigms of action theory and systems theory in the right way, then we could really begin to pursue the questions of Marxism instead of merely defining them out of existence, as both systems theory and action theory have done until now. So the variety of theories which I'm trying to integrate really isn't so large.

But that's another problem that has to be solved, in regard to your theory of emancipation. If I've understood correctly your ideal speech situation in a future society, doesn't that imply the idealistic hope that entire social systems will be altered through changes in the actions of single individuals, in the communicative actions of individuals? That idea must pursue you like the paradigms do Kuhn . . .

That needs to be placed in perspective. I need the ideal speech situation in order to reconstruct the normative foundations of a Critical Theory. The communication theory which I envisage is based on a type of action oriented toward understanding, in which people involved use criticizable validity claims to gain an orientation. The level of understanding is determined by whether or not the validity-claim which is raised by ego is accepted by the other. In this context I have to show what it means to raise and resolve criticizable validity claims—for instance, the truth-claim of an assertion. I believe that there are precisely two validity claims which can be dealt with only on an argumentative basis. That leads me to a 'discourse theory of truth', and in this context I have recourse to the general presuppositions of the ideal speech situation.

One should not imagine the ideal speech situation as a utopian model for an emancipated society. I use it only to reconstruct the concept of reason, that is, a concept of communicative reason, which I would like to mobilize against Adorno and Horkheimer's *Dialectic of Enlightenment*. Horkheimer and Adorno allow reason to shrivel down to the 'unreason' of mimesis. In the mimetic powers the promise of reconciliation is sublated. For Adorno that then leads to *Negative Dialectics*—in other words to Nowhere.

So the standpoint of identity wouldn't be acceptable to you either? The preservation of reason leads us to say that even in a future society there would remain a type of domination. One of Schelling's old problems. If the domination of reason remains in force, then there always remains a domination over objects. Schelling offered the one possible solution to this problem—identity.

I think that's a part of our conceptual heritage that can't be taken over as it stands. There is, if you wish, a bit of Kantianism in me. There remains something unreconciled in our relation to nature.

When we speak of reason, we aren't speaking of decisions concerning basic value postulates. We're dealing with unavoidable premises which are not at our disposition. The aspects of reason which, according to Max Weber, have separated out irreconcilably—the cognitive-instrumental, the moral-practical, and the aesthetic-expressive aspects—these three continue to form a concept of reason which is internally differentiated. Max Weber is wrong, I would say, when he affirms that the autonomous moments of reason transform themselves, so to speak, into irrational powers of belief which compete with one another. No, they remain moments of reason, and the big question is: how can we describe with sufficient precision the way they fit together? What does this pattern of reason mean for the socialization of individuals who speak and work and, because they do those two things, can't help but reproduce their lives with the aid of this three-sided rationality? I certainly don't believe—and here Max Weber is right—that one can capture the unity of reason, the interrelation of the different aspects of reason, on the level of cultural systems of interpretation, in the form of a religious world-picture or a philosophy. That is what is meant, in Marxist terms, by the sublation of philosophy. Nothing is going to come together any more on the level of cultural systems of interpretation. However, the moments of reason fit together in social relations and in everyday communicative practice, albeit in a remarkably distorted way. That is also Marx's concern—the destruction of precisely these rationally based conditions of life through the backlash of an economic-administrative system which, in and of itself, has reached a high degree of system differentiation, yet is so constructed that it has destructive side-effects. It is these which pose the problem.

What constitutes the idea of socialism, for me, is the possibility of overcoming the onesidedness of the capitalist process of rationaliz-ation (to use Weber's terminology). Onesidedness, that is, in the sense of the rise to dominance of cognitive-instrumental aspects, which results in everything else being driven into the realm of apparent irrationality. With the overcoming of that system, these aspects would be shifted to their proper place, so to speak—not that there has ever been a previous phase when they did occupy their proper place. In socialism, too, one would have to live with an economic system which operates exactly like a partial system, a system which is separated out from the political context. But it would not direct this objective, covert, destructive force against communicatively-structured conditions of life. My criticism of Marx is that he failed to see that capitalist production methods ushered in not only a new apolitical form of class domination, but a new level of system differentiation (as Luhmann would say). This differentiation had enormous evolutionary advantages over the level reached in state-organized societies of pre-bourgeois periods. Such evolutionary advantages, if we are to put it like that, are not something we can control. Marx imagined we could just destroy capitalism and the economy would dissolve back into the life-world under our control. He later assessed the matter somewhat more sceptically by separ-ating the realm of necessity from the realm of freedom. Marx spoke of neutral forces of production. I wonder whether there are neutral increases of complexity, or whether this higher level of system differentiation which we have reached in the modern age was achieved only at the cost of some form of class domination. If the latter were the case, then there could be only regressive solutions for socialism. That doesn't necessarily make socialism less attractive, but it does leave it more or less without a future. What kind of condition would we be in if the majority of the population, in order to achieve more humane forms of collective life, were ready to pay the heavy price of a regressive economic system? But there are no a priori arguments for the pessimistic premise underlying that question. For this reason socialization, as a project which is capable of self-correction, undertaken on what could be called a fallibilist basis, is as essential today as ever.

4.

The Dialectics of Rationalization

I
The Tradition of Critical Theory

Honneth: *To begin with, I shall summarize the topics we would like to address: First we want to concentrate on your position within the tradition of Critical Theory in order to, second, examine its deficiencies as you see them. The third and more systematic theme concerns the basic features of your theory, as developed in your latest book. I'm sure that will become very difficult and complicated once we have the comprehensive manuscript before us. In the fourth part our interest switches to the application of the theory to present-day political problems and conflicts. Finally, we'll want to address questions such as science as a vocation, the turning of Marxism and social theory into academic disciplines, and problems of the mode of production of Critical Theory. How can Marxism, which is caught up in an academic system, protect itself against a dangerous loss of experience and academic complacency? In other words: how can we rationally pursue critical scholarship today?*

That's not very clear to me either.

Honneth: *In a journalistic context you are perceived as the modern representative of Critical Theory. Do you accept this characterization?*

I've always felt myself over-estimated. After all, it was the older generation who produced Critical Theory in the 1930. Lukács led me to the young Marx. Adorno played, shall we say, an absolutely electrifying role. It was he who taught me that one need not restrict oneself to a historical approach to Marx.

Knödler-Bunte: *But wasn't that really a philosophical reading of Marx?*

Neither an historicized Marx nor the theory of capitalism was of much importance to me at that time, in the 1950s, but rather the Marx of the *Economic and Philosophical Manuscripts*, of the *Grundrisse* — Marx as the theoretician of reification. Of course, there were also Lukács and Korsch. I didn't take Marx seriously as an economist until 1958, when I read Sweezy's *Theory of Capitalist Development*. Adorno always said, and this is a typically philosophical attitude toward the text: secondary literature is irrelevant. He considered Marx and Freud as classics. He also opened my eyes to the fact that one must first exhaust the primary texts, systematically exhaust them, before one explores their sequels. That was something new to me when I arrived in Frankfurt in 1950. He also led me to stop reading Marx from an 'anthropological' perspective. But, of course, I never considered Marx primarily an economist. He was also a political theorist who took up the traditions of the bourgeois revolutions and their theoretical treatments from the Jacobins to Thomas Paine.

Naturally, one can remain in such traditions only if one criticizes and transforms them. That is a hermeneutic commonplace. The traditions that survive are only those which change in order to fit new situations. The same is true of my relation to the older Frankfurt Circle. I am more than a generation younger than the 'old ones', if I may put it that way, and also come from a different background. For example, I am the first one who is not Jewish, who grew up in Nazi Germany and who experienced the fall of fascism quite differently than the others. For these reasons alone it is not possible for me to have an unbroken identification with Critical Theory. Besides, when I became Adorno's assistant in 1956, the intellectual past of the Institute for Social Research was not accessible to the new students.

Honneth: *What traditions were alive then, if the Critical Theory of the thirties was as good as unknown?*

My philosophical and literary response at that time was to the left traditions of the twenties. For example, I read Lukács very early in the course of my studies, although that wasn't yet a standard thing at the time. The turning point came with the young Hegelian critique as interpreted by Löwith, in an intellectual-historical but nonetheless extremely illuminating manner. The insights of the young Hegelian critique into that which sustains us all, into everything which took place between Kant and Hegel, including Hölderlin, were exciting. In retrospect, I sometimes have the impression that a student can recreate a segment of the critical theory of the thirties if he systematically works his way from Kant through Hegel, including Schelling, and then approaches Marx via Lukács. I wouldn't want that understood as arrogance. If he were then confronted with Adorno in the late fifties and did not just read his writings but also heard him speak of Durkheim, Hegel and Freud, he could easily uncover the origins of this way of thinking, even without knowing the *Zeitschrift für Sozialforschung*. When this sunken continent later resurfaced—in the 1960s with the student protests—and entered the consciousness of us former assistants at the Institute, I didn't have the impression that what was occurring was entirely new.

Widmann: *When you got to Frankfurt didn't you sit down and look up the old papers in the Institute for Social Research?*

But they didn't exist.

Knödler-Bunte: *There was the* Zeitschrift *with the old essays . . .*

That didn't exist. Horkheimer had a great fear that we would get to the crate in the Institue's cellar that contained a complete set of the *Zeitschrift*. Had we had a strong desire to, however, we would have been able to read all of it. I was told at the time, and it was true, that it could have been obtained from Carlo Schmidt at the Institute.

Knödler-Bunte: *How did you actually get to Frankfurt and what did you find there?*

When I arrived in Frankfurt, it struck me that Adorno and Horkheimer did not pay much attention to contemporary philosophy, which I had studied in Bonn. I never got the impression from Adorno that he had read Heidegger intensively. I don't know even today whether he just read isolated sentences. This selectivity—there was no Jaspers, no phenomenology—was something exotic. Only in the 1970s, after Adorno's death, as I read his inaugural lecture and the essay on natural history, did I become clearly aware of all the things Adorno had had in his head as a young man. Subjectively, I saw myself as someone who, in the face of a very narrow, almost dogmatic selection of acceptable texts, carried on philosophical and academic traditions in a less strict manner. Because of my—let us say—more systematic approach, I was also considered by my contemporaries in the philosophical seminar as a kind of foreigner. In addition, it became clear to me that the 1920s, in which I had lived theoretically during my student years, were, after all, the 1920s. That became a stimulus to become interested in American sociology, for example. Analytical philosophy came afterward. Categories such as 'bourgeois science' never meant much for me. In an established science there are either useful things or less useful ones. In principle, I considered worthwhile anything that had a cognitive, structural or hermeneutical element—anything that would allow one to open up objects from the inside.

Honneth: *What was the source of your—even pre-theoretical—affinity with Critical Theory?*

As I mentioned, I had read Lukács. Inspired by the young Hegelians, I looked at the transition from Kant to 'objective' idealism with great interest. Alongside all this were my very strong everyday political interests. I had read *History and Class Consciousness* both with fascination and regret that it belonged to the past. Then I read the *Dialectic of Enlightenment* and the first things published by Adorno after the war. That gave me the courage to read Marx systematically and not simply historically. Critical Theory, a Frankfurt School—there was no such thing at the time. Reading Adorno had given me the courage to take up systematically what Lukács and Korsch represented historically: the theory of reification as a theory of rationalization, in Max Weber's sense. Already at that time, my problem was a theory of modernity, a theory of the pathology of modernity, from the viewpoint of the realization—the deformed realization—of reason in history. So, naturally, the *Dialectic of Enlightenment* became a key. When I met Adorno and saw how breathtakingly he spoke about commodity fetishism and applied this concept to cultural and everyday phenomena, at first it was a shock. But then I thought: try to act as if Marx and Freud, about whom Adorno spoke with the same orthodoxy, *were contemporaries*.

Knödler-Bunte: *Where then did you see the deficiencies of Critical Theory?*

I didn't think of it that way at the time. For me there was no critical theory, no coherent doctrine. Adorno wrote critical essays on culture and held seminars on Hegel. He made contemporary a certain Marxist background. That was it. Only some clever young people in the late 1960s discovered early Critical Theory and made it clearer in my mind that a theory of society should be systematic. In retrospect, what appear to me to be weaknesses in Critical Theory can be categorized under the labels of 'normative foundations', 'concept of truth and its relation to scientific disciplines' and 'undervaluation of the traditions of democracy and of the constitutional state'. With questions about foundations one naturally becomes unpopular in all circles oriented to Adorno.

In the 1930s the old Frankfurt Circle still explicity subscribed to a concept of reason and developed it in terms of the philosophy of history. This was achieved by means of an appropriation through ideology-critique of bourgeois philosophy. We find that in Horkheimer's book on the beginnings of bourgeois philosophy of history, and above all in the many essays in the *Zeitschrift*, including the articles by Marcuse and Horkheimer in 1937, in which both are convinced that bourgeois ideals, with certain limitations, are present in art as well as philosophy, survive as potentials. They could appeal to these potentials because, as Marxist social theorists, they could rely on political groups within the European working class movement—if not the proletariat in the Lukácsian sense—to unleash and realize historically the rational potential of bourgeois society, as a result of the ongoing development of the forces of production. This I call the philosophico-historical concept of reason.

In the 1930s, doubts began to arise about this among the Frankfurt theorists, and the results emerged in the *Dialectic of Enlightenment* and the *Eclipse of Reason*. What I consider Adorno's greatness, what gives him his position in the history of philosophy, is the fact that he was the only one to develop remorselessly and spell out the paradoxes of this form of theory construction, of the dialectic of enlightenment that unfolds the whole as the untrue. In this sense of critical insistence, he was one of the most systematic and effective thinkers I know. Of course, one can draw various conclusions from the results. Either one presses on in the illuminating exercise of negative philosophy, to the insight with which one is forced to endure that, if a spark of reason is left, then it is to be found in esoteric art. Or, on the other hand, one takes a step back and says to oneself: Adorno has shown that one must go back to a stage before the dialectic of enlightenment because, as a scientist, one cannot live with the paradoxes of a self-negating philosophy. If one takes Adorno's *Negative Dialectics* and *Aesthetic Theory* seriously and accepts them, and if one then wishes to advance just one step beyond this scene out of Beckett, then one has to become something of a post-structuralist to conceptualize it. Adorno never took this step. He would have considered it a betrayal of the rational heritage of Critical Theory. I don't think it is possible for Critical Theory in its strictest form to refer to any form of empirical or even discursive analysis of social conditions.

This is related to the second point of criticism, the philosophical concept of truth adopted from Hegel, which the old Frankfurt School never abandoned and which is irreconcilable with the fallibility of scientific endeavour.

The third point has become very relevant to me. On the level of political theory, the old Frankfurt School never took bourgeois democracy very seriously. Those are the three most important deficiencies of the Frankfurt School as I see them today.

II
Deficiencies of Critical Theory

Honneth: *I think we should move from this listing of systematic deficiencies in the tradition of Critical Theory to the constructive means you have employed in these three areas in order to overcome them. Thus, the question is: how have you corrected the normative deficiencies of Critical Theory? In what way have you transformed its concept of truth? How have you evaluated differently the achievements of bourgeois democracy? By what means is it possible to reach a better understanding on these three levels?*

Well, here I can only give some programmatic explanations. For the central intuition that I hope to have clarified somewhat in my *Theory of Communicative Action*, I am indebted to a reception of both the hermeneutic and the analytic strains of linguistic theory and, one could say, to a reading of Humboldt with the insight of analytic philosophy. This is the intuition that a *telos* of mutual understanding is built into linguistic communication. Along this path one comes to the concept of communicative rationality which, by the way, is also at the basis of Adorno's few affirmative utterances concerning the unspoiled [*nicht-verfehltes*] life. When in *Minima Moralia* Adorno actually tries to explain what he means by a mimetic association, not only with nature but also among people, he refers to Eichendorff's 'distant nearness'. So he has recourse to categories of intersubjectivity from which he abstains philosophically. So far this is an attempt to secure a concept of reason by means of formal pragmatics, that is, by means of an analysis of the general characteristics of communication-orientated action. Naturally, that can only be a first step. The next step is to make the concept of communicative rationality applicable to social relations, to institutionalized systems of interaction. Here one must be careful to avoid the pitfalls of foundationalism or linguistic transcendentalism. In the *Introduction to the Critique of Political Economy* of 1857, Marx established in what sense the category of labour is a universal concept applicable to all societies. He shows that only to the extent that the capitalist mode of production has become established are the objective conditions fulfilled that allow him, Marx, access to an understanding of the universal character of this category 'labour'.

With regard to such a theory of communication, one must use the same method to clarify how the development of late capitalism has objectively fulfilled conditions that allow us to recognize universals in the structures of linguistic communication, providing criteria for a critique which can no longer be based on the philosophy of history.

Honneth: *So the categorical means of correcting the normative deficiency of Critical Theory is a concept of communicative understanding based on linguistic theory?*

Yes, and now to the second point. I believe the Frankfurt School cling to a concept of theory—and also to a concept of truth—that was based on the emphatic concept of reason in the philosophical tradition. This is the same concept that reappears in an ironic fashion in the formulation 'instrumental reason'. 'Reason' is not meant to apply simply to truth-intentions, in the narrow sense in which we speak of the truth of utterances. Rather, reason should reveal the unity of the moments of reason separated out in all three Kantian critiques: the unity of theoretical reason with practical-moral insight and aesthetic judgment.

When one does science and, within this framework, philosophy, one has only to do with truth claims in the narrower sense. This generates a dilemma. On the one hand, the conceptions of emphatic theory are tailored to 'truths' from which the moral and aesthetic-expressive aspects have not yet been split off. On the other hand, a critical social theory must also proceed scientifically: it can only make pronouncements with a claim to propositional truth. This is another way of formulating the awkwardness that Hegelianizing social scientists have always felt in relation to empirical procedures. If one doesn't follow Adorno towards a 'negative dialectics', which is a renunciation of the social sciences, it becomes necessary to use theories that specialize in questions of truth in the narrow sense. In this case, one must then see how it is possible, within the social sciences and, first and foremost, in the formation of philosophical theory, to bring into play the experiential domains of both the aesthetic-expressive and moral-practical without empiricist redefinitions, and without endangering the requirements of theoretical descriptions. That is the problem of *non-positivist approaches to theory in the social sciences*. Hermeneutic approaches ensure the connection to the realm of experience of everyday communicative praxis, which is virtually defined by the lack of differentiation between questions of truth, justice and taste (if you don't mind the Kantian divisions).

Freud's theory is another example. This finds inspiration in a concept of 'consciousness' or 'ego'—thus 'conscious control of drives', 'ego strength' and so on—which cannot be explained without simultaneously examining the moral-practical elements of Kant's (or Hegel's) concept of autonomy; and certainly not without referring to aesthetic-expressive elements of an 'id become ego'.

Just as non-objectivist research methods within the human sciences mobilize the standpoints of moral and aesthetic critique without endangering the primacy of basic questions of truth, we can find a similar counter-movement in ethics and aesthetics. Of course, cognitive ethics excludes problems of the good life, leaving over from what is good merely what is just. But the discussion of an ethics of responsibility and of conviction, and the more serious consideration of hedonistic factors, in turn bring into play viewpoints concerned with the consequences of action and the interpretation of needs, which lie in the realm of the cognitive and the expressive. Art, too, which has become autonomous, pushes towards an increasingly pure expression of basic aesthetic experiences. Today, however, post-avant garde art is characterized by a remarkable combination of realistic and politically engaged tendencies with authentic continuations of the classic modernism which had established the independent logic of the aesthetic. Thus, realistic and engaged art forms raise cognitive and moral-practical factors to the level of richness of form which was liberated by the avant garde. It seems as if such movements, which run counter to the radical singlemindedness of differentiated moments of reason, suggest once again a unity. This unity can only be acquired this side of the culture of experts—in a non-deformed daily practice.

The third deficiency—the theory of democracy—is connected with the question of developmental logics. Here I am of the opinion that one can show that the formal features of bourgeois systems of law and constitutions, of bourgeois political institutions in general, demonstrate a conceptual structure of moral-practical thought and interpretation which must be considered superior in relation to the built-in moral categories of traditional legal and political institutions.

Knödler-Bunte: *Superior in what sense?*

Superior in terms of the ability to answer moral-practical questions. This can be seen in the following way: if one reads Marx correctly, one can find certain ideas embodied in the institutions of the bourgeois state which belong to a heritage worthy of preservation in a socialist society. Naturally, one can say that the horizon from which the old critical theory derived its perception of contemporary history was so gloomy that nothing remained of anything that could be reclaimed as reason or—if you like—as utopian in Bloch's sense.

Knödler-Bunte: *Today, on the other hand, the critique of instrumental reason encounters a remarkably urgent situation marked by the expectations of doom and catastrophe-anxieties present in many movements. By contrast, your construction relies on a form of intactness of bourgeois society, at least insofar as it should be capable of developing certain structural mechanisms that bear the stamp of rationality. From a concrete standpoint, and without speaking philosophically, I believe that there are mechanisms which tend to make institutions independent, on account of their size, or through centralization, or by cutting off or obliterating possibilities for feedback. This sets a sort of uncontrolled machinery in motion and brings new risks which E. P. Thompson has called 'exterminism', the logic of self-annihilation.*

Yes, it makes a difference whether you see *any* kind of communicative rationality built into daily practice or the life-world, or into accepted traditional life styles, or whether you simply just relinquish the criteria by which to criticize these tendencies towards independence, or leave these criteria diffusely in the background. It seems to me that the self-contradictions of reason went so far—from the perspective of the dialectic of enlightenment—that Horkheimer and Adorno (Pollock as well, with his theory of state capitalism) found political institutions, all social institutions, and daily practice as well, completely void of all traces of reason. For them, reason had become utopian in the literal sense of the word: it had lost all its locations and thus ushered in the whole problematic of negative dialectics.

For the moment, I simply want to recall that one should always explicate the conceptual structures used to criticize specific features, to avoid falling into embarrassment when the viewpoint, criteria, or context of this critique is challenged. The older Critical Theory fell exactly into this difficulty—even if Adorno was later able to articulate the dilemma fruitfully by recognizing it as such, and attempting to salvage the particular as the intangible, the injured, the victimized—that necessarily falls through the grasp of all discursive or identifying thought. Adorno asked this question but he did it in such a way that it no longer made sense truly to analyze the concrete social phenomena to which you refer, such as the autonomous dynamic of the arms race, economic growth, bureaucratization, and so on.

Honneth: *Even in the Marxist tradition it is not unusual to value the achievements of bourgeois-democratic institutions under the concept of formal democracy. Adorno's perspective, however, is more of a foreign perspective in Marxist theory in that it allows differences among political systems to fade under the pressure of fascism.*

Yes, one could describe that on a scale, to use a positivist device: on the one side are the Second International theorists of continuity, where progress becomes evolutionary in a sense that I wouldn't defend, and on the other side are Benjamin, Bloch, some anarchists —the theorists of total discontinuity. Although I have something against the Aristotelian virtue of moderation and of the mean, I do feel myself drawn to the middle in questions like this. In any case, one has to look at it as an empirical question: in which historical situations could and should fairly strong continuities be preserved with a declining social formation, and in which situations would almost everything have to be rejected to achieve even the smallest step toward emancipation?

III
Dialectics of Rationalization

Honneth: *Perhaps I can now ask the global question: how do these motifs fit together in your book due to appear this fall?[1] How do you tie together the different lines of thought you've been developing for the last ten years in the project of a theory of communicative action?*

Knödler-Bunte: *Adorno always used to say on such occasions: now say that in your own words.*

There are essentially four motifs that I have brought together in this monster. The first motif is an attempt at a theory of rationality. That is especially difficult today, when forms of relativism have the upper hand under the sign of a dubious revival of Nietzsche (or of irrationalism in general). I may be approaching this problem a little too 'straight', though certainly in a confrontation with important counter-arguments. For example, I discuss the rationality debate which took place in England in the early 1970s between some analytic philosphers and anthropologists. One side wanted to strengthen the hypothesis that every culture, every form of life, every language-game, constituted a self-enclosed totality with its own unique criteria of rationality. By connecting up with this kind of discussion I try to make my approach more plausible for all those who find such a theory of communicative rationality a shocking requirement, who cannot swallow such an awkward word as rationality without turning red. I am aware of the fact that the times are not favourable for this type of undertaking, since the tragedy Lukács described as *The Destruction of Reason* now reappears as farce in our liberal cultural weeklies. I develop the second motif (which is not quite so untimely) in the form of a *theory of communicative action*, in order to deal with a series of more theoretical problems, such as the theory of argumentation. Above all, I want to demonstrate that beginning with understanding-

---

1. *Theorie des Kommunikativen Handelns,*, Frankfurt 1981, 2 vols. English translation of vol. 1, *The Theory of Communicative Action, 1: Reason and the Rationalization of Society*, trans. Thomas McCarthy, Boston 1984.

orientated action is useful for purposes of social theory. It did not become clear to me until I was writing—which is why I kept throwing my first drafts away—that Anglo-Saxon discussions about action theory, language theory, and the theory of meaning have become independent as *l'art pour l'art*. One ends up with wonderful, pedantic, conceptually refined ideas of what social interaction is, but has forgotten for what purpose. This prompted me to stick more closely to the history of theory, for example to George Herbert Mead's theory of symbolically mediated interaction, in order to show that the pragmatic tradition already contained this concept of rationality. Further, I took up Durkheim and read him from the viewpoint of a theory of social evolution—which is rather unusual. With the aid of the concept of communicative rationality I decoded the perspective of development from mechanical to organic solidarity. Finally I went back to Max Weber to treat a substantial theme. For I did not just want to show how the theory of communicative action can be useful for social theory. I also had a third motif, namely, the *dialectic of social rationalization*. That was already the main theme of the *dialectic of enlightenment*. I wanted to show that one can develop a theory of modernity using communications-theoretical concepts which possess the analytic precision needed for socio-pathological phenomena, for what the Marxist tradition calls reification.

For this purpose I have developed—perhaps this is a fourth motif—a concept of society that brings together systems and action theory. Because Hegelian-Marxist social theory, developed in categories of totality, has decomposed into its parts, namely, action theory and systems theory, the present task now consists of combining these two paradigms in a non-trivial fashion—that is, not merely eclectically and additively. Thus, one can give new form to the critique of instrumental reason which could not be pursued further using the methods of the old Critical Theory. The appropriate form is a critique of functionalist reason.

Honneth: *Why a theory of rationalization? There would seem to be other ways to a critical social theory, for example, a theory of capitalization, or a theory of specific degrees of the division of labour. Why do you take up the motif of rationality? Why is rationality the key to a critical social theory?*

I could make the answer easy and say that, after all, Adorno and Horkheimer already used the concept of instrumental reason to reformulate the theme of reification. I suggest we first look at the background, in the sense of the psychology of research. The fact that I finally sat down at the end of 1977 to deal seriously with the matter has to do with the following—I'll get back to the theme of rationality later. The tense German political situation, which was becoming more and more like a pogrom following Schleyer's kidnapping in 1977, drove me out of the theoretical ivory tower to take a political stand. For the first time I took seriously neo-conservative ideologies which had become fashionable since about 1973. I did not just shrug my shoulders as if experiencing a sense of *déjà-vu*. Rather, I considered the appearance of these militant late liberals—who followed above all Gehlen and Carl Schmitt in Germany—as signifying a broader change of climate. I attempted to clarify the concept of modernity implicit in these considerations, and the departure from modernity, a departure from radical democracy and enlightenment—those ideas which had given rise to the Federal Republic. That was one side. The other side was that for the first time I felt I better understood the meaning of the new potentials for protest, the new movements with which I had no intrinsic relation. If you take these two phenomena together, you will perhaps understand that at this time the interpretive scheme was formed which guided my concluding observations, if not the whole book. Perhaps I should explain that a little better. Both sides, the neo-conservatives and the critics of growth, the one with greater articulation, the other more diffusely, offer conflicting intepretations of the state into which Western societies have got themselves, with Reagan and the Lady at one end, Mitterrand at the other, and Schmidt in the middle—three decades after the last disaster. Both understandings, ideologies, interpretive schema—whatever you want to call them—manipulate unfortunate consequences of an otherwise successful stabilization of internal conditions. This stabilization was attained on the basis of the welfare-state compromise, of what is in a broad sense a social democratic compromise, as Dahrendorf puts it.

Honneth: *What do you mean by that?*

It is only a catch-word. The mass democracy of the welfare state and state interventionism form a system that maintains to some degree the dynamic of capitalist growth. From this growth it finances compensations in line with the system (money, leisure time, and so on), pacifying traditional class conflicts without disturbing the sanctity of private investment, the structure of private wealth, and so forth. This machine is not running so well at the moment, either *economically* or *socio-psychologically*.

Economically: Some try a refurbished neo-neo-Keynesianism, while others try Friedman and the monetarists, and what results is a fluctuating shift of unsolved problems from the marketplace onto the state, from the state onto the marketplace, and back again. The participants in this zero-sum game have somehow not grasped that the poles 'state' and 'society' are only two sides of the same coin—if viewed from the historical perspective of modernization—namely, systems of action which have become differentiated through the steering media of exchange value and administrative power. These systems have been consolidated into a monetary-administrative complex, and having been disconnected from the communicatively structured life-world (with private and public spheres), have apparently grown *overcomplex*. The state and the economy will necessarily become more complex with economic growth (this is what the neo-conservatives do not see). Connected to this are conflicts that today take a more socio-psychological form: the defence of life-styles threatened by internal colonization. We must also consider the drastic, only temporarily repressed, military dangers of the instability between super powers, with the whole absurdity of the arms race. The conflicting interpretations that have assumed sharper and sharper contours in the last five or six years react against all of this. What most directly interests me is that both sides turn against the heritage of what Weber calls Western rationalism. The one side does this in the name of a robust post-modernism with curiously regressive characteristics—regardless of whether one evokes the social romanticism of pioneering capitalism, as the American neo-conservatives do, or mobilizes the counter-Enlightenment, as in Germany. The other side does it mostly by summoning up anti-modernist emotions. My fear is simply that the two competing and conflicting syndromes are racing toward the destruction of all that I consider deserves to be saved in the substance of Western traditions and inspirations. The post-modernists would like to hold onto the capitalist blueprint of social rationalization at any price—in fact, rather rabidly. They give economic growth priority over the welfare state. This policy attempts to dampen its negative effects on socially integrated areas of life, upon the family, school, political sphere, and so on, by returning to a Biedermeier culture, to uprooted but rhetorically re-harnessed traditions. Luhmann's talk of ideology planning was never as true as today. However, the displacement onto the market of problems which have been shifted with good reason from the market onto the state since the nineteenth century can hardly provide an answer. The problems will survive being shoved back and forth between the media of money and power. And I do not know how one could renew the cushion of tradition that supported capitalist societies for centuries, which was consumed without being regenerated, indeed how traditionalism in any sense could be renewed by a historically enlightened consciousness. The only resource we can still creatively draw on—cultural modernism—is rendered despicable in this perspective.

But this gives rise to an unfortunate convergence with the anti-modernist critique of growth. The demanded de-differentiation is obviously no solution unless clear distinctions are made. One must distinguish between the restraint of the monetary-administrative-military complex and the rolling back of the structural differen-tiation of life-forms. Modern life-worlds are differentiated and should remain so in order that the reflexivity of traditions, the individuation of the social subject, and the universalistic foundations of justice and morality do not all go to hell. Hopefully, this is not leading to an ironic division of labour; between apologetic neo-conservatives who want to give their celebrated functionalist reason a traditionalist twist, and young conservatives who increasingly com-bine their awareness of the high risks of contemporary history, their important and courageous defence of threatened life-forms, and their exploration of new ones with a kind of post-structuralist renunciation of reason itself.

To return to the point of departure: my real motive in beginning the book in 1977 was to understand how the critique of reification, the critique of rationalization, could be reformulated in a way that would offer a theoretical explanation of the crumbling of the welfare-state compromise and of the potential for a critique of growth in new movements, without surrendering the project of modernity or descending into post- or anti-modernism, 'tough' new conservatism or 'wild' young conservatism.

Honneth: *So, in your opinion, the neo-populist potentials fall prey to a misunderstanding of themselves as long as they follow the critique of modernity offered by post-structuralism or* Lebensphilosophie?

I think so. In any case, you must not get the impression that this book is directly political. It is a very theoretical attempt above all to discover how much better the political intentions of these critique of growth movements could be understood, if they were separated from critiques of modernism in general. That is first of all a theoretical problem, and when you read the book you will notice that it has become hopelessly academic.

I wanted to take up the systematic problem again, the question of the normative foundations. Is it not possible—*pace* Adorno—to explicate a concept of communicative reason that can stand against Adorno's negativism, so that it contains what Adorno believed could be made visible only indirectly, by implication, through continual and consistent self-negation? Adorno would certainly not have agreed. All that would have been too affirmative for him. But when one is as involved in scientific research as I am, one must stay away from positions with one foot in post-structuralism; one must seek a theoretical approach that permits connections to productive scientific approaches, in order simultaneously to retrieve the claim of the older Critical Theory and do it justice. What this generates may appear to be a return to positions once aimed for by Critical Theory in the 1930s. Naturally, 'return' must have many quotation marks around it, for I want to make this return without adopting Critical Theory's background in the philosophy of history. That was a rather long-winded answer to your short question: why critical social theory as a theory of rationality?

Honneth: *Two more questions on that: what is communicative rationality and how does it allow an interpretation of the structure of contemporary society?*

As I said, I am trying to work out the normative content of the idea of understanding present in language and communication. That leads to a complex concept that implies not only that we understand the meaning of speech acts, but also that mutual understanding is produced between participants in communication regarding facts, norms, and also experiences. (Each of us has privileged access to experiences, and must reveal them through expressive self-presentation before an audience if they are to be regarded as one's own.)

Here we find the three dimensions contained in the concept of communicative rationality: first, the relation of the knowing subject to a world of events or facts; second, the relation to a social world of an acting, practical subject entwined in interaction with others; and finally, the relation of a suffering and passionate subject (in Feuerbach's sense) to its own inner nature, to its own subjectivity and the subjectivity of others. These are the three dimensions that come into view when one analyzes communication processes from the participants' perspective. To these should be added the life-world, however, which stands behind the back of each participant in communication and which provides resources for the resolution of problems of understanding. Members of a social collective normally share a life-world. In communication, but also in processes of cognition, this only exists in the distinctive, pre-reflexive form of background assumptions, background receptivities or background relations. The life-world is that remarkable thing which dissolves and disappears before our eyes as soon as we try to take it up piece by piece. The life-world functions in relation to processes of communication as a resource for what goes into explicit expression. But the moment this background knowledge enters communicative expression, where it becomes explicit knowledge and thereby subject to criticism, it loses precisely those characteristics which life-world structures always have for those who belong to them: certainty, background character, impossibility of being gone behind.

Widmann: *In this context, alternative life-styles must be of interest to you. Here it is precisely the life-world that is to be criticized. From discussions of personal relations to questions of varying tolerances of uncleanliness, an attempt is being made rationally to discuss questions which are otherwise inaccessible to criticism.*

Knödler-Bunte: *And don't these experiences prove that rational discussion and criticism do not necessarily destroy the life-world, but that new life-worlds can develop?*

Well I certainly do not believe that attempts to develop alternative life-styles result in the destruction of life-forms. I simply think that one can label as a life-world only those resources that are not thematized, not criticized. The moment one of its elements is taken out and criticized, made accessible to discussion, that element no longer belongs to the life-world. I also think it is impossible to create new forms of living by talking and talking about things. One element of these alternative life-styles does appear to differ clearly from more strongly traditional life-styles. That is the wider horizon of what *can* be thematized. That is also very characteristic of what I have called, perhaps using too harsh a term, the 'rationalization of the life-world'. I mean that in a thoroughly positive sense.

One thing you must not forget in any case: for every element of the most explored, well-worn and well-tried life-world that is changed or even consciously accepted, there are untold masses of elements that, even in the course of the most radical weighing of alternatives, never even crossed the threshold of thematization. The life-world is so unproblematic that we are simply incapable of making ourselves conscious of this or that part of it at will. The fact that certain elements of the life-world become problematic is an objective process. It depends on the problems that press in on us from outside in an objective way, by virtue of the fact that something has *become* problematic behind our backs.

Knödler-Bunte: *Do you postulate also, as Agnes Heller does, an ontology of structures of the everyday world that every person has?*

There Agnes Heller is somewhat too anthropological for my taste. I also believe, however, that there are general structures which are essential for life. But they are present only as infrastructures in historical life-forms, which can only exist in the plural—besides which they change in the evolutionary dimension.

One more thing about the problem of thematizing the life-world. The demands of the student movement, that formal rules and institutions, which up till then had been taken for granted, should be questioned, cannot be simply transferred, in my view, to the life-world context in general.

Widmann: *But* Authority and the Family *was after all the theoretical foundation of the alternative schools movement . . .*

Without taking account of what one could have learned about the radically altered life-situation, compared with the twenties and thirties, from the seminars which Oevermann and I were giving at the time. But let's leave that on one side, I don't want to play the professor.

Honneth: *So far the subject has been the concept of communicative rationality. What do you mean, however, by the concept of rationalization? If I understand it correctly, this is supposed to bring a dynamic point of view into the analysis?*

First of all, where history of theory is concerned, Max Weber was my point of departure. What he terms processes of social rationalization—essentially the institutionalization of purposive-rational action, above all in economic and administrative systems—can be understood as the advance of an institutional embodiment of complexes of rationality. Weber himself analyzed this on another level, that of culture, predominantly in the sociology of religion. Social rationalization means, then, that a society remoulds its basic institutions in order to make use of—so to speak—culturally ready-made structures of rationality. In Weber's view, the capitalist economic system could only arise because there was a class of entrepreneurs to be recruited from the puritanical sects, who brought with them the ethical and motivational presuppositions for a methodically rational conduct of life; on the other hand, the capitalist means of production could not have been established and stabilized if a legal system had not been institutionalized, which was tailored to subjects of private law, acting strategically, purposive-rationally, each following his or her own goals. The cognitive structures of a mode of thought governed by principles of an ethic of conviction are embodied in the modern legal system. These structures are embodied by these institutions in the same way that they are 'anchored' in the motives of the strata bearing the spirit of capitalism.

Honneth: *Thus far Weber. But a concept of communicative action would also have to provide another basis for the concept of rationalization.*

Schematically described, my critique of Weber is as follows: he does not see the selectivity in the pattern of capitalist rationalization. He does not see that in the development of capitalism those elements are repressed that he himself analyzed under the heading of the 'ethics of brotherhood'. Nevertheless, for Weber, also, there are moral-practical potentials here which came into play in the radical religious movements, the Baptists, for example, in the attempt to create institutional forms that were not just simply functional for the emerging capitalist economic system. And precisely these potentials did not enter into the dominant institutional pattern of capitalist modernity. It is just these ethical visions—which push towards communicative forms of organization—that are excluded in capitalism.

On the basis of Mead and Durkheim, I attempt to develop an evolutionary perspective for the increasing reflexive fluidity of world-views, for a continuing process of individuation, and for the emergence of a universalistic moral and legal system through the simultaneous detachment and liberation of communicative action from institutionally frozen contexts. Further, I sharply distinguish between the more or less differentiated or 'rationalized' life-worlds that are reproduced by way of communicative action and, on the other hand, formally organized systems of action based on steering media.

Today economic as well as administrative imperatives are encroaching upon territory that the life-world can no longer relinquish. To grossly oversimplify the case, until now the processes of destruction that have paved the way to capitalist modernization have occurred in such a way as to give rise to new institutions. These new institutions transferred social material from the realm of sovereignty of the life-world into realms of action steered by the media and organized by formal law. This went well as long as it only touched on functions of material reproduction that need not necessarily be organized communicatively. In the meantime, however, it seems that system imperatives are encroaching on areas which are demonstrably unable to perform their tasks if they are removed from communicatively structured domains of action. This is true of tasks such as cultural reproduction, social integration and socialization.

The battle lines between life-world and system thereby acquire a new relevance. Today economic and administrative imperatives embodied in the media of money and power encroach on areas that somehow collapse as soon as they are broken off from communication-orientated action and transferred to interactions steered by these media. These are processes that no longer fit into the scheme of class analysis. But one can demonstrate a functional connection between the central conflicts of the life-world and the requirements of capitalist modernization. I have shown this with examples from social, educational and family policy, and also to a degree from the new protest movements.

Honneth: *We have now already entered a new complex of issues. How are the terms of a theory of communicative action used to describe the constitution of contemporary society? Perhaps we should first pose questions of clarification. I would like to have the following question answered: whether it is not more useful to begin with collective agents, with social groups and their organizations, rather than with systems and the logic of institutions?*

From the methodological standpoint my suggestion has the advantage that one can take over something from both structuralism and systems theory. It is worth considering that these two research traditions might have good reason for leaving the realm of action theory. I believe there are such grounds. If one wants to analyze steering crises in the economy, for example, one must bring systems-theoretical methods to bear. We have no choice, since the objective dialectic and the concept of totality of Hegelian theory no longer inspire confidence. What was once bound together is now split asunder: systems theory and action theory.

Widmann: *Fine, what you have said is: here is a sophisticated arsenal of tools, of conceptual means that can be applied. But what domains of reality are revealed by your approach? What cognitive gains do you hope to make?*

One cognitive gain is that the normative contents of a humane social life can be introduced in an unsuspicious way by means of a communication theory, without having to smuggle them in secretly by way of a philosophy of history. With a theory of communication, there is no obligation to proceed only according to action theory, to speak only of agents and their fate, acts and consequences. It becomes possible also to speak of the characteristics of life-worlds in which agents and collectives or individual subjects move. For instance, it is possible to trace the uprooting of a plebeian lower class from a traditional world dating from the time of early industrialization. What are the ideas with which those who have resisted capitalist modernization for centuries have identified?

Well into the nineteenth century it was not so much with the ideals of bourgeois emancipatory movements and certainly not with the ideas of socialism. Instead, such movements drew strength mainly from the potential of traditional ideas, from religious ideas, from religiously-anchored natural law, and so on. I don't mean just the Peasant Wars, rather this extends far into the artisans' movement of the nineteenth century. These movements are driven by directly provoked feelings of injustice as well as the need for spontaneity and expression. But such impulses do not become a historically effective reality if they cannot be publicly expressed. There must be leaflets, there must be someone who will speak out, with whom one can identify. Now, for example, the limits that a traditional life-world places on political movements that objectively aim beyond these life-worlds cannot be comprehended hermeneutically in the intentions and motives of single agents. It is not enough to ask what the agents were thinking of, what their motives were, what they talked about, although these questions have again become perhaps justifiably fashionable in the name of a historiography of everyday life. This is very useful in itself but, as Adorno would have said with more pathos, it is somewhat lacking in concepts. For this reason, a structural analysis of life-worlds, based on communication theory, can be useful if one does not wish simply to load the material from outside with economic interests, political power struggles, and so on. Otherwise, one is swimming in a sea of historical contingencies. Just as a sort of grammar emerges in art through the organization and unfolding of a style, so also differentiations of the life-world can be described from within without recourse to the level of action. What does it mean, for example, when a stable system of institutions, which encapsulates pre-formed patterns of action, differentiates and separates itself, first, from interpretive world-views, which can now also take over functions of legitimation—that's to say, deception —and, second, releases itself from networks of interaction which are now left to the self-definition of individual actors?

Honneth: *I can see that this 'structuralist' element of social analysis does guard against an under-conceptualized approach to social processes. My only reservations are that such analyses may no longer translate back into the field of social conflicts between collectives and agents. Once one has divided up the different dimensions of modern rationality in this way, we must ask what paths of rationalization are pursued by specific collective agents. For instance, one must ask how accumulated knowledge is monopolized by power elites and how social strata themselves are thereby constituted. Doesn't social reality divide in this way into social confrontations in regard to monopolies of rationality?*

There you are sketching a program that I have no reservations about, although I'm sure we would agree that it still requires an extremely long period of development.

Knödler-Bunte: *But must everything really fit together in one theory, as you would have it? Why can't one accept that there are differing types of theories, each with its strengths and weaknesses? Their powers of expression compete with each other, and at times they leave room for whatever has as yet found no clear methodical approach? After all, is it possible to imagine one social theory, founded on evolutionary theory, that can incorporate the pattern of universal history as well as concrete analysis of objects and situations?*

One can be satisfied with a respectable historiography that is candid about its own hermeneutic relativity. But is that enough? One would also like to have a situational analysis, which, if we are lucky, allows us to understand more than a generalizing historiography can. The latter can make it clear to us why, here in Germany, we have such a deformed political culture. It reveals to us the lines of tradition: the empire, Wilhelminianism, the Nazis, the only half-completed bourgeois revolution, and so on. On the other hand, we have theories of language, morality and cognition. All this would just remain in mid-air, without telling us very much, if social theory could not develop the focusing power of a kind of magnifying glass, and throw a bright spotlight on the present.

Knödler-Bunte: *But this bright spotlight could also come from such a view as Benjamin's, which combines disparate contexts in order to make specific, shocking revelations about ourselves.*

If one uses such an approach from the start, one has relinquished a scientific attitude and has gone over to an aesthetic view of history. Let me explain again my own procedure. Naturally, I am somewhat self-conscious about the approach of evolutionary theory. One is plagued on the one hand by the Second International, and by Luhmann on the other, and perhaps even by the ghost of a naturalistic philosophy of history. This must be avoided. But I also see what can be gained from a theory that tries to work out a logic of development. Such an evolutionary perspective is dangerous if one wants, thus heavily armed, to produce a respectable work of social or cultural history, unless one tempers it to the degree I believe is necessary. As far as evolutionistic assumptions are concerned, I restrict myself to certain modes of interpretation for the infrastructure of possible life-worlds, according to general, genetic-structuralist categories.

I have yet to carry out an historical analysis with these instruments of evolutionary theory, but I can imagine that they could reveal new dimensions even of a field as well-researched as the Peasant Wars. One has to give it a try. It is somewhat simpler where the present is at issue. In that context we just let ourselves be guided by everyday intuitions. We are all armchair sociologists who put Hegel's 'realist's morning prayer' into practice, that is: the reading of the newspaper.

Honneth: *Because of the way your conceptual framework is set up, your analysis of the present limits itself to the perception of horizontal frictions in the social system, namely frictions between the life-worlds and the systematically integrated partial systems. By contrast the dimensions of a vertical analysis get short shrift—although not necessarily, since I can easily imagine that one could rework Marxist class theory with your categories, in a way which would reveal more of social reality than can be found in the newspapers.*

One would probably have to produce a combination of class theory and analysis of subcultures, in order to explain the current shifts in areas of conflict and forms of consciousness, but I didn't attempt that in my new book. And as long as this isn't done, one has no way of testing the viability of the approach.

IV
Crisis Theories and Social Movements

Widmann: *In a certain sense, this combination of class theory and analysis of subcultures already exists. Or at least the beginnings of such a combination. Almost nothing is discussed in the ecology movement on a theoretical level as much as the relation between classical Marxist crisis theory and the new crises of complexity evident, for example, in the mechanisms which render the technical and military apparatus autonomous.*

I find it more elegant and plausible to give capitalism credit for being what it is—for what it has actually achieved thanks to its level of differentiation and its ability to control social processes. Let's give our Marxist hearts a shock: capitalism was quite a success, at least in the area of material reproduction, and it still is. Granted, it has indulged from the beginning in an enormous plunder of traditional forms of life. But today the imperatives built into the dynamics of capitalist growth can only be fulfilled through a substantial growth in what we call the monetary-bureaucratic complex.

As a consequence, we now observe, and feel, and suffer an 'over-spill', an encroachment by the system on areas no longer at all related to material reproduction. These areas of cultural tradition—social integration through values and norms, education, socialization of coming generations—are however, ontologically speaking, held together by their very nature through the medium of communicative action. Once the steering media such as money and power penetrate these areas, for instance by redefining relations in terms of consumption, or by bureaucratizing the conditions of life, then it is more than an attack on traditions. The foundations of a life-world that is already rationalized are under assault. What is at stake is the symbolic reproduction of the life-world itself. In sum, crises that arise in the area of material reproduction are intercepted at the cost of a pathologizing of the life-world. I developed this thesis in my book, and I believe that in this way some problems can be solved.

Honneth: *I am more interested in questions that again touch on the conceptual distinction between subsystems, but I would like to begin with empirically oriented questions. Isn't what you have just been saying too much centered on West Germany? Beyond our western borders there are conflicts of a much more profoundly threatening nature, and which can hardly be explained by recourse to a crisis theory of system and life-world. I am thinking of the quite traditional conflicts that today arise mainly from structural unemployment resulting from capitalist accumulation, and from a tremendous wave of rationalization which is approaching us and whose consequences we can only speculate on.*

Where will these conflicts be precipitated as long as the safety net of the welfare state holds up?

Widmann: *When the president of the Swedish Association of Savings Banks predicts that the Western industrial nations will lose one quarter of both their blue-collar and white-collar jobs in the next 15 years, I don't see any safety net of social services that can deal with that. I don't believe crises are automatic, but I see the approach of huge problems that have nothing to do with a conflict between system and life-world.*

The analysis I have worked out presents this alternative: on the one hand, the conditions necessary to the welfare state compromise may be fulfilled—continuous, albeit restrained, economic growth. Then problems would arise that I would place under the heading of colonization of the life-world, an erosion or undermining of realms of communicatively-structured action. On the other hand, the dynamics of growth may not be maintained; then we would see some variant of traditional conflicts.

Widmann: *Can conditions be determined that would once again set off traditional class conflict? Isn't what you have just outlined therefore a theory of the exceptional case?*

Well, first of all, I don't believe in the 'law' of the falling rate of profit . . .

Widmann: *That was the exceptional case.*

But it would be absurd to attempt to exclude the possibility of economic crises. At this very moment we are getting lots of material which illustrates my friend O'Connor's thesis concerning the fiscal crisis.

Knödler-Bunte: *Put quite simply, our problem was this: precisely because we face new zones of conflict, isn't it necessary to reconstruct the old theory of class in light of new experiences, without weakening the concepts of class and class struggle beyond recognition? Don't we need new theoretical approaches that can point out to us the interrelation between traditional zones of conflict and new potential for resistance? The crisis theory assumptions concerning system and life-world remain irrelevant if at the same time new interpretations aren't given to the older problems of class-specific oppression and inequality of cultural opportunity and life-chances. I believe that a theory of social movements, including the classical theory of revolution and class-struggle, must be much more historicized, and must be disconnected from the determinations of political economy, and from conceptions of a universal history. What we know as the workers' movement arose in a specific phase of capitalist industrial development, with many internal time-lags and contradictions. The workers' movement became most radical where the transitional situation, in which it found itself in Germany in the second half of the nineteenth century and the first quarter of the twentieth, was experienced most dramatically. Large parts of the working class could not return to agricultural production or to small artisanal enterprises, but neither were the conditions present which would have permitted an integration into bourgeois culture. This basic outlook can be reconstructed with the model of system and life-world, except that—in contrast to today—the life-worlds of workers were organized in a much more traditional way by shared schemas of interpretation. These were later eroded under the pressure of the internal differentiation of both proletarian and bourgeois culture, up to the point of the present privatization of life-worlds. I've outlined all that in a very general way, but I don't see such a sharp break between the traditional lines of conflict of the working-class movement and the social movements of today.*

It could be that radicalization came about through an influx of cultural conflicts. You said it yourself: there is no comparison between the world of the Social Democrats of 1890 or 1910 and that of today. That was still a political party which provided a sense of identity. It also had no stabilizing function comparable to social democracy today. The old Social Democratic Party was truly an 'enemy of the *Reich*'.

Honneth: *But since there is no such thing anymore as the working-class movement in its traditional form, we have to confront problems that didn't even exist in, say, the time of the Weimar Republic. I just think that the potential for conflict and protest that you speak of in terms of 'neo-populist movements' has to be seen in a different light. One could say that these are the potentials for protest which are given publicity enough in the press these days, but that they are the tip of an iceberg rising out of a broad spectrum of persisting class-specific problems and conflicts. These, however, do not find an appropriate voice because a working-class movement that previously provided cultural means of expression no longer exists.*

That would be a decisive point only if the groups that today present the medium of resonance and articulation for the now questionable class-specific base were to react to some kind of class-specific problems.

Honneth: *The first thesis would be that there are states of conflict and potential for protest that are or have been forced to remain voiceless, for different historical reasons and for reasons traceable to cultural reproduction. The problems that accumulate here and which are related to class-specific conditions of life . . .*

But why then should the class-specific problems of workers forced into silence find their voice precisely in the complaints of the sons and daughters of the bourgeois strata?

Honneth: *No, no, that is a misunderstanding of my thesis. I simply suspect that next to these explicit protest formations, which of course have also been encouraged by the press, there exists another, more traditional set of conflicts, which does not have this kind of cultural means of expression. Your thesis of cultural impoverishment could therefore be taken seriously in another way. I admit that in order to name such forms of conflict one certainly cannot rely on what you referred to as empirical data. One therefore can't rely on questionnaires, that privilege certain economic . . .*

I wonder if that isn't an ahistorical view. Isn't it true that you can discover these deficiencies because you belong to an entirely different current of protest? Isn't it so, that with your completely different background and socialization, you experience the imperatives—of consumption, administration, bureaucracy—that penetrated into highly differentiated life-worlds from the outside as a conspiracy? Aren't you ascribing your viewpoint to someone who sees things differently?

Honneth: *Yes, it is always difficult to answer the objection that one is projecting one's own sensibilities onto social groups and strata that may not be affected by them. I believe one can avoid this by hypothetically testing the type of conflict or experience of deprivation that is in question, and by being able to show that this has nothing to do with one's own sensibilities and experiences. The core of what I could expect here would be a repressed and culturally silenced potential for protest in dimensions of social respect and social recognition. Those may be antiquated concepts, but they are still capable of recording a persistent experience that we really do have of the deprivation of social respect. I don't believe that is a projection. There would be historical indices of that, which a new historiography of the working-class movement would have to investigate. Precisely this motive of the 'struggle for social recognition' is perhaps a central and also always latent impulse.*

Knödler-Bunte: *I would also say that it is in parts of the middle class that the psychological framework for sensitization, for experiencing cultural disenfranchisement, finds its breakthrough point, so to speak. That still says nothing about the genesis and the validity of these conflicts, although it does oppose the thesis of a suspended class struggle, in which the working class is considered culturally integrated. Is it actually true that the entire proletariat has been bound to the system by internalizing the norms of abstract labour? Or is it not the case that in truth large portions of the proletariat, the majority of the working population, have simply not participated to a great extent in this system—bourgeois culture as a structuring of the subject? Perhaps they have not subscribed, after all, to the normative concepts of bourgeois ideology along with its self-understanding and its world view, but have kept it at arm's length, always conscious that in very basic issues the system operates independent of their own wishes and needs. That is the question as I see it, whether the 'alternative movement' does not to a degree continue this experience in a non-class-specific way. Within the dominant system it, too, finds no cultural recognition, no way of establishing a satisfying organization of its own life.*

All right, you know the scene better than I do. Earlier, at least, it was simpler to see the student movement as a catalyst providing energy for the real class struggle. Perhaps one should now realize that the 'alternative scene' arises from the sensibilities of those who are able to experience as deprivations things which a middle-aged Social Democrat worker or employee would not experience in that way.

Knödler-Bunte: *There I would still disagree with you, for several reasons. First, as I see it, the predominant type of person in the 'alternative scene' is by now no longer someone from an educated bourgeois family and often has not completed any programme of higher education. For such a person, to drop out is less symbolic as an experiment with new living patterns than it is as an alternative to life in a factory or office, with clear and concrete advantages and disadvantages. The aesthetic stylizations come from outside, from the culture apparatus (also on the Left), which projects onto the 'alternative scene' its own wishes and fears. Within the workings of 'alternative' projects there are few illusions about what one is doing, and many concrete experiences of the difficulty of organizing life and work. That brings me to a second point. Recently, I have taken part in many discussions between young unionized workers and members of 'alternative' projects. It was remarkable how quickly and directly the two groups understood each other. And that is actually not surprising, since both have to deal with similar problems of the work situation—division of labour, hierarchies in the workplace, and the right to work. Only the possible solutions are different. The need to live and work differently, therefore, seems to extend far into the core of the industrial workers' community. 'Alternative' projects would be attractive to many young workers if concrete dialogue would take place and if 'alternative' projects could make certain guarantees regarding income, continuity and social services. Finally, a third point. Your criticism is aimed too high, because you assess our argument by very traditional standards. You apply a concept of class struggle and class analysis that in recent debates, especially in social history, has long since been opened up and expanded. Perhaps the theory of class we have ascribed to Marx has itself become historical, applicable at best to a short phase of industrial capitalism in the second half of the nineteenth century. Fine, you say, that is a cultural reinterpretation of the theory of class. But I think that one must analyze social conflicts in a widened spectrum of cultural theory, without letting the concept of class lose its expressive power.*

Honneth: *I would ask if it is possible to define the dimensions of social class relations on the basis of the concept of the social lifeworld, which is what you are actually doing. I am thinking here not only of the dimension of class-specific living situations and certain, let us say, biographically central sets of problem. These can be empirically observed in specific opportunities for social mobility, opportunities for securing an identity, risks to life and damage to health. But I am also thinking of the dimensions of cultural reproduction—a concept that is also central to your model—that is, a socially stratified system of cultural opportunities for expression and rights to social definition. Can what Gramsci describes with the concept of cultural hegemony—the elevation of one social class's form of expression by means of a culturally prescribed network of dominant forms of expression—simply be separated from the idea of cultural reproduction? To put it simply, what can be learned for the concept of the social life-world from this cultural turn in Marxism? Can one simply exclude it?*

No, of course not. But Lukács had already used reification as a general term for deformations of consciousness. In Critical Theory's critique of mass culture this is even more pronounced.

Widmann: *I tend more to the opinion that your model is to a certain extent a general theory, of which the theory of class struggle describes a particular sharpening at a certain point in time. The theory of class struggle would then be a special case of the antithesis of system and life-world, which permeates all of history.*

You mean that the classical conflicts between peasants, proletariat and bourgeoisie also reflect a defensive reaction against the destruction which was caused by capitalist modernization. I can accept that without hesitation. The only thing which is missing from this picture is the transformation of the life-world itself. Marx could not sufficiently distinguish between traditional life-worlds, which are worn away through modernization processes, and a structural differentiation of the life-forms which are today threatened in their communicative infrastructure. As a result of capitalist modernization disruptions occur, which imply the downfall of traditional forms of life. Where modern societies arise this breakdown is indeed always unavoidable. This does not mean that one should bring it about intentionally or consider it as morally acceptable.

Knödler-Bunte: *I agree with that. The question is only: can the destruction of life-worlds by the imperatives of a capitalist system in each case only be constructed on the basis of concrete historical material, or is there something like a logical progression of steps for the differentiation of life-worlds? There I am very sceptical.*

Well, there are certainly communicative structures, which all life-worlds have in common. These are very formal elements like the relation of personality structures to social institutions and to contexts of tradition. The dimension of developmental logic concerns only how these elements differentiate themselves and how the differentiation passes through individuation processes, through the abstraction and generalization of norms and through the increasing reflexivity of cultural traditions. That is what Durkheim or Mead described. That does not mean that these processes are irreversible, but just that they take place when any form of modernization begins.

Honneth: *I do not believe that one can introduce the above mentioned categories in a class-neutral fashion. One cannot argue on the basis of an internal evolutionism that asserts a linear destruction of the life-world. Is it not more the case that when one looks at the family, for example, then the proletarian family is a product of the historical conflicts surrounding the shortening of the working day?*

These communicative life-relationships should therefore not be seen as remnants of a precapitalist life-world, which was untouched by the constraints of capitalist rationalization, but rather as a product of social conflicts and not as a remainder of a precapitalist form of production which will gradually be corroded by capitalism.

That is also the case.

Knödler-Bunte: *I also believe that destruction and deformation are interlaced with new growth and new formations.*

Widmann: *It makes a difference, however, whether one understands the current protests as a form of reaction of a closed life-world to administrative and monetary intervention or whether one conceives of the life-world itself as functional for the administrative system, so that in the course of development both spheres must determine anew their relation to one another and thereby also their inner structure. From this perspective an intact life-world does not simply stand opposed to the capitalist system. Instead, today's conflicts are a medium through which a new balance must be found between these spheres and within themselves. Thus, they fulfill the same function as the classical crisis of capitalism. It did not signal the collapse of the system, but rather the mechanism by which the system maintained itself through change. That is a different view, a different perspective, than yours. According to you the communicative life-world is a block against which capitalist rationalization scratches.*

Yes, I really do believe that it is a question of injecting communicative everyday praxis into institutions. This was once a conservative view.

V
Science and Life-Praxis

Knödler-Bunte: *I admit that I have the most difficulties with the structure of your theory and with the attitude that I surmise is behind it, and considerably fewer problems with your political programme and your political and theoretical self-understanding. What libidinous images does a theory evoke, which is so abstract and which stands under an unbelievable compulsion to synthesize? Where in the intellectual work linked to it are the moments of happiness, of satisfaction, without which one can hardly understand such effort? In your explanations of your concerns the word* anschlussfähig *[making connections] appears again and again: one's own intellectual work must connect with the standards and expectations represented by the academic system. But how do you justify the centrality of this academic system that is practically your only reference point? The other—historically alternative—reference point, namely a prole-*

*tarian political organization, has since disappeared from the scene,
but are there really only these two possibilities? The scientific-
educational system and the organized labour movement have one
thing in common, that they have made themselves institutionally
autonomous and have isolated individuals from exactly those experiences which they require for intellectual stimulation. As a result,
the best that the tenured academic and the political functionary can
still offer is a kind of ethic of craftsmanship. That is, if it has not
already been buried by industriousness and officiousness, and by the
accommodation to short-term requirements which maintains the system
and keeps things going. Radical attitudes and scientific innovations
require changes in life-praxis, a restructuring of the priorities according to which one structures one's life. Can a social theory such as you
propose also prove that this confidence in the ability of the academic
system to produce results is objectively justified?*

There are two questions here. The first has to do with the impulses
and motives behind my work, and the second with a certain, shall we
say, faith in science. Concerning the first question I have a conceptual motive and a fundamental intuition. This, by the way, refers
back to religious traditions such as those of the Protestant or Jewish
mystics, also to Schelling. The motivating thought concerns the
reconciliation of a modernity which has fallen apart, the idea that
without surrendering the differentiation that modernity has made
possible in the cultural, the social and economic spheres, one can
find forms of living together in which autonomy and dependency can
truly enter into a non-antagonistic relation, that one can walk
tall in a collectivity that does not have the dubious quality of
backward-looking substantial forms of community.

The intuition springs from the sphere of relations with others; it
aims at experiences of undisturbed intersubjectivity. These are more
fragile than anything that history has up till now brought forth in the
way of structures of communication—an ever more dense and finely
woven web of intersubjective relations that nevertheless make possible a relation between freedom and dependency that can only be
imagined with interactive models. Wherever these ideas appear,
whether in Adorno, when he quotes Eichendorff, in Schelling's
Weltalter, in the young Hegel, or in Jakob Böhme, they are always
ideas of felicitous interaction, of reciprocity and distance, of separation and of successful, unspoiled nearness, of vulnerability and
complementary caution. All of these images of protection, openness
and compassion, of submission and resistance, rise out of a horizon of

experience, of what Brecht would have termed 'friendly living together'. *This* kind of friendliness does not exclude conflict, rather it implies those human forms through which one can survive conflicts.

Knödler-Bunte: *My questions were rather concerned with what kind of impulse, what structure of experience underlies this explicit self-understanding. Perhaps I can illustrate this by a contrast of extremes. I can have the basic feeling that, fundamentally, the world is in order as it is, and for this reason I can relate to individual domains of reality in an experimental and adventurous way. Chaotic multiplicity does not disturb me at all, because I can relate to it from an affectively secured distance. I detect this attitude in the typical Brechtian gesture, Brecht being, so to speak, a virtuoso of radicalized adaptation. The other fundamental structure consists in experiencing chaos as threatening, and in therefore attempting to structure it by means of conceptual systems, in order to have some firm ground under one's feet. This type would rather correspond to that of the surveyor, who must first create structures before he begins to move.*

Well, I do not have this primitive trust in my environment, but neither do I have the attitude of someone who must bring a satisfying order into chaos. There is nothing at all to which I have an unambivalent attitude, at least apart from very rare moments. For this reason even my naive connection to social relations is not really naive, but profoundly ambivalent. This has to do with very personal experiences, which I would rather not speak about, but also with critical moments—for example with the coincidence of great events and my own puberty in 1945. I am also ambivalent because I have the impression that something is deeply amiss in the rational society in which I grew up and in which I now live. On the other hand, I have also retained something else from the experience of 1945 and after, namely that things got better. Things really got rather better. One must use that as a starting-point too; and I then go on to look for a prehistory which is too lightly disposed of with the concept of 'Enlightenment'.

Now for the question about confidence in the established system of scientific knowledge. I am myself still not certain whether what I truly intend and what intuitively directs my work can be accommodated in its essential elements within this system. When one grows up as we have, one tries somehow to do something in life into which one can bring, and in which one can clarify, one's basic intuition. For me, this occurs through the medium of scientific thought or philosophy. When one is oriented to questions of truth and does not misunderstand oneself in the process, then one should not try, as Heidegger and Adorno both did, to produce truths outside of the sciences and to wager on a higher level of insight, on the thinking of Being or on a mindfulness of tormented nature. It is my deep conviction that one should not do that when one ventures on thinking.

Widmann: *Why not?*

If one wants to live and write from a fund of ultimate, self-evident truths, then one should not try to achieve what one would like in a tenured professorship or at a research institute. That reminds me of experiences I have had at the rostrum or in the seminar room. When I realize that students are totally uninvolved emotionally with what I am doing, what we are doing together, then I am dissatisfied because I know that all learning depends on the formation of deeper motives. On the other hand, when I realize that students can no longer stand back from their emotions, that a symbiotic relationship is being developed, then I become tremendously nervous. I want to preserve a sense that questions of truth can be isolated, to keep a sense for discourse alive in a situation which objectively forces one not to mix questions of truth with questions of justice or taste. That is a stubbornly Kantian way of putting things; but I have accustomed myself to this neo-Kantian jargon in recent years, and I am somehow relieved that I can say it so casually. I have never before dared to say it in this manner—'this bureaucratic departmentalization of moments of reason', Adorno would have said. Precisely this, however, is the mark and the thorn in the side of modernity. How we cope with this situation is perhaps the problem.

In what I intend—one never really knows what one is up to—I meet Max Weber half-way by trying to keep various spheres separate: first of all these political-journalistic things, then 'real' philosophizing (which paradoxically I can only pursue intermittently, even though it is here that my intentions are most consistently realized). After that, scientific work in a narrower sense; and finally teaching and, when the time is ripe, a political praxis which goes beyond journalism. In the last ten years I have also had to play the role of institutional director. I keep these various kinds of work separate, but I am not saying that this is the kind of division of labour in which one thing has nothing to do with another, or in which it is a matter of a combination of various roles. I would much rather play each of these roles in such a way that the others remain visible at the same time. What annoys me terribly, what gets to me, is the aggressivity of people who do not see the role-differentiation in me, let alone respect it, and mix everything together. I have experienced that again in the last few weeks. I am not speaking about the routine persecutory articles, about the degenerate products published under the editorial direction of the Bavarian minister for culture in the *Rheinsche Merkur*; I mean the sheer opportunism of the so-called liberal milieu.

I would like to maintain a certain differentiation, and indeed, if it does not sound too lofty to say so, for moral reasons—or perhaps also out of fear? In contemporary society there are certain criteria that separate responsible from irresponsible minds. As a professor or scholar, with the authority of one who examines questions of truth, one should not say things that affect other people without at least trying to bring one's work up to the standards set by institutionalized research.

Widmann: *Don't the reasons for this lie much more in yourself? Namely, that you would not like to be caught holding on to something against all reason?*

There is also a dogmatic core to my convictions, of course. I would rather abandon scholarship than allow this core to soften, for those are intuitions which I did not acquire through science, that no person ever acquires that way, but rather through the fact that one grows up in an environment with people with whom one must come to terms, and in whom one recognizes oneself.

Widmann: *Why do you consider the geographic site of the university to be the place where rational argumentation and meaningful analytic procedure are guaranteed?*

I only think like this when I get annoyed with people who persist in talking about 'bourgeois science', as if they had commandeered a sweeping insight. Theories can in any case no longer be sorted out according to such criteria. But that is only a genetic explanation. With that one has not yet said why exactly the choice of the university . . . But is there then another location?

Widmann: *You always link up with dominant theories or good outsiders . . .*

Perhaps what you mean by that is: are you not a coward who always makes himself secure by means of authorities and what is currently in vogue? It is certainly true that in the 1960s and 1970s, and this annoys the empiricist crowd, I played a large role in bringing certain theoretical methodologies into discussion, which others still had to work through—such as Wittgenstein, Piaget, Chomsky, Kohlberg, Searle, and so on. The difference is only that I still hold on to what I have learned from all of them, even when academic fashion has moved on. When I have learned something from someone I remain to a certain extent faithful to him in this respect. I do not follow the fashions of the academic industry. I do not know whether this answers your question.

Widmann: *Do you have the feeling that you need these constructs, this speaking in different tongues, this terrific willingness to be receptive, in order to articulate your own concerns?*

I think I make the foreign tongues my own in a rather brutal manner, from a hermeneutic point of view. Even when I quote a good deal and take over other terminologies I am clearly aware that my use of them often has little to do with the authors' original meaning. What is then the peculiar pleasure to be had in the process? Even if I sweat a lot over my work and use a lot of my life history for it, I enjoy it when I have the impression: 'Ah, you have seen something. There you can further develop something with arguments'. Then I am satisfied because I think that is the only way. Those are certainly small joys. The thinker as life-style, as vision, as expressive self-portrait is no longer possible. I am not a producer of a *Weltanschauung*; I would really like to produce a few small truths, not the one big one.

When I have found an interesting flower or herb I try to figure out how it will fit together with others, whether it can create a bouquet or pattern. This is constructive puzzle-work. I take over other theories. Why not? One should accept others according to their strengths and then see how one can go from there. One thing should support another, for theoretical truths actually exist only in the form of plausibilities.

For my own part, in any case, I have said goodbye to the emphatic philosophical claim to truth. This elitist concept of truth is a last remaining piece of myth, and you know that I do not want to return to where the *Zeitgeist* is leading today.

Knödler-Bunte: *Are there experiences of happiness and of satisfying situations in your intellectual praxis?*

There are minds which are more analytic and minds which are more synthetic, and I certainly belong on the synthetic side. As a result, my satisfactions lie more in a synthesis of argumentation. Earlier, I used to enjoy fabricating texts. This aspect of the 'pretty tongue', as Grass once said about Adorno, has retreated more and more. More recently, I have put up with rougher discourse in order to develop something even when a text is not the result. You can see it in my new book. Of course, there is still the ambition that there should be a text with introduction, exposition, interpolations, and so on, but the setting up of perspectives on problems is now more important.

I experience the problems that occupy me at any given moment in an almost physical way, so I am happy when something seems to be working out for me. I am very seldom euphoric . . . I must have paper in front of me, blank paper, written-on paper, books around me, but I am not someone who works with card indexes. One needs to invest oneself in the work, and then the problems begin to move with the writing. This way, having problems is a matter of personal history. It disrupts your life, and then you are happy, when you have found a solution and can carry on writing.

Knödler-Bunte: *What is the next mountain you need to climb?*

Hills, only little hills. I might go to the University of Frankfurt, and I do not know how much time my responsibilities there will leave me. I am planning a series of lectures about theories of modernity. That will certainly be fun. With colleagues from other disciplines I would like to practise what I always insist on, the cooperation of philosophy with the individual scientific disciplines. It must be possible to show with empirical material that one can introduce reason into science. The other aim would be once again to write something like *Strukturwandel der Öffentlichkeit*, from my current perspective. So much fog lies around everywhere today. I am not giving up the hope that this fog can be lifted. It would be nice if I could still make a contribution to this task.

5.

Conservative Politics, Work, Socialism and Utopia Today

In recent decades philosophy has increasingly contented itself with a defensive position. This is a role which you justified in your 1971 essay, 'Does Philosophy Still Have a Purpose?'.[1] Today, it is true, you once more entrust it with bigger tasks—and yet there is a growing chorus which laments or even invokes the 'end of philosophy'. There are certainly reasons for, and indeed a long tradition behind, this attitude. With the Enlightenment philosophy consciously forfeited its power as a positive world-picture. Later, as a means of interpreting the world, it lost out more and more to the individual sciences.

You have always defended a concern with the linking of philosophical and scientific—in particular sociological—thought, with proving them and testing them against each other, in the intention of holding onto philosophical goals which can no longer be straightforwardly defended in their own terms. For a good ten years you were the Director of the Max Planck Institute for 'Research into the Life Conditions of the Scientific-Technical World' in Starnberg. The activities of the Institute included both research into theoretical foundations and empirical programmes.

What opportunities does such a demanding linkage open up for philosophy, against the background of such a fragile situation; where does its impulse derive from; what cannot be relinquished in this tradition?

Philosophy today is no longer in possession of metaphysical truths.

---

1. Jürgen Habermas, 'Does Philosophy Still Have a Purpose?' in *Philosophico-Political Profiles*, London 1983, pp. 1–19.

It is involved, almost to the same extent as the sciences, in the fallibilism of a research process which takes place on the shaky ground of argumentation which is never immune to revision. Nowadays it is philosophizing animal behaviour specialists, or physicists, who push towards popular syntheses which have something of the character of world views, and with regard to which philosophers are unable to conceal a certain scepticism. To this extent the traditional roles have rather been reversed. On the other hand, philosophy still retains a more intimate relation to common human understanding and to the life-world than do the sciences. It still has to play the role of an interpreter in the exchange between autonomized cultures of experts and everyday life.

Because science, morality and art have acquired a considerable independence as specialist cultures and developed an institutional life of their own, the need—in reaction to this splitting-off—to mediate theory and practice, morality and customary ethics, art and life, has become ever more urgent—in this context it is the same reference point of everyday communicative practice which is intended under different titles such as 'practice', 'customary ethics', or 'life'. At an earlier stage this was called the need for enlightenment, for enlightenment concerning collective interests and one's own; and philosophy still seems better equipped for this purpose than other disciplines. Furthermore, philosophy can play the role of a stand-in within the human sciences, holding open possibilities of universalistic questioning, encouraging bold theoretical strategies, and contributing to the analysis of the rational foundations of knowledge, speech and action.

In recent years we have seen certain philosophical currents exert a more powerful influence on the life-world, not only in France, with its stronger cultural traditions, but also in Germany. Here what is at stake are questions of how one should live one's life, questions of the significance and the dangers of reason. It is quite astonishing that in many of these projects, which are also controversial in other respects, Nietzsche plays an important role. In 1968, as editor of a volume of Nietzsche's epistemological writings, you remarked laconically that Nietzsche was no longer contagious[2] . . .

. . . I was mistaken there . . .

---

2. See 'Zur Nietzsches Erkenntnistheorie', postscript to Friedrich Nietzsche, *Erkenntnistheoretische Schriften*, Frankfurt 1968. Reprinted in Jürgen Habermas, *Kultur und Kritik: Verstreute Aufsätzse*, Frankfurt 1973, pp. 239–263.

Doesn't this Nietzsche renaissance awaken extremely ambivalent memories, for example of the history of his influence within National Socialism, even though it was already noted at the time that a few Nietzschean motifs had been substituted for the 'whole Nietzsche'?

It is through the reception of authors such as Foucault and Derrida that Nietzsche has once more become a virulent influence on ways of looking at the world, for the first time in the history of the Federal Republic. Of course, he has always been present on the academic scene in recent decades, but now he is influential not through particular insights in the domain of epistemology or the critique of ideology, but as the author of *Zarathustra*, above all as the author of *The Birth of Tragedy*, in other words as the Dionysian thinker who settles accounts with the West. How far the Nietzsche of *The Will to Power*, or rather of the aphorisms from the *Nachlass*, which could certainly only have had the historical effects they did in the compilation prepared by Elizabeth Förster-Nietzsche, how far this ideologically exploited Nietzsche is playing a role today I would not venture to judge. Presumably a few of the old Nietzsche fans are creeping out of their holes, and now publicly expressing the elitist phantasies which they always had in their heads. But the Nietzsche who comes to us mediated through France is rather the aestheticist, playful Nietzsche, thoroughly critical in posture, even if the implications are ultimately hostile to reason. This, of course, is a different Nietzsche from any the Nazis could have lived with. I take this reception of Nietzsche entirely seriously. This is one of the reasons why I am about to begin a series of lectures in France on the 'discourse of modernity', in which I want to engage with French colleagues, who have indeed been extremely productive. During the last ten years of my life in a research institute, I have not taken all this as seriously as I should have. But that was a mistake.

The question of the possible influence of philosophy can also be posed from another, more primitive, but not necessarily less effective angle. After and in addition to the abandonment of universal interpretations of the world, there is a further test for critical thought: the new conservatism which—along a broad front, above all in the Federal Republic—expresses its wish to revoke the claims of the Enlightenment through what are at times militant demands, and would prefer most of all no longer to permit any critical understanding of problems— whether in everyday life or in science—at all. The strivings of this counter-enlightenment are directed towards a ban on thought. Critical thought is seen as a kind of sickness, a pathology, which always appears whenever people no longer think in conformity with the rules.

Such turnarounds in the intellectual climate, of the kind which have taken place in the whole Western hemisphere since the mid-seventies, are not autonomous developments, but rather reflections of shifts in the political and social order.

What arguments are employed in this context to stake out the terrain of permissible thought?

There are extreme examples. I remember the autumn of 1977, when the 'League for Freedom in Science' made public a list of names of university teachers, who were denounced, in phantasy terms, as being liable to establish links with the terrorist underground. Such things serve as an aid to the *Verfassungsschutz*, which neo-conservatives generally provide with somewhat more subtle means, and in less dramatic circumstances than at that time. Furthermore, the neo-conservative theses which have become influential through the press are tailored to justifying the form of life created by capitalist modernization. The ideology-planning which is envisaged for this purpose has been summarized by Peter Sloterdijk as: a halt to reflection and solid values [*Reflexionsstopp und feste Werte*]. I find it difficult at the moment to warm over this whole theme, which I have in fact treated extensively elsewhere.

Let me ask what the change of regime in the Federal Republic means, about the social and political background to these neo-conservative trends. Is it an alteration of social attitudes which is expressed here, an alteration of political orientation? What kind of explanation can we give for the slide to the right in parliament?

First of all, it has to be said that changes of regime in periods of major economic difficulties are perfectly normal. Without Strauss's candidature, the changeover would probably have taken place two years earlier. What is more interesting is the weakening of the social democratic party. I do not consider its internal divisions at all reprehensible. It is the only one of the established parties whose sense-receptors are still open; it is still sensitive to the kinds of problems which agencies concerned simply with acquiring and retaining power push to one side. The weakness of the SPD is also a consequence of its democratic strength, which consists in the fact that it does not hush up a central social conflict, but at least experiences it in its own body, even if it cannot resolve it. In one respect, the SPD represents the successes of post-war development in the Federal Republic, insofar as—with its right hand—it stubbornly defends the welfare-state compromise, which has indeed secured internal peace in a practical way during the last three decades. In another respect it is doing penance for the unwanted side-effects of these successes, insofar as—with its left hand—it even intensifies the neo-conservative critique of the welfare state, without being able to counterpose a productive answer to the false prescriptions of the other side. I don't have any answers either, by the way. But let me at least attempt to explain the problem as clearly as possible.

From the subjective perspective of the economically active citizen, the welfare-state compromise consisted in the fact that one earned enough and received sufficient social security to come to terms with the stress of more or less alienated labour, with the frustration of a more or less neutralized political role as a citizen, with the paradoxes of mass consumption—for example during an annual holiday spent as a tourist—and with the uneasiness of a client relationship to the bureaucracies. This compromise is at present endangered from two directions. It is obvious that neo-Keynesian economic policies are no longer sufficient to ensure the growth which is necessary to secure full employment, and to inhibit conflicts over distribution. A loss of real income for the mass of the population, unemployment and poverty for a growing minority, the collapse of companies, and at the same time improved conditions for investment, even rising rates of profit, for a small minority—these are the obvious signals of the abandonment of compromise. In a less obvious way, however, the welfare-state compromise is also being abandoned from another direction.

What I am thinking of here are the problems which have been taken up by the Greens, in the counter-cultures, and in the new social movements—namely the costs of capitalist modernization, and the breakdown of a policy of war-prevention based on strategic calculation rather than on the generalization of consensus. These two things are more and more experienced as *absurd* threats, as *bewitched* dangers, the more each grows and grows and grows: both the forces of production and abstract wealth, as well as the forces of destruction and the stockpile of weapons. This seems all the more absurd, the more our experiential capacities, our fantasy, our imagination, our sense of responsibility, our understanding, our feelings—the range from love to hate for example—lag behind our technical power to control and destroy nature, and behind the complexity of the mesh of social relations. When the substance of the foundations of life, which had up till now been taken for granted, comes into question, whether in nature, in the urban environment, in the family environment, or in the school, then phenomena of withdrawal and experience of deprivation result, around which new lines of conflict emerge.

Thus, the welfare-state compromise is being put into question from these two directions—and Social Democracy, as both the advocate of this compromise and the diagnostician of its growing costs, is being pulled in different directions. It must either justify a defiant continuation of these policies—that is the perspective of the conservative apparatchiks in the SPD; or it must find a productive answer—without relying on the patent remedies of Reaganomics or Thatcherism. Let me add a couple of words about this.

Instead of too much state, a return to a bit more market—how could the problems suddenly be shifted back onto the market, when the long-term trend of increasing state income and state expenditure is only the symptom of a successful policy for the pacification of class conflict?

So are the old prescriptions to be taken up again, against new problems like unemployment, conflicts over distribution, the possible outbreak of class conflict, against the threatened disintegration of mass loyalty and the safety net of welfare? What shape are these prescriptions in?

The old prescriptions, which our present regime is working its way through more and more energetically, basically require four additions. *Firstly,* a demand-oriented economic policy, which must be able to cope with mass unemployment, even in the long term. This could lead to a new segmentation of society into 'ins' and 'outs', in which the 'ins' are composed of socially privileged minorities, who form a majority over against those who have been expelled from the labour-process. The mentality of a majority of basically middle-class character, which is prepared to exclude a severely underprivileged minority, will one day only be describable in the vocabulary of social Darwinism, a vocabulary which even today has acquired a surprising new lease of life in the enthusiasm for elites, and in the invocation of a readiness for competition and for making one's own way.

The *second addition* consists in a traditionalism which—in the domains of cultural, educational and family policy, but not in media policy, which directly affects economic interests—backs secondary virtues, the positive features of the past, common sense, unbroken historical consciousness, conventional religiosity, in short which backs the natural order of things [*Naturwüchsigkeit*], a halt to reflection and solid values. Cultural modernity, by contrast, is experienced as subversive. Spiritual-moral renewal means a return to before the eighteenth century, which is seen as promising a wondrous regeneration of certainties, a cushion of tradition—in other words—which can take the strain wherever monetary and bureaucratic forms of direction break down.

The *third element* is, as it were, the opposite of Willy Brandt's slogan, 'Dare more Democracy'—not a direct dismantling of democracy, but attempts to free the state from the onerous constraints of legitimation, attempts to contract the circle of themes of public debate, to de-problematize the political consciousness of the populace, to disburden it of socio-political questions, with which either negative or utopian investments of future perspectives could be connected. The limitation of the right to demonstrate which has just been decided on must be set in this context. *Fourthly*, there belongs to this prescription, if not a deliberate sharpening of international tensions, at least the stimulation of the awareness of a growing external threat. Of course, the defence policies against outer and inner enemies must work in tandem. Both are dramatized at the same time: the threat posed by the Red Army, and by the troublemakers within the country. Nervous journalists in our country have been busy for months assimilating the forms of non-violent protest to the same legal status as the use of violence.

What chance do you think such a strategy has?

I would not dare to make a definitive judgement as to whether and to what extent such a neo-conservative politics can be successfully implemented. In the last decade and a half a remarkable change of attitude has taken place, not only among marginal groups, but also among the mass of the population. For example, the difficulties which Herr Genscher ran into during the change of regime can only be explained by the fact that demands for legitimacy are being made which are different from those of the fifties.[3] A change of regime

3. Hans-Dietrich Genscher, the leader of the Free Democrats and Helmut Schmidt's coalition partner, switched his support to Helmut Kohl in September 1982, bringing about a change of regime without an election for the first time in the history of the Federal Republic. The result was a split in the Free Democratic party, and the resignation of its general secretary, Günther Verhengen.

which took place legally was not experienced as legitimate. The resistance to the census was a similar symptom.

The question of possible strategies for a solution can basically be posed in the context of a different set of themes: as a question of what socialism means under contemporary conditions, in a high-technology society with structural unemployment. Socialism, particularly in its Marxist version, made not only ethical and socio-political, but also scientific and historico-philosophical claims. In the nineteenth century there was an obvious basis for this, which made socialism's pathos and its force effective: an excess of available labour, new technologies, the setting up of factories, the breaking-down and mechanization of the labour process, and so on. This made necessary the uprooting of workers from the context of their daily lives, and led to a visible impoverishment of human beings. The pitiless exploitation, the brutality of factory and machine, the increase of labour time, without even the guarantee that the basic necessities of life would be provided, the extremely low life expectancy, injuries caused by negligence—all this reveals the dark side of immiseration very clearly. Socialism as the revolutionary solution to these grievances was obvious, and needed no additional justification: only proletarian revolution could offer workers the prospect of securing their own survival through the control of production. This transparency of the whole system entered into Marx's theory. The experience of misery forces the exploited and deprived into solidarity, and brings it about that oppression becomes an educative process.

The contemporary situation is not only the outcome of different developments, but shows that the conflicts have been held in check, the class struggle frozen. Disagreeable labour is tied up through the welfare system with more than just the satisfaction of primary needs; consumerism beckons in the form of a range of goods which package happiness and satisfaction for every need.

Today we also face the menace of another development which strikes at the basis of such a clear opportunity for socialism: work is becoming increasingly scarce, is itself becoming redundant, and with this the model of the oppressed worker, who is forced into an educative solidarity, dissolves. Unemployment due to increases in productivity and automation, a stabilized international division of labour, which more and more 'exports' disproportions and inequalities —these developments in the highly industrialized societies force us to consider more precisely what socialism means at the level attained by modern standards of living, and their attendant dangers, against

the background of much increased 'free time', and of the unmistake-
able consequences of industrialization, of forms of economy whose
necessary growth has never been truly or fundamentally challenged
by Marxists. Are there new forms of solidarity? Is there an indignation
which is aroused not by conditions of material need, but by the total
moral condition of such an economy? Or do we quite simply face the
threat of a forcible and violent—albeit controllable—division of
society, centred on the sharing out of a limited supply of work, and
the privileges generated by a new scarcity?

The substance of those expectations which were connected with the
concept of socialism in the workers' movement has not been realized.
But one should only say that when one has taken note, with due
respect, of what has nevertheless been achieved historically. Merely
because we have the side-effects of a terribly brutal process of
modernization before our eyes, we should not forget what have today
become trivial acquisitions—by this I mean not only the level of
subsistence of the masses, but also the democratic and constitutional
achievements of citizens. Indeed, the fact that one only becomes
aware of these acquisitions when they are threatened is a circum-
stance which merits philosophical attention. What I am thinking of
is the peculiar tracelessness of a particular type of progress, as a
result of which progress does not become something bad, but rather
something subjectively unreal. Material improvements—for the generations who lived through the economic upswing of the post-war
period, these have a biographical obviousness of course—bear,
so to speak, the sign of a loss of historical memory on their brow.
Thirty days annual holiday or the first car once meant an eminent
increase in private mobility and satisfaction—they were goals for the
sake of which we accepted struggle, even sacrifice. But a level of
satisfaction, once attained, eliminates, as it were, the traces of the
history of its own appearance. Specific achievements, real emancipation from constraints of nature or society, must obviously be
symbolically preserved if they are to be snatched from the fate
of forgetfulness, of absorption into the stifling, ahistorical, 'bad'
present of an endless pressing forward. Utopias are important,
perhaps we will even speak about this later; but memory is just as
important, anamnesis, even if not in such a demanding sense as
Benjamin's anamnetic solidarity. We need a symbolic form of representation for those things for which we have fought, for which a
collective effort was required. What is terrifying about material
progress, even about political and constitutional progress among

people who have not fought through a revolution, is this traceless disappearance of the historical path. It is terrifying both for past suffering and past sacrifice, which, without the possibility of a re-conciling rememoration, is as good as lost, and for the identity of those who come later, who, without an awareness of the heritage which they have entered into, can have no idea of who they are.

*The work-based society [*Arbeitsgesellschaft*] prioritized the develop-ment of labour as a technical system. The solidarity acquired through shared experiences is disappearing more and more, and is replaced by other domains organized on technological lines (for example, consumerism, the mass media). And yet it is still the case that the problem of progress is explained either in terms of the compulsion peculiar to technology, or simply in terms of inadequate control, so that technology then appears as a neutral force which merely needs to be applied in a rational way in order to have a liberating effect. What you are saying points towards an unexplored and unconsciously functioning domain: that progress is achieved through the extinction of remembrance, and is consolidated by means of it. In this sense there would be no 'neutral' technology.*

Yes, 'extinction of remembrance' is a good expression. In the list of questions you sent me, you spoke about the 'lack of images of happiness', and asserted that 'on the iconographic level, images of happiness are not to be found in the industrial, but only in the artisanal and the familial domains.' This is perhaps a key to the extinction of remembrance in all societies based on industrial labour. Industrial labour is haunted by the telos of its own abolition. If you go into the assembly-shop of a factory which produces television sets nowadays, you will see that the few tasks which are still carried out by (female) labour power are already moribund—a residue left over from the tempestuous advance of technical rationalization. And you can also already identify the tasks which, in a few years' time, will no longer be carried out by living labour. Where the physical move-ments of the human organism become appendages of electronically controlled installations, tasks are performed in the anticipation that they will disappear without trace. Perhaps human labour has been confronted with the prospect of its own elimination ever since the first breaking-down of labour processes in manufacture. This objec-tive state of affairs will probably only enter the consciousness of the broader public when not only sociology conferences, but the mass media, tackle the fact which Dahrendorf has reduced to a pregnant formula: that work is disappearing from the work-based society. At the last German sociology conference in Bamberg Claus Offe addressed this question. He demonstrated very convincingly that the facts of work, production and income are less and less determining the state of society as a whole.

Is the sphere of work and production losing its structurational force? Can one say, despite the continuing wage-dependence of the overwhelming majority of the population, that, on the individual and on the global level, work is losing its central significance?

If, like Offe, you give a positive answer to this question, then there are consequences for the theory of society, which has in fact been centred, since Marx, around concepts such as praxis and labour. It is for this reason that I have proposed the use of the concept of communicative action as a key to theory-construction, so that we can get a better grip on the structures of the life-world. And above all on the menacing of this life-world by bureaucratic and economic imperatives, dangers which arise from the fact that ever more personal relations, services and phases of life are being transformed into objects of administration, or into commodities. Even what the Greek philosophers once honoured as the founding elements of nature— water, earth, air, sun and shade—one must buy for oneself, as a tourist, by the slice.

The end of the work-based society, if I can use this slogan, is throwing up problems which so far have not been properly analysed. But they are experienced as problems by everyone.

I have already mentioned the first problem. Two colleagues, Herr Esser and Herr Fach, have indicated developments which suggest that the Federal Republic is moving towards a 'split' society, with a productive core of the employed, and an expanding margin of the poorly fed and neglected, who are forced into subcultures and ghettos. The decisive political question of the next few years will be whether this process can be kept out of the public gaze, or will become the focus of political confrontations—and which side, if the problem is explicitly dealt with, will win out: the selfish interests of a majority which is prepared to defend its possessions tooth and nail—we have had a foretaste of this in the struggle around the maintenance of the tripartite school system in recent years,[4] or in the doctors' protest in Paris; or rather the solidarity of those who are still on the inside with those who have been left out. This will also — and perhaps in the first instance — depend on whether the trade unions go in for a 'closed shop' policy on the American model, or whether they take up the solidaristic traditions of the workers' movement. In this case, too, political culture could be more important than political economy. Will our society insist on preserving its existing structures, and prefer to put up with what Gorz calls a 'nonclass of non-workers', or — as Marx puts it — 'to feel at ease in alienation'? Or has the rat-race society, has capitalism, through the unleashing of competitive struggle, of an orientation towards achievement, and of self-assertive energies, fulfilled its historical mission — namely, the creation of an ensemble of productive forces which has long ago surpassed the utopian imaginings of the last century?

What is crucial here is how one analyses this set of questions. The *second problem* is therefore of a more theoretical nature. Is the potential for development of the work-based society in the advanced industrial countries of the West also exhausted in the sense that the process of transforming traditional domains of activity into organized occupational systems with monetary rewards is coming up against a critical limit? Curiously enough, up till now there have always been domains where capitalism has not intruded — thus, for example, the professionalization of the role of mother or housewife could monetarize the enormous domain of childcare and housework within the family. And yet one has rather the impression that the mechanism of the labour market is breaking down in the face of the social need for certain types of activity. At present, for example, we have neither too few teachers, nor too many superfluous teachers, but too few paid teachers, who are able to do the work they would like to do, and which is also needed. This picture can quickly alter as a result of demographic developments. But the problem remains. For one thing, the need for socially necessary labour seems to be shifting into domains which are unfamiliar with activities modelled on industrial labour, which rather demand communicative interaction with persons; for another, this need is shifting into domains which do not fit

---

4. Up until recently, secondary education in the Federal Republic has been divided between three types of school, with selection at the age of ten: the *Volksschule* for those destined for manual trades, a *Mittelschule* for those likely to take up clerical jobs, and the *Gymnasium* preparing pupils for higher education. Attempts to alter this system, mainly in social-democratic *Länder*, through the introduction of a *Gesamtschule*, have encountered middle-class resistance.

into the organizational forms of industrial and administrative enterprise.

Here I am thinking of social and educational tasks, also political ones, which cannot be transposed into formal occupational structures, because they do not offer a profit; but which also cannot be organized as services, because this would deliver up the life-world even more to the clutches of experts. Nowadays, for example, we speak of work concerned with relationships, also of 'political work'—just think of the time-consuming, highly intensive decision-making processes which would be needed in tenants' associations, in neighbourhoods, in communes, in order to arrange the collective life of different generations—for example—in such a way that the negative effects of nuclear family structures, whose advantages we would not wish to abandon, could be compensated for—in relation to the elderly, to children, to the handicapped and frail, to those afflicted by loneliness, and so on. I mean this in a quite unsentimental way: I doubt whether the market is still appropriate for identifying the work which is really needed, and for satisfying this need within socially recognized forms of labour.

What has up till now been productive labour from the capitalist standpoint, therefore, stands opposed not only to social recognition, but also to the value of social activities which no longer fit into the available forms of recognition and evaluation.

This is connected with the *third problem*, the revaluation of activities. So called 'free time' [*arbeitsfreie Zeit*] is increasing, not only on a weekly basis, but also over the span of the individual's life-history, and yet the areas of life which lie outside of formal occupations are still only defined privately, in relation to a sphere of labour which is becoming more and more obsolete. How can society be reconstructed from the foundations up so that, not only from the perspective of the economy as a whole, but also from the standpoint of the individual life-history, a shift of emphasis can take place? As Offe suggests, what counts as productive labour is above all remunerative activity in an economic enterprise, which takes the form of a processing of things, and can be divided up into abtract operations. In contrast to this, one should consider the type of 'work' in which energies of which we are scarcely aware, and yet which are not inconsiderable, take on a meaningful form, of the kind which today come together in a women's group, for example, or in a local social democratic party, where—despite all good intentions—they tend to be damped down, in other words, both canalized and neutralized.

So, different and differently characterized forms of distribution would be necessary, another basis for the social recognition of necessary and neglected activities. What does socialism mean, then, when its strategy can no longer start from production, as was obviously necessary in an earlier period?

I have the impression that, judged in terms of real needs and capacities, the allocation mechanisms for the distribution of socially recognised labour are no longer working. Nor do I have any answers which could be treated as recipes. I merely think that one can only achieve a clear image of socialism under present conditions when one thinks such questions through. Socialism used to mean making an attempt, which was as fallibilist and as open to self-correction as possible, to at least reduce identifiable suffering, identifiable injustice, avoidable repressions, in other words, to resolve through collective efforts, and from a specific perspective, problems which have to be dealt with and resolved as one goes along anyway. This perspective can be easily characterized in abstract terms: namely, to arrest the destruction of solidaristic forms of life and to generate new forms of solidaristic collective life—in other words, life-forms with possibilities for expression, with space for moral-practical orientations, life-forms which offer a context within which one's own identity and that of the others can be unfolded less problematically, and in a less damaged way. This is a perspective which has emerged from the self-criticism of the life-forms which were established by capitalist modernisation, and which are predominant today.

Well, there is at least a long tradition of decisions concerning development based on different convictions: the utopias. It is precisely socialism, however—particularly in the scientific forms defended by followers by Marx—which has had a broken and negative relation to the utopian. Eventually technological development, the state of the productive forces, overtook the images of utopia. Even Herbert Marcuse has pointed to the 'end of utopia' in this context. Our relation to utopias is characterized in both these respects by a kind of prohibition of images. More recently, however, the necessity of utopian orientations has been increasingly appealed to, and from an irritating variety of directions. Utopian thought is recommended as a form of correction, although with regard to such corrections it is difficult to know whether the utopian image has a right to be tested through an attempt to put it into practice. What kind of function does the drawing up of utopias have today?

Utopias have a practical function to the extent that they enter into social movements in the form of orientations. Bloch, for example, used the formula 'walking tall' with the gaze of a utopian. Society should be such that everyone can walk tall, even the long-suffering and the heavy-laden, the deprived and the degraded. In this context the use of utopian image serves to introduce a precisely defined concept, namely that of human dignity. Dignity was once, of course, a feudal category. Dignity meant that one possessed a certain status within a hierarchical order, and behaved in a manner appropriate to this status—it is in this mediaeval sense, for example, that the Pope has dignity. Compared to this, one could perhaps characterize the show-business style of an itinerant tamer of the masses as un-dignified.

By contrast, human dignity has been more abstractly conceived in rational natural law, and in modern philosophy in general. Every individual should be unmolested in his or her autonomy, protected in his or her physical and spiritual integrity. This universalistic concept can be derived from the metaphor of walking tall through a process of conceptual sharpening. This is an example of the critical function of promissory images in theoretical contexts. Promissory—dignity must be taken over from the feudal world where only representative figures walk tall, and transposed into the bourgeois and socialist world, where even the deprived and heavy-laden may walk tall, here and now, and not just in the beyond.

Ernst Bloch always said that utopia gets a bad press. Today we are rather confronted with an inflationary use of the word . . .

. . . by Ernst Bloch, amongst others . . .

. . . which is not made conceptually viable, but which apparently links up with new forms of sensibility. A sensibility, for example, for what you term the dessication of life-worlds and communicative traditions. On the other hand, it is becoming clear how insidious appeals to utopia can be. Utopia is taken as justifying the individual's projection of phantasy worlds, which aim at nothing less than a boundless whole. This seems to be something different from the critical, and therefore self-critical, potential of utopian thought.

In specific historical moments, where we can recognise a real so-cial movement, real historical struggles, we also become aware that people do not fight for abstractions—despite the three great and ineradicable goals of the French Revolution. People do not fight *for* abstractions, but *with* images. Banners, symbols and images, rhetorical speech, allegorical speech, utopia-inspired speech, in which concrete goals are conjured up before people's eyes, are indeed necessary constituents of movements which have any effect on history at all. Everything else, by comparison, is re-working and stasis.

Even in conceptual thought, however, most obviously in the domains of philosophy, of the social and human sciences, but even in physics, the language of theory is not free of pictorial, metaphorical, or indeed mythical elements. There is no language which is exclusively conceptual. This is what could be called the mythical kernel of even scientific discourse, although here the image is conceptually tamed. A philosopher like Bloch can then make out a strong case for the necessity of moving back and forth between theoretical language, where the intention is to proceed purely discursively, simply because there are problems to be solved, and a receptivity to the pictorial language which is more central to everyday life, which is at any rate rooted in everyday experiences.

When constructive utopian thought aims at the interpretation of totalities, there remains a lingering critical suspicion that this totality covers over deficiencies and side-effects. Doesn't this critique, in its emancipatory intention, turn against the very idea of utopia?

There are good reasons for that, I think. Utopias are often depicted forms of life. In other words, they are outlines of totalities. As such, they cannot be theoretically retrieved. I do not believe there are any theoretically-based utopias. Whenever one portrays totalities, whole forms of life, whole life-histories, whole areas of life in their concretion, and suggests that these can be directly politically realized, the result can easily be the kind of consequences which our neo-conservative friends have indicated. This is why, in the socialist tradition, a certain abstinence has been practised with regard to the depiction of concrete forms of life. One should only speak of socialism in the sense of an attempt, in the historical conditions in which one finds oneself, to indicate the necessary conditions which would have to be fulfilled in order for emancipated life-forms to emerge— whatever they may be. Totalities only appear in the plural, and this pluralism cannot be anticipated in theory.

Is an understanding of utopia sufficient for this purpose which

*aims at a system of freely developed conceptions of the good life, at a
kind of minimal state which allows individuals to realize their own
utopias, and to enter into agreement with one another by way of
regenerative life-forms?*

Those are liberal ideas, which have an honourable history. I would
in fact retain an element of this tradition. That degree of legal
equality should be achieved which will allow at the same time the
greatest possible measure of individualism, and this means space for
individuals to shape their own lives. However, one cannot simply
forget the kinds of criticism of these individualistic constructions of
law which have been brought forward ever since Hegel. Freedom,
even personal freedom, freedom of choice in the last instance, can
only be thought in internal connection with a network of inter-
personal relationships, and this means in the context of the communicative structures of a community, which ensures that the
freedom of some is not achieved at the cost of the freedom of others.
Interestingly, abstract right is not sufficient for this purpose. One
must make the effort to analyse the conditions of collective freedom,
which remove the dangers of individual freedom, its potential for
social-Darwinistic menace.

The individual cannot be free unless all are free, and all cannot be
free unless all are free in community. It is this last proposition which
one misses in the empiricist and individualist traditions.

6.

A Philosophico-Political Profile

I

Could you tell us something of the sequence of the principal intel-lectual influences on your work? You are often represented as an heir of the Frankfurt School who gave its legacy a 'linguistic turn', with a move from a philosophy of consciousness to one of language. Is this an accurate image—or did your interest in, at least, the American pragmatism of Dewey and Peirce actually predate your encounter with the work of Adorno and Horkheimer? In what period did you start to reflect on the ideas of Wittgenstein or Austin? Similarly, in the social sciences, was your concern with Weber or Parsons subse-quent to an earlier, primarily Marxist, orientation—or did these coexist from the outset? What were the seasons of your engagement with the phenomenological tradition of Schütz, or the genetic psycho-logy of Piaget and Kohlberg?

Apart from the summer semester in Zurich, I studied in Göttingen and Bonn between 1949 and 1954. As far as my areas of study were concerned, there was an almost unbroken continuity of subject-matter and personnel stretching back through the Nazi period to the Weimar Republic. It is not at all the case that the German universi-ties were opened up to outside influences immediately after the War. Thus, from the academic standpoint, I grew up in a provincial German context, in the world of German philosophy, in the form of a declining Neo-Kantianism, of the German Historical School, of phenomenology, and also philosophical anthropology. The most powerful systematic impulse came from the early Heidegger. As students we were familiar with Sartre and French existentialism, perhaps also a few works of American cultural anthropology. While working on my dissertation on Schelling I naturally read the young Marx. Löwith's *From Hegel to Nietzsche* encouraged me to read the young Hegelians; Lukács's *History and Class Consciousness* also made a strong impression on me. These first intrusions of 'left-wing literature' did have the result that I rounded out my dissertation, which was strongly influenced by Heidegger, with an introduction setting late German Idealism in relation to Marx. Directly after my studies I became familiar with industrial sociology. I was then given a grant to do work on the concept of ideology—this gave me the chance to penetrate somewhat deeper into Hegelian Marxism and the sociology of knowledge, and I also read Adorno's *Prisms* and the *Dialectic of Enlightenment*. In Frankfurt, from 1956 in other words, Bloch and Benjamin were added, along with a few articles from the *Zeitschrift für Sozialforschung*, Marcuse's books, and a discussion— which was very lively at the time—around the so-called philosophical and anthropological Marx. A little later I tackled *Das Kapital* seriously, and in this connection I also ready Dobb, Sweezy and Baran. I also learned sociology in these early Frankfurt years; above all I read empirical things on mass communications, political socialization, political sociology. At this point I first came into contact with Durkheim, Weber, and very cautiously with Parsons. More important than this were the Freud Lectures in 1956—since hearing the international elite, from Alexander and Spitz to Erikson and Binswanger, I have considered psychoanalysis, despite all the dire predictions, as something to be taken seriously.

During these years as Adorno's assistant, between 1956 and 1959, there evolved what later crystallized in the empirical investigations of *Student und Politik*, and in my first two books (*Strukturwandel der Öffentlichkeit* and *Theory and Practice*)—the attempt to continue the Hegelian and Weberian Marxism of the nineteen-twenties with other means. All this remained within the context of a very German tradition, or at least of one rooted in Germany—even though at the time, through my contact with Adorno and Horkheimer, and later with Abendroth and Mitscherlich, I lived with a sense of having grown into different, decisively broader horizons of experience, of having been freed from provincial narrowness and a naively idealistic world.

In Heidelberg, from 1961 on, Gadamer's *Truth and Method* helped me to find my way back into academic philosophy. Hermeneutics interested me, on the one hand, in connection with questions of the logic of the social sciences, and on the other in comparison with the later philosophy of Wittgenstein. This was the period, therefore, of my first more intensive involvement with linguistic philosophy and analytical philosophy of science. Encouraged by my friend Apel, I also studied Peirce, as well as Mead and Dewey. From the outset I viewed American pragmatism as the third productive reply to Hegel, after Marx and Kierkegaard, as the radical-democratic branch of Young Hegelianism, so to speak. Ever since, I have relied on this American version of the philosophy of praxis when the problem arises of compensating for the weaknesses of Marxism with respect to democratic theory. This inclination was also the basis of my later friendship with Dick Bernstein. In any event, when I returned to Frankfurt to take up Horkheimer's chair in 1964, I had a firm enough footing in Anglo-Saxon discussions to be able to distance myself from an overstrained concept of theory derived from Hegel.

In the mid-sixties Cicourel and ethnomethodology led me back to Schütz. At that time I viewed social phenomenology as a proto-sociology, carried out in the form of analyses of the life-world. This idea connected up with influences from another direction: I was fascinated both by Chomsky's programme for a general theory of grammar, and by Austinian speech-act theory, as systematized by Searle. All this suggested the idea of a universal pragmatics, with the aid of which I wanted above all to deal with the awkward fact that the normative foundations of the critical theory of society were entirely unclarified. Having rejected the orthodoxy of the philosophy of history, I had no wish to lapse back either into ethical socialism, or into scientism, or indeed into both at once. This explains why I hardly read Althusser. In the second half of the sixties, thanks to collaboration with accomplished co-workers like Offe and Oever-mann, I worked my way into specific areas of sociology, primarily socialization and family research on the one hand, political sociology on the other. In the process I got to know Parsons better. I was already reading Piaget and Kohlberg, but it was only at our Starn-berg Institute, that is, after 1971, that I became an adherent of genetic structuralism. It was also here that I first began a more intensive study of Weber.

So you can see that from the outset my theoretical interests have been consistently determined by those philosophical and socio-theoretical problems which arise out of the movement of thought from Kant through to Marx. My intentions and fundamental convictions were given their stamp by Western Marxism in the mid fifties, through a coming-to-terms with Lukács, Korsch and Bloch, Sartre and Merleau-Ponty, and of course with Horkheimer, Adorno and Marcuse. Everything else which I have made my own has only acquired its significance in connection with the project of a renewal of the theory of society grounded in this tradition.

In the twenty-five years since Strukturwandel der Öffentlichkeit, *you have produced a very large body of work, of increasing complexity and range, with impressive continuity of direction. At the same time, your thought has obviously also undergone certain alterations of substantive emphasis or conviction during this period. What do you regard as the most important such changes?*

The books which I published at the beginning of the sixties implicitly express the conviction that the things I wanted to do could be accommodated more or less within the inherited theoretical framework—in this respect I felt a special affinity with the existentialist, i.e. the Marcusean variant of Critical Theory. What is more, Herbert Marcuse, with whom I became friends in the nineteen-sixties, felt the same way. I still remember the day when he dedicated a copy of *One Dimensional Man* to me with a flattering quote from Benjamin—'to the hope of those without hope'. However, the engagement with analytical philosophy, and also the positivist dispute, then reinforced my doubts about whether concepts of totality, of truth, and of theory derived from Hegel did not represent too heavy a mortgage for a theory of society which should also satisfy empirical claims. At that time, in Heidelberg and then back in Frankfurt, I believed that this problem was an epistemological one. I wanted to do away with it through a methodological clarification of the status of a doubly reflexive theory (reflexive with respect to its context of emergence and of application). The result was *Knowledge and Human Interests*, which was written between 1964 and 1968. I still consider the outlines of the argument developed in the book to be correct. But I no longer believe in epistemology as the *via regia*. The critical theory of society does not need to prove its credentials in the first instance in methodological terms; it needs a substantive foundation, which will lead out of the bottlenecks produced by the conceptual framework of the philosophy of consciousness, and overcome the paradigm of production, without abandoning the intentions of Western Marxism in the process. The result is *The Theory of Communicative Action*. In a brilliant article soon to be published in Britain,[1] Dick Bernstein expounds the particular problems which have forced me immanently to make repeated changes of position—away from 'knowledge and human interests' to 'society and communicative rationality'.

What is your sense of the current intellectual conjuncture in the West? In 'Does Philosophy Still Have a Purpose?' you suggested that Germanic philosophical intensity and originality were migrating to the United States, while Europe relapsed into a placid 'Swissification'.[2] Would you still hold to this judgement? More generally, most of your references in recent years have been along a German-American axis of comparison—as lately in your criticism of the different forms of neo-conservatism in the two countries. Is this due to biographical reasons, or does it express an underlying judgement about the predominance and relevance of these two cultures for the West as a whole in the late twentieth century? Would one be right in thinking that France and England, for example—central poles of reference in your treatment of bourgeois civilization in the 18th and 19th centuries in Strukturwandel—*have lost salience in your subsequent work?*

The reasons for this orientation towards developments in the USA are undoubtedly trivial—it is typical for the post-war generation of German philosophers and sociologists in general. Of course, there is also a background in power politics: the Federal Republic has come so close to being the 51st State of the Union that the only thing we still don't have is the right to vote. This total dependence has never before appeared so undisguisedly as it did in autumn 1983, with the stationing of missiles that was forced upon us. Nevertheless, I do in fact prefer a political culture which, like the American, dates from the eighteenth century. I marvel at the intellectual openness and readiness for discussion, this mixture of impartiality and engagement, that I find in American students more than here in Europe. For a German of my age and outlook there may also be the fact that in American universities we could follow very readily in the footsteps of German emigrants who had acquired a considerable reputation. In addition, the Institute for Social Research, where I have worked, eventually returned from the USA. And those members of the Institute who did not return—Marcuse, Löwenthal, Kirchheimer,

---

1. 'Introduction', in R. J. Bernstein, ed., *Habermas and Modernity*, Oxford 1985, pp. 1–32.

2. *Philosophical-Political Profiles*, London 1983, p. 8.

Neumann and others—have made a big contribution to the dense web of personal and academic ties between here and over there. Today this web is in fact extending to a third generation of younger scholars. Speaking of the younger people, it is evident that the influence of the French has been growing steadily for the last ten years or so. In questions of social theory, the most inventive impulses are coming from Paris—from people like Bourdieu, Castoriadis, Foucault, Gorz, Touraine and so on.

Finally, so far as England is concerned, you yourselves admit that I have been influenced by analytical philosophy. However, I would not wish to deny that there is a certain difference of climate between England and the Continent. There are no deep elective affinities between the spirit of empiricism, which is still dominant in your country, and German Idealism. A fermenting agent is lacking in the philosophical metabolism, which could mediate between the two mentalities—as pragmatism does, for example, in America. I believe I can detect this estrangement in basic philosophical convictions. For example, I observe a certain incomprehension in the way in which distinguished colleagues like Quentin Skinner or W. G. Runciman, even my friend Steven Lukes, write about my concerns. In their case the ontology of empiricism has become second nature. Of course there are also counter-examples such as Tony Giddens.

Recently you have argued that Horkheimer and Adorno can only find resistance to a totalized purposive rationality in the irrational mimetic powers of art and love, or in the 'impotent rage of nature in revolt'.[3] Although these strictures do pinpoint a certain tendency of classical Critical Theory, it is not clear that they can be applied without qualification to the thought of Adorno, who always remained conscious of the danger of appeals to an unmediated nature. Is it possible that in your desire to distance yourself from an unremitting negativism, and to rehabilitate the collaborative and constructive conception of Critical Theory current during the 1930s, you have been led into polemical exaggerations, and have underplayed the extent to which Adorno remained fundamentally committed to the ideals of autonomy and enlightenment, even at his most desperate?

I agree with you: at no point does Adorno and Horkheimer's critique of reason darken to a renunciation of what the great philosophical

---

3. *Theorie des Kommunikativen Handelns*, II, Frankfurt 1981, p 491.

tradition, and in particular the Enlightenment, once intended, however vainly, by the concept of reason. Like Nietzsche, they both radicalize the critique of reason to the point of self-referentiality, in other words until this critique begins to undermine even its own foundations. But Adorno differs from the followers of Nietzsche, from Heidegger on the one hand and Foucault on the other, precisely in the fact that he no longer wishes to break out of the paradoxes of this critique of reason, which has now become as if subjectless—he wishes to endure in the performative contradiction of a negative dialectics, which directs the unavoidable medium of identifying and objectifying thought against itself. Through the exercise of endurance he believes himself to be remaining most nearly faithful to a lost, non-instrumental reason. This forgotten reason, belonging to prehistory, finds an echo only in the powers of a wordless mimesis. The mimetic can be circled around by negative dialectics, but it cannot—as Heidegger suggests—be revealed. The mimetic does allow one to sense what it is performing the role of stand-in for, but it permits no knowledge of a structure which could be characterized as rational. To this extent, Adorno cannot appeal to any structure heterogeneous to instrumental reason, against which the force of totalized purposive rationality must collide. In the passage that you mention I am in the process of pinning down such a resistant structure, namely the structure of a rationality which is immanent in everyday communicative practice, and which brings the stubbornness of life-forms into play against the functional demands of autonomized economic and administrative systems.

Can Adorno, in his evocations of reconciliation, justly be accused of surreptitiously employing categories of intersubjectivity from which he abstains philosophically, and can what he terms 'love towards things' be simply reformulated in terms of undistorted communication? One might consider, for example, the following passage from Aesthetic Theory, *where Adorno seeks to evoke a reciprocal relation between nature and human technology, without in any way suggesting that nature could be legitimately viewed as a subject: 'After the abolition of scarcity, the expansion of the productive forces could occur in a dimension which is different from the quantitative increase of production. There are intimations of this in functional buildings that have been adapted to forms and lines in the surrounding landscape; or in old architecture where the raw materials for buildings were taken from the surrounding area, and fitted in with it, as is the case with many castles and châteaux. What is called "culture landscape" in German is beautiful as the schema of this possibility. A rationality which took up such motifs could help to close the wounds of rationality.'*[4] *In the light of such passages, would it not be plausible to suggest that there is a relation of complementarity—rather than of substitution—between Adorno's explorations of the subject-object relation, and your own theory of communication?*

If I may say so, I find your suggestion, that Adorno's *Aesthetic Theory* and my theory of communication should be viewed simply as supplementing each other, a little too innocuous. On the other hand, neither can one theory simply replace the other, if for no other reason than that I have said very little about aesthetic matters.

Albrecht Wellmer, who has a far more thorough understanding of these questions, has shown, in an outstanding discussion of 'Truth, Illusion and Reconciliation',[5] how Adorno's aesthetic utopia 'turns sour', so to speak, once its connection with the philosophy of history of the *Dialectic of Enlightenment* is dissolved. If this is done, Adorno's aesthetic insights become independent of the metaphysical thesis that, with every new advance of subjectification, humanity becomes ever more deeply entangled in reification. To this negative view belongs the perspective, extended into a positive, of a reconciliation of human productivity with nature, which you recall in your quotation. Adorno's appeal to *'die Liebe zu den Dingen'* is not without irony, and yet in earnest. This love is a utopian counter-image to the despairing belief that subjectivity 'works towards its own extinction by the force of its own logic'. A theory of communication which breaks with the conceptual framework of the philosophy of subjectivity undermines this 'logic', this apparently indissoluble internal relation between emancipation and subjugation. More specifically, it discovers that there is already a mimetic moment in everyday practices of communication, and not merely in art. Allow me to put this in Wellmer's words: 'This must remain hidden to a philosophy which, like Adorno's, understands the function of concepts in terms of the polarity of subject and object; it cannot recognize, behind objectifying functions of language, communicative performances which are the condition of its own possibility. For this reason, it can only understand mimesis as the other of rationality . . . In order for the prior unity of the mimetic and the

---

4. *Aesthetic Theory*, London 1984, pp. 69–70 (translation modified).

5. L. v. Friedeburg, J. Habermas, eds., *Adorno-Konferenz 1983*, Frankfurt 1983, pp. 138 ff.

rational moment in the foundations of language to be recognized, a paradigm-shift is required . . . For if intersubjectivity of understanding, communicative action are no less constitutive of the sphere of mind than the objectification of reality in contexts of instrumental action, then the utopian perspective which Adorno seeks to elucidate with the concept of an unforced synthesis derived from the philosophy of consciousness, migrates into the sphere of discursive reason itself: undamaged intersubjectivity, the unforced togetherness of many, which would make possible a simultaneous nearness and distance, identity and difference of individuals, indicate a utopian projection whose elements discursive reason derives from the conditions of its own linguisticality.'[6]

In a number of recent essays you have passed sharp judgements on post-structuralism, suggesting that the French post-structuralists must be seen as 'Young Conservatives' who 'on the basis of modernistic attitudes . . . justify an irreconcilable anti-modernism'.[7] Could you expand on this assessment, if necessary drawing distinctions between different post-structuralist thinkers? And could you explain the discrepancy between your condemnation of post-structuralism, and your comparatively friendly reception of the work of Richard Rorty, which provides parallels to, and has in some cases been directly influenced by, post-structuralist themes?

As you will see from my lectures on the philosophical discourse of modernity, which are due to appear shortly, 'condemnation' is not the appropriate word for my attitude towards post-structuralism. There are, of course, many similarities between negative dialectics and the procedures of deconstruction on the one hand, between the critique of instrumental reason and the analysis of formations of discourse and power on the other. The playful-subversive element of a critique of reason which is conscious of its own paradoxical self-referentiality, and the exploitation of experiential possibilities which were first revealed by the aesthetic avant-garde—these two things characterize a Nietzschean style of thought and presentation, which founds the spiritual kinship of Adorno with Derrida on the one hand, and with Foucault on the other. What separates him from these two figures, as from Nietzsche himself—and this seems to me

6. Ibid., p. 150.
7. 'Modernity versus Post-Modernity', *New German Critique* No. 22, Winter 1981, p. 13. Reprinted as 'Modernity—an Incomplete Project', in Hal Foster, ed., *Postmodern Culture*, London 1985, p. 14.

to be politically decisive—is simply this: Adorno does not merely bale out of the *counter*-discourse which has inhabited modernity ever since the beginning; rather, in his desperate adherence to the procedure of determinate negation, he remains true to the idea that there is no cure for the wounds of Enlightenment other than the radicalized Enlightenment itself. Unlike Nietzsche and his disciples, Adorno has no illusions about the genuinely modern origins of aesthetic experience, in whose name modernity falls victim to a levelling, undialectical critique.

As far as Richard Rorty is concerned, I am no less critical of his contextualist position. But at least he does not climb aboard the 'antihumanist' bandwaggon, whose trail leads back in Germany to figures as politically unambiguous as Heidegger and Gehlen. Rorty retains from the pragmatist inheritance, which in many, though not all, respects he unjustly claims for himself, an intuition which links us together—the conviction that a humane collective life depends on the vulnerable forms of innovation-bearing, reciprocal and unforcedly egalitarian everyday communication. This intuition is even more alien to Derrida and Foucault than to Adorno (who also remained a romantic of course, and not just as a composer).

The question of post-structuralism has an obvious importance at the present time, given the increasing penetration of this style of thought into the Federal Republic. What do you consider to be the reasons for this success, and what are your feelings about the repatriation of the thought of Nietzsche and Heidegger in post-structuralist form?

The influence of post-structuralism on the German universities is undoubtedly also connected with the situation in the academic job-market. The horizon of expectations of the younger intellectuals has become so gloomy that a negativistic mood has become widsespread, which in part even flips over into apocalyptic anticipations of revival. Social reality is doing something further: it is not miserly in the creation of ever new dangers which, even on calmer consideration, appear as side-effects of purposive-rational action, thus as dangers which we have brought upon ourselves. For this reason theories which grasp the whole as the untrue, and offer the affirmation of the impossibility of escape as the only affirmation possible, not only match the mood of the critique of civilization—they also have an increasing reality-content. After all, how ought one to respond to the spectacle of the last American election, in which all levels of reality triumphantly intermingled: in which a play-actor president reveals to an enrap-

tured public that, despite all asseverations of leadership and he-man-
ship, he is merely playing at being president, and is promptly
returned to office? To that kind of thing one can only reply with the
cynical antics of the deconstructionists.

The situation is a little different with Heidegger, who still tends to
inspire a holy terror in this country. The latest return of a felici-
tously de-Nazified Heidegger is, of course, based on the ahistorical
reception of Heidegger in France and America—where he stepped
on stage after the War, like a phoenix from the ashes, as the author of
the 'Letter on Humanism'.

*The suspicion of system in philosophy is characteristic of many
currents in twentieth century thought. Scepticism about the possibility of
philosophy as an ordered body of truths is characteristic of thinkers as
diverse as Wittgenstein, Merleau-Ponty and Adorno. How would you
defend the need for, and possibility of, systematic philosophy against
these deeply rooted objections?*

Since Hegel's death philosophical systems are no longer to be had
with good conscience. Any thinker who, in the twentieth century,
has asserted and practised the death, the supersession, the end, or
the disbanding of philosophy, has therefore simply been belatedly
carrying out a decree which was issued by the first generation of
Young Hegelians. Ever since then philosophical thought has sought
to step over into another medium. In this respect we have all
remained contemporaries of the Young Hegelians—all post-modern
ambitions notwithstanding. 'After Philosophy'—the title of a collection of essays which Tom McCarthy is planning—characterizes a
situation which, for me, has become so self-evident that I consider
the grand gestures of the anti-systematists to be pretty superfluous.
Any philosophical work implicitly renounces thinking in systems
which weaves itself into the ramified network of the human and
social sciences, without fundamentalist claims and with a fallibilistic
consciousness, in order to contribute something of use whenever the
problem of the presumptively universal features of knowledge,
speech and action arises.

*One of the most obvious general developments in your work has been
the increasing prominence of the arguments and procedures of analytical philosophy. Could you explain the reasons for this transformation? What resources are offered by analytical philosophy which cannot
be provided by other traditions, including the major German traditions?*

In general, the example of analytical philosophy has been a salutary force in post-war German philosophy for no other reason than that it demanded a higher level of explicitness. I have learned most from Wittgenstein, Austin and Searle—as you know, I find instruments in their work for the investigation of general pragmatic presuppositions of the use of propositions in utterances.

One of the most prominent developments in English-speaking philosophy over the last ten years or so has been the emergence of new, substantive works of political philosophy (Rawls, Nozick, Dworkin, Walzer) and of a widespread debate around them. How significant do you consider this development? And do you feel that it would be appropriate for you to make a more direct intervention into this debate than you have so far, given that the concerns of these thinkers in many respects overlap with your own?

Besides speech-act theory, I could also have mentioned moral philosophy, at least the line of thought (from Baier and Singer to Rawls) in which the substance of Kantian ethics is retrieved in a certain way in terms of linguistic philosophy. More recently, I myself have explained the discourse ethics approach, which Apel and I favour, more thoroughly.[8] This approach is an attempt to reconstruct Kantian ethics with the help of the theory of communication. The suggestions which I have reworked in this process derive above all from Rawls and Kohlberg. When I initiated a discussion of civil disobedience last year, in response to contemporary events, the work of Rawls and Dworkin provided the most important points of reference. If you are under the impression that I have not been sufficiently engaged on this front, this may be the result of my somewhat restricted understanding of the task of philosophical ethics.

According to my conception, the philosopher ought to explain the moral point of view, and—as far as possible—justify the claim to universality of this explanation, showing why it does not merely reflect the moral intuitions of the average, male, middle-class member of a modern Western society. Anything further than that is a matter for moral discourse between participants. Insofar as the philosopher would like to justify specific principles of a normative theory of morality and politics, he should consider this as a proposal for the discourse between citizens. In other words: the moral

8. 'Diskursethik—Notizen zu einem Begründungsprogramm', in *Moralbewusstsein und kommunikatives Handeln*, Frankfurt 1983, pp. 53–125.

philosopher must leave the substantive questions which go beyond a fundamental critique of value-scepticism and value-relativism to the participants in moral discourse, or tailor the cognitive claims of normative theory from the outset to the role of a participant. In this way we gain a larger space for the contribution of social theory to the diagnosis of the present. Admittedly, ethical considerations are frequently of great methodological value in the construction of such theories. I have discussed this question in *Legitimation Crisis*, in connection with the problem of distinguishing particular from universal interests.

In your own recent writing stylistic considerations appear to have retreated in favour of a more functional mode of expression, a shift which seems to be correlated with the increasing importance of analytical philosophy in your work. Given your remarks, in 'Does Philosophy Still have a Purpose?', about the end of 'great philosophy', the transformation of philosophy into a branch of 'research', and the demise of the 'style of philosophical thinking tied to individual scholarship and personal representation',[9] would you consider a concern with style in the work of a contemporary philosopher to be a diversion or a regression? Is what is of value in a philosophical position always susceptible to direct statement?

The type of text changes in accordance with purpose, addressee, place and time—according to whether I am dealing with the theme of the *Berufsverbot*, or of civil disobedience in the public-political sphere, or whether I am giving a speech in honour of Gadamer, polemicizing against Gehlen, writing an obituary for Scholem, or whether I am attempting to justify a moral principle or to classify speech-acts. The rhetorical constituents vary in relation to these different purposes. We are now well aware, since Mary Hesse at the latest, that even the language of the sciences is shot through with metaphors; this is plainly true of the language of philosophy, which can never of course be entirely absorbed into its role as a stand-in for scientific theories with strong universal claims. But one cannot, like Derrida, conclude from the unavoidably rhetorical character of *every* kind of language, including philosophical language, that it is all one and the same—that the categories of everyday life and literature, science and fiction, poetry and philosophy, collapse into each other. For Derrida all cats are grey in the night of 'writing'. I

9. *Philosophical-Political Profiles*, pp. 1–2.

would not wish to draw this conclusion. The use of language in the practices of everyday life stands under different restrictions from the language used in theory or in art, which is specialized for the solving of problems, or for an innovative disclosure of the world.

How would you summarize your present conceptions of truth? If any adequate approach to truth should include a theory of evidence and a theory of argument, would it be fair to say that your work so far has given much more attention to the latter than the former? Today, would you still maintain the categorical separation between 'objectivity' and 'truth', [10] *the experiential and the veridical, of the postscript to* Knowledge and Human Interests?

The core of the discourse theory of truth can be formulated by means of three basic concepts: *conditions of validity* (which are fulfilled when an utterance holds good), *validity-claims* (which speakers raise with their utterances, for their validity), and *redemption* of a validity-claim (in the framework of a discourse which is sufficiently close to the conditions of an ideal speech situation for the consensus aimed at by the participants to be brought about solely through the force of the better argument, and in this sense to be 'rationally motivated'). The basic intuition, then, is simply this. Validity-claims are explicitly thematized only in non-trivial cases, but it is precisely in these cases that there are no rules of verification available which would make it possible to decide directly whether certain conditions of validity are fulfilled or not. When claims to truth or justice become really obstinately problematic, there are no neat deductions or decisive pieces of evidence which could *enforce* an immediate decision for or against. Rather a play of argumentation is required, in which motivating reasons take the place of the unavailable knock-down arguments. If one accepts this description, it becomes clear that the following difficulty arises in the attempt to explain what it means to say that an utterance is valid. An utterance is valid when its conditions of validity are fulfilled. According to our description the fulfilment or non-fulfilment of conditions of validity, in problematic cases, can only be ascertained by means of the argumentative redemption of the corresponding validity-claims. The discourse theory of truth, then, explains what it means to redeem a validity-claim by an analysis of the general pragmatic presuppositions of the attainment of a rationally-motivated consensus. This

---

10. *Knowledge and Human Interests*, London 1978, pp. 360–366.

theory of truth provides only an explication of meaning, it does not provide a criterion; in the end, however, it undermines the clear distinction between meaning and criterion.

To what extent is the notion of an ideal speech situation as a regulative principle of truth a circular one? If truth is defined as the consensus that would be reached by the speakers in an ideal speech situation, how could the existence of such a situation itself ever be truthfully ascertained? In other words, isn't the idea susceptible to the same kind of critique that Hegel made of Kant's theory of knowledge, and you of Hegel's, in Knowledge and Human Interests *—the 'aporia of knowing before knowlege'?[11] Perhaps one could reformulate such a criticism another way. How could any speech situation be ideal, save in terms of the symmetry and sincerity of its speakers? But even at their most perfect, these conditions could normally only yield agreement rather than truth—that is, in abstraction from evidence, the opportunities for which can themselves never be ideal, since they always depend in some measure on historically changing techniques. Even the most flawlessly democratic and equal community of classical Greeks could not have discovered the laws of thermodynamics in the absence of modern optics. Isn't this one of the limits of any consensus theory of truth?*

The discourse theory of truth only claims to reconstruct an intuitive knowledge of the meaning of universal validity-claims which every competent speaker has at his or her disposal. 'Ideal speech situation' is somewhat too concrete a term for the set of general and unavoidable communicative presuppositions which a subject capable of speech and action must make every time he or she wishes to participate seriously in argumentation. In answering your previous question I wanted to recall the fact that this intuitive knowledge of universal presuppositions of argumentation is linked with the preunderstanding of propositional truth and moral truth (or rightness). Of course, we know from philosophy and from the history of science that these ideas can be operationalized in very different ways; what counts at any given time as a good reason, as a proof, as an explanation, obviously depends on historically-changing background convictions, and also, as you suggest, on the associated techniques for controlling and observing nature; in short, on changing paradigms. But the paradigm-dependence of theories can be more readily

---

11. *Knowledge and Human Interests*, p. 21.

harmonized with a discourse theory of truth than with a realist theory. The discourse theory is only incompatible with a Feyerabend-style paradigm-*relativism* because it sticks to the idea that paradigm-dependent ideas of truth and rightness nevertheless point towards a universal core of meaning.

How do you conceive the relation between philosophical and scientific truth-claims? Are philosophical truth-claims cognitive claims, and would a rational consensus ultimately guarantee the truth of the consensus theory of truth itself?

This is an interesting question, on which I have been working for a good while, although so far I do not have a conclusive answer to hand.

What is your attitude to psychoanalysis today? In Knowledge and Human Interests *you eloquently present it as the paradigm of a critical science serving an emancipatory interest. At the same time, you remark that Freud's metapsychology was a misunderstanding of his own project, whose instinct theory has never yielded 'a single statement that has ever been tested experimentally'.*[12] *But how far does this stricture apply to the main body of analytic theory itself? Even if the evidential weaknesses—widely aired—of psycho-analysis are set aside, doesn't the theory in fact present peculiar difficulties for a consensus theory of truth, insofar as the transactions between analyst and analysand are inherently confidential— i.e. non-extendable to others? In the gap between the 'clinical' and the 'ideal speech' situations, isn't there a temptation in your original account to fall back on essentially a pragmatic justification of Freud's theory—whose test becomes a change in the conduct of the patient, a 'continuation of the self-formative process' indeterminable in direction or duration? This could seem close to the kind of Deweyan instrumentalism that you reject in the postscript. But the success rate even in these terms is not very high. In sum: isn't there much more question about the scientificity of many of Freud's claims, scrutinized in a large literature, than you allowed in the late sixties?*

My friend Mitscherlich once summed up his experience as a psycho-analyst in the following terms: therapy often achieves 'no more than the transformation of illness into suffering, but into a suffering

---

12. *Knowledge and Human Interests*, p. 253.

which enhances the status of *homo sapiens*, because it does not extinguish his freedom'. I would like to make use of this statement to express my scepticism about critieria based on statistics of so-called success.

It certainly seems to be the case today that psychoanalytic research has come to a standstill, not only in Germany but on an international scale, and that intelligent young people prefer to go into other disciplines. But how definitive is this? Many disciplines have survived similar periods of stagnation. Even sociology is going through thin times at the moment. I have not done any work myself on Freud's metapsychology since the end of the sixties. But I find the attempts to bring Freud and Piaget together, which have been undertaken in various contexts, both exciting and fruitful. Beyond that, my interpretation of Freud in terms of communication theory still seems to me to be plausible. I cannot entirely accept your objection. I have never understood the therapeutic discourse as discourse or argumentation in the strict sense, because of the asymmetries between doctor and patient which are built into it. Of course it is inhabited, so to speak, by the *telos* of working to remove those asymmetries. For these reasons the patient also acquires in the end, at least in the ideal case, a freedom to say 'yes' and 'no' which immunizes him or her against the suggestive obtrusion of functional interpretations, which are, in a superficial sense, 'life-assisting'. What should be involved is, of course, the continuation, made possible *through reflexive insight*, of an interrupted, neurotically-inhibited process of formation of the self.

The Theory of Communicative Action *contains a fascinating reconstruction and critique of Weber's account of 'rationalization' as a world-historical process. In it, you tax Weber with abandoning his own starting-point—the advent of substantive reasoning with the major religions—in his final focus on formal rationality alone, as the necessary matrix of modern capitalism; and you also point to significant lacunae in his regional theory of the origins of capitalism—his omission of the rise of modern science, and more generally its bearers during the Renaissance. These are compelling demonstrations. What is not so clear, on the other hand, is whether you accept the main thrust of his thesis concerning the importance of the Protestant Ethic itself, as the engine of a rationalized life-world and so motor of early capitalism. Many historians have been highly sceptical of Weber's claims for Calvinism—one need only think of a critical survey of the evidence like Kurt Samuelson's* Religion and Economic Action, *or*

Trevor-Roper's essays on Erasmianism. Did you feel that these doubts fell outside the province of your treatment of Weber?

I did indeed neglect the wide-ranging discussion around the question of whether and to what extent Weber's analysis of capitalism has proved correct. There were, above all, practical reasons for that—it would have required, if not another book, at the very least an additional chapter. It is also for these reasons—to reduce the burden of work—that I planned *The Theory of Communicative Action* as an intertwining of history of theory with systematic investigations. In Weber's case this had the additional advantage of illustrating a favourite idea of mine. Weber perceives with great acuity the narrowness of the Calvinistic doctrine of grace, and the repressive traits of the forms of life which bore the stamp of this doctrine; but Weber refuses to see this protestant ethic as a *one-sided* exploitation of a potential which was built into the universalist ethics of brotherhood. In fact, it is the selective model of capitalist rationalization as a whole which is mirrored in the protestant ethic.

Of course, such interests attached to the form of presentation should not be allowed to get the upper hand; otherwise one would become cynical about questions of truth. Insofar as I am familiar with the literature, I believe that Weber's thesis must be expanded and revised with regard to *other* social strata who were bearers of early capitalism. However, I doubt whether such revision would be forced to tamper with the general correlation of an ethics of conviction, worldly asceticism, and economic behaviour.

More generally, what is your view of the position and contribution of history as a discipline within the social sciences? You have always argued that 'history as such is not capable of theory', because it is always a retrospective narrative—'whereas theoretical statements allow the derivation of conditional predictions of events that will occur in the future'.[13] You contrast this incapacity for theory and prediction with the competence in these respects of sociology or evolutionary discourses. This distinction seems quite close to the neo-Kantian dichotomy between ideographic and nomothetic sciences. But is it warranted? It is difficult to see why historians like Taylor or Hobsbawm should be unable to make forecasts at least as reliable—

---

13. *Zur Rekonstruktion des historischen Materialismus*, Frankfurt 1976, pp. 204, 207.

to put it no higher—as those of sociologists like Bell or Dahrendorf,
whom you cite as valid diagnosticians of the time. Don't warnings of
the increasing dangers of nuclear war, for example, have a special
weight when they come from a historian of the authority of Edward
Thompson? Once such a sharp division is made between 'history' and
'theory', aren't the effects on historical materialism itself necessarily
paradoxical—in the sense that to reconstruct it as theory, it has to be
drastically reduced as history, in the evolutionary version presented
in Communication and the Evolution of Society? *It would appear*
prima facie more plausible to imagine that Marxist (and other)
historians would have more to contribute to the enterprise of recon-
structing historical materialism than child psychologists. Couldn't
one cite your Strukturwandel *against yourself here, as a memorable*
example of a work at once and indivisibly historical and theoretical,
and diagnostic to boot?

The prognostic capacity of social theories was and is very limited—
that could hardly be otherwise, given the high level of abstraction at
which these statements concerning complex states of affairs are
formulated. Nor do I doubt that a shrewd and politically-seasoned
historian, with his or her experience-steeped intuitions, often judges
contemporary developmental tendencies with an astonishing sure-
ness of touch. It is for methodological reasons that I have insisted on
a distinction—but not a distinction of rank—between historiography and social-scientific theory. If one introduces the viewpoint
of social evolution into history without mediation, it is easy to fall
victim to patterns of thought familar from the philosophy of history,
above all the danger of thinking in terms of historical teleology,
which Marxists in particular have often enough succumbed to. The
reflections which you refer to belonged in the context of the critique
of historical objectivism, and of its unfortunate consequences for the
political practice of so-called vanguard parties. I am not in any sense
opposed to the necessity of theoretically-guided historical research.
Theories, especially those of Marxist inspiration, ultimately only
prove their worth by making a contribution to the explanation of
concrete historical processes. I myself find it unfortunate that for the
last two decades (if one disregards some shorter political writings)
my interest has been taken up exclusively with problems which can
be characterized in a broad sense as problems of theory construction.
I must accept the criticism which, most recently, Tom Bottomore
has directed at me in this respect.

What are the methodological grounds for the homologies you postulate between individual growth and social evolution? In The Theory of Communicative Action, *you remark that most adults in* all *societies can achieve the higher levels of moral and cognitive competence, as described by Piaget and Kohlberg.*[14] *If this is so, how can the maturational sequence they posit help to explain the huge differences between such societies, when arrayed along a scale of rationalization of the world-views they exhibit?*

Empirical investigations come out strongly against the idea that all adult members of a society, even of modern Western societies, have acquired the capacity for formal-operational thought (in Piaget's sense) or for post-conventional judgements (in the sense of Kohlberg's theory of moral development). I maintain only (for example, with reference to tribal societies) that individuals can develop structures of consciousness which belong to a higher stage than those which are already embodied in the institutions of their society. It is primarily subjects who learn, while societies can take a step forward in the evolutionary learning-process only in a metaphorical sense. New forms of social integration, and new productive forces, are due to the institutionalization and exploitation of forms of knowledge which are individually acquired, but culturally stored and capable of transmission and so, in the long term, accessible to the collective. However, the process of social implementation only takes place as a consequence of political struggles and social movements, of the outrider-role of innovative marginal groups, and so on. Thus I start from the trivial assumption that subjects capable of speech and action cannot help but learn, and use this to support the assumption that ontogenetic learning processes acquire pacemaker functions. However, this thesis is contested by Klaus Eder in his *Habilitations-schrift* on the development of German constitutional law since the eighteenth century. He traces the innovative impulses back directly to *social* learning processes in the framework of new forms of association, namely to new experiences of egalitarian social relations, initially in the Masonic lodges, secret societies and readers' unions, later in the early socialist workingmen's associations.

Can a theory of emancipation avoid the idea of progress? You stress in The Theory of Communicative Action *that we cannot judge the worth of societies by the degree to which their life-worlds are rational-*

---

14. *The Theory of Communicative Action*, I, London 1984, p. 44.

ized, even in the sense of an 'encompassing' rationality that is not only formal but substantive; suggesting that at best we can speak perhaps of the relative 'health' or 'sickness' of a given social order.[15] *Earlier, however, in* Legitimation Crisis, *you criticized the use of such terms, drawn from biology, as fundamentally inapplicable to society.*[16] *Have you definitely changed your views here, or is this still a relatively unresolved issue for you? The difficulty seems to be to resist historical triumphalism—an Enlightenment complacency that devalues all anterior or alien social forms—without falling into political agnosticism. For if all epochs and societies are equally close to God, in Ranke's sense, why fight for a better one? A consistent cultural relativism must be conservative. In what direction do you think a solution to these dilemmas is to be looked for?*

I have not revised my conception in this respect, but continue to think that statements concerning the level of development of a society can only relate to *single* dimensions and to *universal* structures: to the reflexivity and complexity of social systems on the one hand, and to the social forces of production and forms of social integration on the other. One society may be superior to another with reference to the level of differentiation of its economic or administrative system, or with reference to technologies and legal institutions. But it does not follow that we are entitled to value this society more highly *as a whole*, as a concrete totality, as a form of life. You know that, in relation to objectifying knowledge and moral insight, the position I represent is one of cautious universalism. We observe tendencies towards a 'progressive' rationalization of the life-world—not as a law, of course, but as a historical fact. Again and again those tendencies have been confirmed which distinguish modern societies from traditional ones—the increasing reflexivity of the cultural tradition, the universalization of values and norms, the freeing of communicative action from tightly circumscribed normative contexts, the diffusion of models of socialization which promote processes of individuation and the formation of abstract ego-identities, and so on. But all these 'advances' concern the universal structures of life-worlds in general; they say nothing about the value of a concrete way of life. This value must be measured by other things, of the kind which we look for in clinical judgements: whether people in such and such circumstances have a 'hard' life,

---

15. *The Theory of Communicative Action*, I, p. 73.
16. *Legitimation Crisis*, London 1976, pp. 175–177.

whether they are alienated from themselves. For the intuition of an unspoiled life we apply yardsticks which are valid in the first instance in the context of our culture or plausible in the context of our tradition, which in any event cannot be generalized in the same way as the standards which we use in judging processes that involve learning—knowledge of nature or moral and legal ideas, which, despite their paradigm-dependence, are not *entirely* incommensurable. So far I have no idea how the universal core of those merely clinical intuitions—if indeed they have one at all—can be theoretically grasped.

Can a morality of enlightenment skirt a commitment to happiness? If not, what is the bearing of a 'discursive ethics' on it? In your essay on Benjamin, you evoke the possibility of a society at once freed of domination and devoid of meaning—rationality without felicity. Doesn't such a prospect undermine the argument that every truthful statement is 'an anticipation of the good life'?[17] *Another way of putting the question would be this: you have argued on a number of occasions that ethics is a 'reconstructive science'—while elsewhere you define such sciences as those, in contradistinction to critical theories, which are without practical effects on the conduct of agents.*[18] *But isn't the idea of a* post facto *ethic, an anodyne codification of existing practices, virtually a contradiction in terms?*

Let me start with a couple of general propositions. Morality has certainly to do with justice and also with the wellbeing of others, even with the promotion of the general welfare. But happiness cannot be brought about intentionally, and can only be promoted very indirectly. I prefer a relatively narrow concept of morality. Morality refers to practical questions which can be decided with reasons—to conflicts of action which can be resolved through consensus. Only those questions are moral in a strict sense which can be answered in a meaningful way from the Kantian standpoint of universalization—of what *all* could wish for. At the same time, I prefer a weak concept of moral theory. We have already touched on this: it should explain and justify the moral point of view, and nothing more. Deontic, cognitive and universal moral theories in the

---

17. *Philosophical-Political Profiles*, pp. 115–158; *Knowledge and Human Interests*, p. 314.

18. *Knowledge and Human Interests*, p. 378; *Theory and Practice*, London 1974, p. 23.

Kantian tradition are theories of justice, which must leave the question of the good life unanswered. They are typically restricted to the question of the *justification* of norms and actions. They have no answer to the question of how justified norms can be *applied* to specific situations and how moral insights can be *realized*. In short, one should not place excessive demands on moral theory, but leave something over for social theory, and the major part for the participants themselves—whether it be their moral discourses or their good sense. This merely advocatory role sets narrow limits to theory: whoever takes a risk upon him or herself, must be allowed to make his or her *own* decision. But now to your questions.

Moral theory proceeds reconstructively, in other words after the event. Aristotle was right in his opinion that the moral intuitions which theory clarifies must have been acquired elsewhere, in more or less successful socialization processes. However, I would also expect a critical theory to perform the task of making possible enlightening interpretations of situations, which affect our self-understanding and orientate us in action. Even social theory would overstep its competence, however, if it undertook to project desirable forms of life into the future, instead of criticizing existing forms of life. In so doing, it can refer to historically superfluous repressions, and to that untapped potential for rationality which can be read off from the state of the productive forces, the level of legal and moral ideas, the degree of individuation, and so on. For this reason Marxist theory cannot cash out the expression 'socialism' in terms of a *concrete* form of life; at most it can indicate necessary conditions under which emancipated forms of life would be possible today.

How far is the realm of 'inner nature' a source of potential values for you? You've written of a necessary 'fluidification' of this nature in any post-conventional morality or society, and have suggested that art has a particularly significant role to play in such redispositions.[19] *Could you give some examples of the kind of process you have in mind?*

Our needs are only ever accessible to us in an interpreted form. In other words, language is constitutive for needs, in the light of which situations—which are always affectively tinged—are disclosed to us. Up till now the transformation of evaluative, need-interpreting languages has taken place in a nature-like manner; the changing of

19. *Communication and the Evolution of Society*, London 1979, p. 93.

this vocabulary has taken place as part of the changing of linguistic world-pictures. To the extent that art and literature have become differentiated into a sphere with a logic of its own, and in this sense have become autonomous, a tradition of literary and art criticism has been established which labours to reintegrate the innovative aesthetic experiences, at first 'mute', into ordinary language, and thus into the communicative practice of everyday life. In the medium of this criticism the formerly sluggish, nature-like process of revaluation of our evaluative vocabulary, our world-disclosing and need-interpreting language in general, becomes more and more reflexive; the whole process becomes, as it were, discursively fluidified. Central concepts such as the happiness, dignity, integrity of the person are now changing as if before our very eyes. Diffuse experiences, which crystallize out under transformed life-circumstances produced by changes in social structure, find their illuminating, suggestive, visible expression through cultural productivity. This is what Castoriadis means by 'imagination'. Benjamin, for example, investigated through Baudelaire those experiences of a mobilized, concentrated, metropolitan life-world which surfaced like a new continent in nineteenth-century Paris, the 'capital of the nineteenth century', as he called it. Kafka and Musil can be seen as literary exemplifications of the experiential space of the collapsing Austrian Imperial and Royal Monarchy, Celan and Beckett of a world transformed by Auschwitz. Our moral-practical reflections and discourses are affected by this productivity, precisely to the extent that it is only in the light of such innovations that we can say what we *really* want, and above all: what we *cannot* want. Only in this light do we find a precise expression for our interests.

In recent years you have polemicized against theories of post-modernity, associating them with concepts of post-history and with the neo-conservative implications of post-structuralism. It is not entirely clear, however, whether you intend to deny that there are any developments to which the concept of post-modernism corresponds, or whether you are merely contesting the appropriateness of the designation. Would you deny, for example, that the shift away from the esotericism of high modern art to fusions of high and mass culture is a development to which the term 'post-modernism' could be applied? In The Theory of Communicative Action *you hint at the emergence of a 'post-avant-garde art' which would be 'characterized by the simultaneity of realistic and engaged tendencies with the authentic continuation of that classical modernity which separated out the distinctive meaning of the aesthetic'.*[20] *What examples would you give of works of art which are moving in this direction? And, given your refusal to deny all progressive potential to mass culture, would fusions of high and mass culture be one aspect of such a 'post-avant-garde art'?*

Peter Bürger sees post-avant-garde art, art after the failure of the surrealist revolt, the contemporary scene in general, as being characterized by the juxtaposition of styles, which draw either on the formalist languages of the avant-garde, or on the inheritance of realistic or political-didactic styles and literatures. You can find examples in the museum of any large city. This juxtaposition also includes the by now ritualized forms of the *'Aufhebung'* of esoteric art. I would not interpret the contemporary scene in the sense of so-called postmodernism as a sign of the exhaustion or the 'end' of modernism in art and architecture. Our situation testifies, rather, to the fact that the aesthetic experiences revealed by the twentieth century's avant-gardes find no access to a onesidedly rationalized everyday practice, but circle around restlessly before its portals in split-off specialist cultures. I share Adorno's reservations about mass culture, against Benjamin's overhasty hopes for its 'profane illuminations', only to the extent that the fusion of high and trivial culture has, up till now, fallen short of its programmatic goal. Desublimated mass-art does not penetrate in a transforming, illuminating and liberating way into life-forms reified by capitalism, and deformed and distorted by consumerism and bureaucracy, but rather helps to advance these tendencies. It was not the hopes of the surrealists which were false, but their path—the *Aufhebung* of aesthetic illusion—was counter-productive.

One of the significant developments in your work over the last decade has been the progressive attenuation of the claims made for the 'ideal speech situation'. In The Theory of Communicative Action *you admit the utopian nature of the project of an ideal speech community, and you have also emphasized that the procedural rationality of argumentative grounding cannot provide the substance of a form of life as such. Even after having made the concessions, however, there might still be a tension between the telos of universal consensus and the human (and epistemological) value of conflict and diversity. It is this kind of tension to which Mill, whose conception of truth in some ways resembles your own, reveals himself to be sensitive when he writes, in* On Liberty: *'The loss of so important an aid to the*

---

20. *Theorie des kommunikativen Handelns*, II, p. 586.

intelligent and living apprehension of truth as is afforded by the necessity of explaining it to, or defending it against, opponents, though not sufficient to outweigh, is no trifling drawback from the benefit of its universal recognition.' In Strukturwandel *you suggest that Mill disguised his 'resignation before the rational insolubility of competing interests in the public sphere' by means of a 'perspectivist theory of knowledge'.*[21] *However, as the above quotation makes clear, this is not entirely accurate. Mill does not doubt that truth ultimately entails consensus, but nevertheless perceives unanimity as purchased at the cost of other human values. Are you at all susceptible to this kind of consideration?*

I think I am—after all, my Marxist friends are not entirely unjustified in accusing me of being a radical liberal. I can only repeat what I have already stressed elsewhere. 'Nothing makes me more nervous than the imputation that because the theory of communicative action focuses attention on the social facticity of recognized validity-claims, it proposes, or at least suggests, a rationalistic utopian society. I do *not* regard the fully transparent—let me add in this context: or indeed a homogenized and unified—society as an ideal, nor do I wish to suggest any other ideal—Marx was not the only one frightened by the vestiges of utopian socialism.'[22] The ideal speech situation is, as I have said, a description of the conditions under which claims to truth and rightness can be discursively redeemed. In communicative action these validity-claims remain for the most part implicit and unproblematic, since the intersubjectively shared life-world holds in reserve a solid background of culturally self-evident truths, taken-for-granted assumptions. The action-coordinating role of processes of reaching understanding, which proceed by means of the criticism of validity-claims, does not conflict therefore with the pluralism of life-forms and interest. The fact that modern societies are differentiated in terms of life-forms and interest-positions, and are becoming increasingly differentiated, is a fact which does not put action orientated to reaching understanding out of service; of course, the need for understanding, which increases in step with this process, must be satisfied at higher and higher levels of abstraction. For this reason the consensual norms and principles become ever more general.

---

21. *On Liberty*, Harmondsworth 1982, p. 106; *Strukturwandel der Öffentlichkeit*, Neuwied 1962, p. 150.

22. 'A Reply to my Critics', in J. Thompson and D. Held, eds., *Habermas—Critical Debates*, London 1982, p. 235.

There is also another way of meeting a need for understanding which goes beyond the available possibilities of reaching consensus; this need in fact disappears entirely as soon as socially-integrated domains of action are switched over to system-integration. That is precisely what happened to many areas of life in the wake of capitalist modernization. Money and power—more concretely, markets and administrations—take over the integrative functions which were formerly fulfilled by consensual values and norms, or even by processes of reaching understanding. Of course my thesis, which I develop in the second volume of *The Theory of Communicative Action* through a discussion of Parsons' theory of media, is this: that those domains of action which are specialized for the transmission of culture, social integration or the socialization of the young, rely on the medium of communicative action and cannot be integrated through money or power. A commercialization or bureaucratization must therefore generate—this is the thesis—disturbances, pathological side-effects in these domains. But here I am straying from your question about the rights of pluralism.

In your discussion of the structures of domination typical of capital-ism, you stress the way in which these act to occlude and suppress 'generalizable interests', as opposed to 'particular interests' which they themselves covertly represent. You argue that difference be-tween these two kinds of interest can in principle be established by a species of thought-experiment you call 'simulated discourse'.[23] Could you give an illustration of how this might work? One of the problems the distinction seems to raise is the status of interests that are not generalizable but are nevertheless perfectly valid—in other words, the question of the 'natural' heterogeneity of interests, even in socialist society, in which different agents or groups will have a plurality of specific needs or exigencies, all in their own terms quite legitimate—regional, occupational, generational, and so on. How would your proposed model of 'discursive will-formation', which appears to put a premium on consensus around generalizable inter-ests, arbitrate conflicting demands of this sort?

The model of repressed generalizable interests is of course only a proposal for a way of criticizing interests which unjustly pass them-selves off as general interests. This goal is also pursued by Marx in his critique of bourgeois legal forms, or in his critique of the

---

23. *Legitimation Crisis*, p. 117.

doctrines of Smith and Ricardo. The model which I propose is designed to demonstrate the non-generalizability of interests which are presumed to be general. For example, an argument which arouses this suspicion today often crops up in social-democratic pronouncements: such and such a stimulus must be given to investment 'in order to secure jobs'.

Your objection is directed against an assumption which I do not in any way make. In no sense do I begin from the basis that in all, or even in the majority of political decisions, legal or administrative regulations, a general interest is at stake. Modern societies are not like that. Often, maybe in the majority of cases, the social matters which are nowadays regulated through state intervention concern only particular interest-groups. In such cases moral discourse could only have the aim of withdrawing legitimacy from the privileging of one side, which falsely claims to represent a general interest. When only particular interests are at stake, conflicts of action cannot be settled, even in ideal cases, through argumentation, but only through bargaining and compromise. Of course, the *procedures* of reaching compromise must for their part be judged from a normative standpoint. A fair compromise is not to be expected when—for instance —the parties involved do not have at their disposal the same positions of power or capacity to make threats. To give an example: when the complicated question arises of the effects of constitutional rights on third parties, one is entitled to expect that the ruling of the court will be supported by arguments; when it is a matter of the straightforward, but politically delicate question of the location of a nuclear power station, the most that can be expected is that a fair compromise will be arrived at. Compromises are not only widespread as a matter of fact, but also, from the normative standpoint, occupy a position which is not in any way to be despised. This is why I do not have any difficulties with the pluralism of interests. After all, we anticipate that the pluralism of life-forms and the individualism of life-styles would increase at an exponential rate in a society which deserves the name socialist.

One of the novelties of your work as a whole, viewed against the background of classical forms of Marxism, is a shift from 'production' to 'communication', both as an analytic focus and as a source of value. At the same time, you have always emphasized that you regard yourself as a materialist. Could you specify the terms of the materialism you defend?

Right from my earliest publications I understood 'materialism' in the Marxist sense, as a theoretical approach which does not simply affirm the dependence of the superstructure on the base, the life-world on the imperatives of the accumulation process, as an onto-logical constant, so to speak, but which simultaneously explains and *denounces* this dependence as the latent function of a particular, historically transitory social formation. The transition from a pro-duction to a communication paradigm, which I advocate, does of course mean that the critical theory of society must no longer rely on the normative contents of the expressivist model of alienation and reappropriation of essential powers. The young Marx borrowed this model from the production aesthetics of Kant, Schiller and Hegel. The paradigm-shift from purposive activity to communicative action does not mean, however, that I am willing or bound to abandon the material reproduction of the life-world as the privileged point of reference for analysis. I continue to explain the selective model of capitalist modernization, and the corresponding pathologies of a one-sidedly rationalized life-world, in terms of a capitalist accumu-lation process which is largely disconnected from orientations towards use-value.

How far does the emergence of ecology, as a theory and a movement, qualify your earlier view that there is 'only one theoretically fruitful attitude towards nature'—that informed by an interest in technical control?

The awareness of ecological cycles, of biotopes, of human-environment systems has certainly brought forward new themes, new questions, perhaps even new disciplines. As far as I can tell, however, from the methodological point of view these ecologically inspired investigations move entirely within the inherited frame-work. So far nothing seems to suggest that alternative natural sciences can be developed in a non-objectifying attitude, for example in the performative attitude of a partner in communication—theories in the tradition of the romantic or alchemistic philosophies of nature.

II

What is the balance of your judgement on the political evolution you have witnessed, and lived through, from the fifties to the eighties, in the

178

West? The conclusion of Strukturwandel, *your first major book, contains a kind of ambiguity. The overall direction of your account of the 'structural change' in the public domain in the advanced capitalist countries was a deeply pessimistic one—etching an unforgettable portrait of a degraded public life, in which the substance of liberal democracy is voided in a combination of plebiscitary manipulation and privatized apathy, as any collectivity of citizenry disintegrates. Yet you also evoked the possibility (more briefly) of a 'restoration' of the public domain, by the democratization of parties, voluntary associations and media within it—but without giving much grounds for hope that this would occur. Looking back over a quarter of a century, do you feel things since have got worse or better, or have remained more or less the same?*

It is a perilous undertaking to recast the intuitive life-experiences of a political contemporary in the form of calculations of loss and gain. On the other hand I must admit that a proper theory of society, and a diagnosis of the present based upon it, can have no other point than to sharpen our perceptions for the ambivalent potential of contemporary developments. Let me try to give a very tentative and sketchy account from the perspective of the Federal Republic. On the one hand I have the impression that the tendencies to disintegration of a public sphere of the liberal type—a formation of opinion in discursive style mediated by reading, reasoning, information—have intensified since the late fifties. The mode of functioning of electronic media testifies to this, above all the centralization of organizations which privilege vertical and one-way flows of second and third-hand information, privately consumed. We are witnessing an increasing substitution of images for words, and also that intermingling of categories such as advertising, politics, entertainment, information, which was already criticized by Adorno. Adorno's critique of mass culture should be both extended and rewritten. The display aspect of the centres of our large cities has indeed absorbed elements of surrealism in an ironic way, and promoted the neon-lit re-enchantment of a de-realized reality. The banal coalesces with the unreal, hellenistically de-differentiated customs blend with high-tech style, and the ruins of popular cultures with the highly personalized, consumeristically polished bizarre. The refuse dumps of civilization are camouflaged with plastic. The substance of the universal is dissolved into a narcissism which has forfeited everything individual, and become a stereotype. As I have suggested, Derrida and a capering deconstructivism give the only appropriate answer to this really existing surrealism. This is matched, somewhat more seriously, by another tendency which is also well advanced: a manipulation of mass loyalty which is both perfected and passed off as respectable, administered by political parties which have migrated from the life-world into the political system. At an earlier stage it was still said that the parties and their exponents procured the *acclamation* of the voting public. That is a touchingly old-fashioned expression for the staged performances, barred against all spontaneity, which run according to scenario and bring literally everything under control. At all events, *that* was the new quality which the last American presidential election attained—with an actor playing a president whose office is increasingly restricted to presenting this office to the outside world as a fictive reality. Reality is overtaking the systems-theoretic description which Luhmann gives of it: the political system *extracts* from the public sphere the legitimation it needs. That is the one side.

On the other side, the reactions to this evacuation of the public-political sphere are getting stronger. After all, our observations of how the provision of legitimacy is running into difficulties, and the mirror-image laments of the neo-conservatives about 'ungovernability', are not totally mistaken. I wrote *Strukturwandel* before the protest movement of the sixties—what is more, without having in any way foreseen it. In the Federal Republic at the present time there are increasing indications of locally fragmented, subcultural resistances, of defensive movements at the 'base', as well as of spectacular mass demonstrations which abruptly flare up, and then die down again. The peace demonstrations in the autumn of 1983, immediately prior to the stationing of the missiles, reached dimensions previously unimaginable in the history of the Federal Republic; they also had a previously unknown quality of, shall we say, disciplined aggressive-ness. The sensitivity to threats to the protection of personal inform-ation, which was manifested in successful resistance against the planned census, against the introduction of a 'forgery-proof' identity-card and so on, is a further, admittedly less dramatic, symptom. Psephological monitorings of the erosion of traditional party ties, and of the increasing number of floating voters, also belong to this context. It is not only the successes of the Greens which are a sign of what we call over here 'party peevishness'. It seems to be generally the case that the ground is getting slippery. More or less unpredictable potentials for reaction are building up, which are mobilized by chance events.

These two contrary tendencies, of which I have given a few

illustrations, testify to a polarization of the public sphere into official, desiccated sectors directed from above, and into local sub-cultures, which are difficult to define in socio-structural terms, in part connected with the old middle-class, in part 'post-materialistic-ally' aligned, but in any event resistant, which have become the core of autonomous counter-public spheres—the old and the young, feminists and homosexuals, the handicapped and active unemployed, radical professionals, suburban housewives and so forth.

In work subsequent to Strukturwandel, *there emerges what might be called a counter-theme—that of a creeping 'legitimation crisis' of the prevailing order, with a decline, not of the public domain, but of the 'substitute programme' for it, or civil privatism and the 'ideology of achievement'. This more optimistic reading of the time was de-veloped in* Towards a Rational Society *and* Legitimation Crisis. *How do you view this diagnosis today, from the vantage-point of the long recession and the neo-conservative wave that has accompanied it?*

Let's say that at that time I was already reacting to experiences with the student protest movement.

In the central essay of Towards a Rational Society, *you maintained that the dominant ideology in the West draws its lexicon from 'technology and science'—the socio-political order being funda-mentally legitimated in the name of technocratic efficiency and necessity.[24] Couldn't one argue that it is rather 'democracy' that is the basic legitimating code of Western capitalism? If one analysed the speeches of Reagan, Thatcher, Kohl or Mitterrand, wouldn't one find that while the discourse of 'efficiency and prosperity' is a very important one, it is structurally subordinate to that of 'liberty and democracy'? How else, for example, are the stationing of missiles, the rollback of welfare programmes, the curbing of trade unions, justified?*

One could nevertheless defend the thesis that Reagan won his last election as the orchestrator of a mood of 'efficiency and prosperity'. On the other hand, it is certainly true that today a continuing technocratic practice, under the banner of neo-conservative atti-tudes and slogans, is no longer justified with technocratic ideologies.

---

24. 'Technology and Science as "Ideology"', in *Towards a Rational Society*, London 1971, pp. 81–122.

Technology and science, as an ideological programme, have lost much of their public effectiveness. My analysis of 1968 cannot be simply extended today; I already began to supplement it in 1973, in *Legitimation Crisis*. And in *The Theory of Communicative Action* I explore the 'crisis of the welfare state' which has developed in the meantime. The project of the welfare state has also become problematic in public consciousness, insofar as the bureaucratic means with which the interventionist state aimed to bring about the 'social restraint of capitalism' have lost their innocence. It is no longer merely the monetarization of labour power, but also the bureaucratization of the life-world which is experienced by broad strata of the population as a danger. Political-administrative power has lost the appearance of neutrality for the clients of welfare-state bureaucracies. These new attitudes are exploited by neo-conservatism, in order to sell the well-known policy of shifting the burden of problems back from the state onto the market—a policy which, Lord knows, has nothing to do with democratization, which rather effects a further uncoupling of state activity from the pressure for legitimation emanating from the public sphere, and understands by 'freedom' not the autonomy of the life-world, but a free hand for private investors.

How would you compare the 'new social movements' of the eighties with the student movement of the sixties, in terms of the direction and durability and likely effect of their protests against the established order?

Once again, I can only attempt to answer that with reference to the Federal Republic. Under the conditions of the boom, with a false understanding of the situation largely borrowed from orthodox Marxism, and in the narrow catchment area of the universities, our student movement already expressed, and in part made effective in the form of cultural revolution, a change of outlook which has continued to be manifest in the New Social Movements since the middle of the seventies. These movements, in conditions of persistent recession and increasing unemployment, have a more defensive posture, are less articulated than the students were in their day; perhaps they are more realistic in their understanding of the situation; above all, they recruit from broader social catchment areas. For example, the differences between the younger workers, apprentices, students and unemployed have been eroded within the framework of a youth culture whose unity is not simply a matter of image and appearances. Admittedly, this broader social basis does not yet indicate a power of veto strongly anchored in social structures. At the moment this 'anti-productivist' alliance is proving to have a certain socio-psychological contagiousness, but occupies no vital functional domains of industrial society. However, neo-conservative policies are the best way to secure a further influx to this alliance. Even if there are unforeseeable ups and downs in the manifestation of this capacity for resistance, I consider to be false the prognosis that people's anger will just as soon evaporate. The anger is structurally generated.

Do you continue to think that it was a mistake for the Greens to form a political party in West Germany, and to participate in electoral competition? How would you assess their prospects now?

Perhaps my warning at the time was fainthearted, but it was not unjustified. The predictable struggle between fundamentalist and reformist wings may still destroy the party of the Greens. The experiment has a prospect of success only so long as this dialectical tension is not discharged onesidedly. Above all internally, in relations with themselves, the Greens must improve their ability to compromise. For this is precisely the problem which would have to be solved: how can the relative capacity for action, indeed the very existence of a political party be secured, which must resolve within itself the contradiction between social movement and political system? Allow me to make a short detour in order to clarify this contradiction.

Recently the Federal Republic has been afflicted with the financial scandal of the Flick company. The scandal does not consist in the corruption of members of parliament, party leaders and ministers, who pocket illegal contributions for their party in return for favouring interests of big capital. The privileged influence of the owners of capital on the state apparatus is secured in such a way, through functional connections and structures, that these risky and antiquated methods of corrupting individuals are not at all necessary. The Flick method is out of date and untypical. However, the procedure reveals something else, and indeed something quite trivial: the political parties are no longer able to finance themselves from members' contributions, and yet are only allowed to supply half their needs from taxation, since otherwise they would be obliged to admit publicly the extent to which they are already divorced from their base, and have become autonomous as organs of the state. Thus, measured by our normative self-understanding, the real scandal, if it is still experienced as a scandal at all, consists in the following: the parties engage with good conscience in the legitimation process almost exclusively from above—that is, from the perspective of an integral part of the state apparatus. In any event, they act so little from the perspective of a mere mediator in the process of forming public opinion, that they overrun the public-political sphere with their interventions, instead of reproducing themselves out of it.

According to their own declarations, the Greens wish neither to be nor to become such a party. On the other hand, neither should they become submerged in the wake of the many subcultural and local counter-public spheres. As a party they must force the self-assured particularism of dissidents unconcerned with norms of civic equality through the filter of generalization, of equal consideration of interests. Perhaps this experiment should have been initiated after the capacity for self-organization had developed more strongly in different autonomous public spheres. Perhaps the experiment will succeed anyway—salutary effects are already stemming from it, for example on the internal life of the SPD, without which, if we are realistic about it, nothing can be moved.

How do you view the German national question, and the relationship between the two Germanies? Can the issue of 'reunification', or alternatively 'confederation', be raised from the Left today?

Willy Brandt has just made an impressive speech on this subject in Munich. Its tenor was: the German question is no longer open. I consider talk about a new German nationalism to be nonsense—it feeds more on inventions in the *New York Times* than on feelings here in Germany. The longing of many intellectuals for a lost German identity is as kitsch as the reunification rhetoric of CSU orators is mendacious. Long ago Kurt Schumacher, on his return from the concentration camps, was obsessed by the idea that he had committed an error at the end of the Weimar Republic—for this reason he wished, as Adenauer's opponent, to incorporate preventively right-wing feelings which in fact no longer existed. The West German Left should not repeat Schumacher's mistake today.

In Strukturwandel, *you point out Kant's failure to provide any theory of how the political power that could institutionalize the moral unity of a free civil society might itself be won—in other words, for ignoring (as you put it elsewhere in the book) the 'hard struggle against the ancient power' of Absolutism which was the price of the victory of a sovereign legislature.*[25] *Mutatis mutandis, could something similar be said, at any rate so far, of your own theory of 'domination-free communication'? How is the power that issued from the bourgeois revolutions Kant sidestepped to be transformed in its turn—through what kind of material struggles?*

'Freedom from domination' is presupposed by those who engage in *argumentation*. It would be a concretistic fallacy to assume that an emancipated society could consist in nothing but 'communication free from domination'. People who impute this to me make it a bit too easy for themselves. The release of a potential for reason embedded in communicative action is a world-historical process; in the modern period it leads to a rationalization of life-worlds, to the differentiation of their symbolic structures, which is expressed above all in the increasing reflexivity of cultural traditions, in processes of individuation, in the generalization of values, in the increasing prevalence of more abstract and more universal norms, and so on. These are trends which do not imply something good in themselves, but which nevertheless indicate that the prejudiced background consensus of the life-world is crumbling, that the number of cases is increasing in which interaction must be co-ordinated through a consensus reached by the participants themselves. Otherwise they must be transposed to media such as money or power, or controlled by a pseudo-consensus. This, in turn, is becoming less and less obtainable through ideologies, and is rather secured through the fragmentation of consciousness, and through barriers to communication which distort everyday practice in inconspicuous ways.

I recall these sociological considerations, which are developed in the second volume of *Communicative Action*, in order to make clear that I am no transcendental philosopher. I would not speak of 'communicative rationalization' if, in the last two hundred years of European and American history, in the last forty years of the national liberation movements, and despite all the catastrophes, a piece of 'existing reason', as Hegel would have put it, were not nevertheless also recognizable—in the bourgeois emancipation movements, no less than in the workers' movement, today in

25. *Strukturwandel der Öffentlichkeit*, pp. 124–125; 96–97.

feminism, in cultural revolts, in ecological and pacifist forms of resistance, and so forth. One must also bear in mind the rather more subcutaneous transformations in patterns of socialization, in value-orientations—for example, in the diffusion of expressive needs and moral sensitivities, or in the revolutionizing of sexual roles, in an altered subjective significance of waged work, and so on. Such long-term displacements in the motivational and attitudinal economy of the population do not hang in mid-air. Structurally they are above all based on the fact that the second industrial revolution augments labour productivity at a breakneck tempo while drastically reducing socially necessary labour time; for this reason it will require more and more absurd efforts, as Gorz, Offe and Negt argue, extending an old notion of Marcuse's, to hold the growing mass of those excluded and pushed to the margins in reserve for the role of full-time worker, which is set up as a norm by the capitalist labour market, instead of uncoupling income and social security from occupation, and doing away with the fetishism of the labour market.

The introduction to Theory and Practice *contrasts 'communicative action' with 'strategic action'—the arts of persuasion as against those of manoeuvre or constraint. The political distinction is very close to Gramsci's couplet of 'direction' and 'domination'. Your own commitment to the fullest possible exercise of the first, as the guiding principle of political practice, has always been unequivocal. Do you think that there are any grounds for supposing there to be limits to the suasive force of communicative action in advanced capitalism— possible or probable boundaries of enlightenment, so to speak? Or do you lean to the view that in principle a transition to socialism could rally the democratic assent even of those whom it deprived of their capital?*

You must be trying to have me on!

You have generally resisted a shift from procedural to institutional theories of democracy—criticizing, for example, proponents of 'council democracy' for confusing the two. But isn't the move an essential—even urgent—one if socialism is to be a credible project in the West? After all, if you could describe the transformation of the bourgeois public domain within capitalism, from greater to lesser substance and vitality, as a 'structural change', wouldn't it seem evident that the transformations involved in passing beyond capitalism must involve far greater 'structural' changes in democracy, which can only be specified institutionally?

I think that one must distinguish between the idea of a democratic justification of political power and the institutionalization of this level of justification, which changes according to circumstances. The idea of a process of will-formation in which all those concerned participate freely and equally is one thing, the organization of opinion- and will-forming discourses and deliberations, which would come closest to this idea under given circumstances, is another. For example, one can only appropriately criticize bourgeois parliamentarianism, in its different phases and national contexts, if one keeps these two things separate. But from this it does not follow, as you seem to suggest, that the transition to socialism, however one may imagine this today in societies such as ours, would change nothing about the existing political institutions—or should change nothing. I am convinced that the competition of parties which have become more and more independent of their bases, and which carry on the business of providing legitimation in an essentially manipulative way, must be changed. I suspect that *another* kind of separation of powers would have to be introduced. Of course I also think that such transformations of political institutions should only be carried out in the light of the constitutional principles recognized today—by drawing on the universalist content of these principles. The whole wretchedness of so-called actually existing socialism can basically be traced back to a reckless disdain for the principles of the constitutional state—as if these principles did not also primarily belong to those productive forces, to those results of the bourgeois emancipation movement, which make socialism possible in the first place.

In the second volume of The Theory of Communicative Action *you suggest that 'in bureaucratic socialism crisis tendencies result from the self-blocking mechanisms of administrative planning, just as they do, on the other hand, from endogenous interruptions of the accumulation process.'*[26] *Given these formal limitations of both the market and planning, how do you envisage the operation of the economy in a democratic socialist society?*

How can I answer that in a few sentences? After fifty to sixty years of Soviet Russian development, no one can now fail to see that Max Weber was right, in other words: that the abolition of private

---

26. *Theorie des kommunikativen Handelns*, II, p. 565.

ownership of the means of production in no sense does away with class structures as such. Personally, I no longer believe that a differentiated economic system can be transformed from within in accordance with the simple recipes of workers' self-management. The problem seems to be rather one of how capacities for self-organization can be sufficiently developed in autonomous public spheres for the goal-oriented decision-making processes of a use-value oriented life-world to hold the systemic imperatives of economic system and state apparatus in check, and to bring *both* media-controlled subsystems into dependence on life-world imperatives. I cannot imagine that this would be possible without a gradual abolition of the capitalist labour market, and without a radical-democratic implantation of political parties in their public spheres. The secondary, although in no sense trivial, question then arises of how, under such altered initial conditions, plan and market are coordinated with each other, how their relative weights in the interaction of state and economy can shift. This would be difficult for me to anticipate, even if I had a better knowledge of economics. For every intervention in complex social structures has such unforseeable consequences that processes of reform can only be defended as scrupulous processes of trial and error, under the careful control of those who have to bear their consequences.

The Frankfurt School tradition as a whole has concentrated its analyses upon the most advanced capitalist societies, at the comparative expense of any consideration of capitalism as a global system. In your view, do conceptions of socialism developed in the course of anti-imperialist and anti-capitalist struggles in the Third World have any bearing on the tasks of a democratic socialism in the advanced capitalist world? Conversely, does your own analysis of advanced capitalism have any lessons for socialist forces in the Third World?

I am tempted to say 'no' in both cases. I am aware of the fact that this is a eurocentrically limited view. I would rather pass the question.

Is there any significance in the modulation from your initial programme of a 'theory with practical intent' to your current description of your work as a contribution to 'the self-understanding of modernity', or does this simply reflect the variable kinds of work that you've produced over the years? Whom do you conceive as the addressees of your successive books—presumably these have varied too? Do you

*feel closer or more distant from your readership today than in the
sixties?*

Everyone changes during the cycle of his or her life-history; however, I am, if anything, one of those stubborn types, to whom a rigid bourgeois identity is attributed. For this reason I do not believe that I have changed any more in my fundamental orientations than was necessary to hold true to them in altered historical circumstances. I work as a philosopher and sociologist, and therefore the people to whom my work is addressed primarily occupy positions in the scientific and educational system; now and again I dabble in political journalism and write in daily and weekly newspapers, or in so-called cultural periodicals. In both cases it tends to be the left intellectuals who are interested in what I write—and of course my old sparring-partners on the other side. I don't think of myself as avant-garde, nor do I dream of a revolutionary subject. At the moment I am more distant from the attitudes of the politically active young people, including many students, than I was at an earlier period. In my view, they have become less political, more conservative in their ways of feeling, less theoretical, and at the same time more open to the inheritance—so dubious in our country—of political romanticism, of young conservatism, and so on. But please rather consider these as the usual prejudices which mark the general ageing-process of the New Left—they do not diminish my unrestrained delight in discussions with my students, and discussions in general.

*Could the Left expect from you some more direct treatment of
socialism, a notion that remains at once relatively marginal in your
writing (in the sense that it is never explored in its own right), yet
presumably central to its overall purpose? Aren't you in a way
logically committed to some programmatic account of the social order
your work is concerned to bring about, beyond your diagnostic
analysis of the present order which you reject? Could one contemplate
your producing one day an equivalent for us of Hegel's* Constitution
of the German Nation *or Kant's* Scheme for Perpetual Peace—*a
cross between the two today would virtually give us a sketch for a
democratic socialism in a disarmed Europe! Hasn't the highest
philosophical vocation traditionally embraced this kind of concrete
thought too?*

The examples are too grand, but I must take your admonitions to heart. I should not talk about socialism only in interviews—even though there is otherwise hardly anyone who still does so. In a speech which I am delivering to deputies of the Spanish parliament next week,[27] you will see that, besides the things for which I am paid, I also reflect about normative questions, about questions of political and practical principles.

Could you conceive of reassuming a more active political role, as you did in the time of the Sozialistischer Bund *in the late fifties, under other circumstances?*

Were I to rule that out, I would be someone other than the person I would wish to be.

27. See 'Die Krise des Wohlfahrtsstaates und die Erschöpfung utopischer Energien', in *Die Neue Unübersichtlichkeit*, Frankfurt 1985, pp. 141–163.

7.

Life-forms, Morality
and the
Task of the Philosopher

*Could you tell us something of the earliest direction of your interests?
In particular, what was the relationship between your initial philosophical and sociological concerns?*

There was no sociology at Göttingen, Zurich or Bonn, the universities where I studied. I took two or three terms of economics but my
main courses were in philosophy, history and psychology. By the
time I finished my dissertation, however, I was fed up with intellectual work generally, and philosophy particularly. In reaction, I
maintained myself for the next two years as a freelance journalist.
There I mostly just picked out problems as they came up—traffic
control, civil service test procedures, or what have you. But I also
developed one more persistent focus, the sociology of labour and
industrial relations. Georges Friedman's work was translated into
German at that time, which I read. It so happened that in the mid
fifties this field was re-established as an area of professional research
in West Germany. Nearly all my later friends, in fact, got interested
in it too. The result in my case was an essay I wrote on rationalization of industry and rationalization of human relationships, which
was published in *Merkur* in 1954. The key ideas in this article
contain the kernel of much of what I later came to write in *The
Theory of Communicative Action*. By chance Adorno read this
article. One day one of my employers told me that he knew Adorno
and offered to introduce me to him. I had no permanent job at the
time. So that was the way I came to Frankfurt. I was already
interested in sociology. So when I got a chance of the combination of

Frankfurt and sociology, I was enthusiastic. There I learned statistics and did some empirical research—producing several studies during the three years when I learned sociology on the job, only one of which was published: *Student und Politik,* in 1961.

How much of Adorno had you read before you met him? How far were you aware of the tradition of the Frankfurt School?

I had read *Dialectic of Enlightenment* and Adorno had the feeling that some of his (or their) ideas had gone into my article on rationalization. I must confess that I wasn't thinking of them when I wrote it. But probably there's some truth in this—I've never really checked it. The context in which I had assimilated *Dialectic of Enlightenment* had been a quite different one. I had come across it when studying the early Lukács. I found *History and Class Consciousness* a marvellous book. But it was like a historical document for me—I felt, what a pity one can't take it up systematically. Whereas reading *Dialectic of Enlightenment* was a revelation: I suddenly realized that there were people who had been using Marx's theorems for their own systematic purposes, in the present. Nobody did that in West Germany, where there was a bad Restoration climate at that time. It is difficult for you to imagine how totally closed a world the Federal Republic was then.

Have you ever felt any tension in your subsequent career between your different interests?

Not any more. I don't really like the distinctions between the disciplines. I have never understood how one can distinguish between, say, political science and political sociology, or between social theory or political theory and related work in philosophy. It really makes no sense. Popper makes the nice comment somewhere that disciplines are historical accidents. That's more or less true. We never had any political science as such in Germany before about 1947–48, for example. People like Carl Schmitt or Hermann Adler taught *Staatsrecht* or public law. Today, I am in a philosophy department, but the reasons are rather external and institutional.

Turning to your philosophical formation, you've said that you found in pragmatism a corrective for the deficiencies of democratic theory in Marxism. Could you expand on this?

It was always my feeling that there was no adequate theory of democracy in Marxism. The orthodox accounts of it were function-alist analyses—which struck me as incomplete, at the limit even tautological. I also read Austro-Marxist authors like Karl Renner (who was certainly an influence on me) and Otto Bauer, and then the English Labour version of the same sort of approach in Strachey. They confirmed my impression that the orthodox analysis was insufficient. But more important was the deep, everyday experience we lived through after 1945: things got better with the reintroduc-tion of democracy, and even simply of the rule of law (although I detest those people in Germany who play down democracy in favour of the rule of law). In these conditions, where was I to look for alternative accounts? One very important influence for me in the late fifties was Wolfgang Abendroth. He had several sides to his person-ality, but he was among other things a *Staatsrechtler*, and this reformist side appealed to me—especially his interpretation of human rights and the welfare state.

It was only later, in the mid sixties, that I became familiar with Peirce. Then I discovered that there was a missing branch of Young Hegelianism, one that led to a more or less radical-democratic humanism. You find this already on a philosophical level in Peirce. What stemmed from it was—I don't know whether the phrase was coined by Peirce himself—'logical socialism'. What this meant was that not only Peirce's theory of signs, but also what he calls his analysis of categories, or his crazy ontology, led him to the idea that communities, and what occurs within them, have an internal impact on scientific research and on social conditions generally. This idea then turns up in the pragmatist tradition in various versions and on various levels. Royce, whom I don't know very well, developed a religious or transcendentalist version of the role of community. In Mead it took the fundamental form of the idea of universal dis-course. In Dewey, it became an immediately political conception of democracy.

You've remarked that you were particularly attracted to Marcuse because of the existentialist strand in his thought. But there doesn't seem to have been any element of existentialism in your own formation?

When I arrived in Frankfurt and listened to Adorno lecturing or giving seminars, I was immediately struck by the fact that contem-porary philosophy—as I knew it, two years after my dissertation—was completely ignored. The most recent thinkers ever cited were

Bergson and Husserl—and the Husserl of the *Logical Investigations* alone. If Adorno mentioned Heidegger—which didn't happen very often—I had the impression that he had scarcely read him. It was not until a few years ago that I read his Inaugural Lecture of 1931, published posthumously, and realized that he must have known *Being and Time* at that time. But afterwards you couldn't discern any deeper knowledge of Heidegger, let alone Jaspers. Against this background, you may understand better what it meant for me, as someone who had been a thoroughgoing Heideggerean for three or four years, to read Marcuse for the first time. It was while I was working on the concept of ideology that I came across Marcuse's early articles. There you could see the exact breaking-point between an orthodox Heideggerean and a Marxist. I still can show you the lines where Herbert made *the* substantive, *the* strategic criticism of Heidegger— namely where he rejects not just the ontological difference but the difference between history and historicity. So I can recognize my own point of departure, so to speak, from Heidegger in these texts of Marcuse. Then came *Eros and Civilization*. That touched me because of its direct political resonance. I always felt much closer to the practical attitudes of Marcuse. Not only to the practical attitudes, but also to the idea that the life of theory is a project of practical reason, or conducted in its name.

But you have been very critical of existentialist theories of morality —as versions of decisionism.

I was critical of decisionism from the very beginning—from the minute when I read Schmitt, for instance. I must say, however, that I didn't put Sartre so much in the category of decisionism. That may be surprising for you. But Sartre I like for different reasons. For me he did not represent an existentialist ethic. He was just this marvellous phenomenologist who introduced you to extreme situations. I had been brought up in a high school between '45 and '49, where Sartre's theatre was a tremendous excitement. He was a door-opener to the world for us. That was how we looked out from our dusty closet. Sartre was a great figure for my generation.

You're critical of what you call the ahistorical way in which Heidegger was taken up in the United States. How do you feel a knowledge of Heidegger's political involvement should influence one's understanding of his philosophy?

In my next book, I have a chapter on that and I can give you the idea in a nutshell—though this will now become a very rough and one-sided idea. My thesis is that the whole Heideggerean notion of a history of Being cannot be derived from the internal development of his philosophy prior to 1934 or 1935. There is no real problem in his thought up to that date which would have made him rethink his whole project. The transition to his later philosophy—a process which took exactly ten years, from 1935 to 1945, between *An Introduction to Metaphysics* and the *Letter on Humanism*—was thus largely determined by external events. Heidegger had treated the whole framework of *Being and Time* without any obvious change up to 1933. Then he suddenly gave it a collectivist turn: *Dasein* was no longer this poor Kierkegaardian-Sartrean individual hanging in the air, in *Sorge*. But now *Dasein* was the *Dasein* of the people, of the *Volk*. I can show that line by line. All his election speeches—and he made lots of them; he wrote for a local paper; he made a speech in Leipzig where there was a rally of scientists for the Führer, on a platform bedecked with Nazi flags (we have pictures of it); he made speeches at the University (all of them for the November elections) and also, of course, his Inaugural Address as Rector at Freiburg, although that is the least revealing—all of these publications and utterances show that he gave to *Being and Time* a national-revolutionary reading. In fact, he reinterpreted one substantive point in his theory, without touching any single category of the whole framework. Now, after a year or two—and I suppose it was only two years after and not just three months or so—he started to become hesitant about the whole cause with which he had been identifying. You must understand that he had really been fighting at the front of it. He had the nutty idea that he, as a spiritual leader, could set himself at the head of the whole movement. You have to be brought up in a German *Gymnasium* to have such notions. But now he became disillusioned. What was he to do? What if the whole philosophical project of *Being and Time*—identified with the movement from which he now retreated—were to be affected and discredited by it? Given Heidegger's personality structure, one solution was to interpret what had happened as an objective, fatal mistake, one for which he was no longer responsible as a person—an error which revealed itself like fate in a Sophoclean tragedy. You can trace the lines where he took this way out. But he also, of course, changed his interpretation of the role of fascism itself. As late as 1935, he had still seen it as a movement which accomplished the destiny of the national revolution, including the use of technology as

Ernst Jünger had extolled it in *Der Arbeiter*. Later he turned this interpretation upside down: and by the late thirties and early forties fascism had become the epiphenomenon of a fate which had turned out to be not the salvation from, but the last act of, nihilism. It is these external reasons that lie significantly behind the emergence of the later idea of the history of Being. Internally, this idea is only related to his work on Nietzsche. You can trace back this idea via Nietzsche to Hölderlin, but in Hölderlin and in Nietzsche as well it was of course not an idea that had been linked to metaphysics, but to an idiosyncratic perception of the myth of Dionysos. Heidegger now used that Nietzschean-Dionysiac messianism for his own quite different purposes.

Why do you think Heidegger lost enthusiasm for Nazism after 1935—when the regime was actually stronger because of its success in overcoming economic crisis and mass unemployment?

I can only speculate. The immediate reason is that he didn't succeed institutionally. But of course that was not the only reason. It was quite usual for German intellectuals to lose their enthusiasm for the regime in the second half of the thirties. Carl Schmitt became disillusioned a little later than Heidegger. He still wanted to write a constitution for the Third Reich in 1938. Gottfried Benn, on the other hand, I think became disillusioned rather earlier, perhaps soon after 1934. You can see this in his *Doppelleben*. You cannot imagine what this legacy did to bourgeois students after the war—there were no other students—who encountered an essential continuity in the universities: there was no break in terms of persons or courses. The two pre-eminent thinkers—who determined the direction of my philosophical interests—were Heidegger and Gehlen. The expressionist poet with whom everybody identified was Benn. Nobody told us about their past. We had to find out step by step for ourselves. It took me four years of studies, mostly just accidentally looking into books in libraries, to discover what they had been thinking only a decade or a decade and a half ago. Think what that meant. My own two teachers, under whom I wrote my dissertation—Ernst Rothacker and Oskar Becker—were cases in point. There I could have short discussions, because of personal relations and even, in the case of Oskar Becker, who was a nice man, because of personal attachments. But in the cases of Heidegger, Schmitt or Jünger—who was never a Nazi, but was an outright anti-semite in the Weimar Republic— there was never a single sentence of regret afterwards. There was no apology or remorse afterwards by any of these people. The moral and psychological implication was devastating.

Turning to your own work now, could you comment on the relation between your theory of cognitive interests and your theory of communicative action? Is the theory of cognitive interests in some sense still in force, simply waiting for a reformulation, or has the theory of communicative action replaced it?

The role of *Knowledge and Human Interests* has changed in my mind, since I came to the conclusion that it was of secondary significance to defend or establish critical social theory in epistemological terms. That is what I didn't see when I wrote the book. Nor, for that matter, did Adorno or even the earlier Horkheimer—they too were fascinated by methodological problems, and gave them great importance. I don't any more. But that doesn't mean I dismiss them. Today, I think one should go ahead from a different angle, substantively, and then if people ask you, one might also argue the case methodologically. The theory of cognitive interests I more or less shared with my friend Karl-Otto Apel—he has written further on it—and I continue to think that it's basically sound. But I would be a bit more cautious now. We have all the new arguments on the table from the post-empiricists. If only for that reason, one would have to reformulate the account more carefully and leave room for historical change. Nevertheless, I hold by the fundamental idea that there are constitutive relationships between scientific enterprises and everyday orientations. These internal relationships are so strong that they can predetermine—via the formal pragmatics of research—the possible channels of application or implementation of different types of knowledge. The correlation between these knowledge-types and the various disciplines is the weakest part of the theory. There one has to admit to several sins. But I think this too could be remodelled. However, I'm no longer interested in that—at least not just now. The intellectual situation has changed so much since I wrote the book. At that time, all these secondary, victimized minds of the postwar generation in Germany, including myself, were looking to Oxford and the London School of Economics and Cambridge, and even more so to America: and what did they tell us? You remember the empiricist and positivist climate. People like us in Frankfurt were so marginal in that discussion that we had step-by-step to reconquer certain dimensions. The first dimension was the quasi-transcendental questions of the constitution of knowledge. For that Peirce was helpful. Today, everyone takes it for granted that theories are paradigm-dependent and paradigms are in some sense socially constituted and historically changeable. Analytical philosophers have done a wonderful job here. But for myself, I don't want to follow them too far in a historicist direction . . .

One feature of your original theory that perhaps aroused most conventional resistance at the time was your notion of an 'emancipatory interest', constituting the specifically 'reflexive sciences' like psychoanalysis. Do you hold to this today?

There is one difficulty in the general theory which McCarthy showed me. Namely, once you accept that there is a category of sciences which I now, for purposes of convenience, call reconstructive, where do you place them? They are, in a way, successors to good old transcendental philosophy, although in a pretty de-transcendentalized and desublimated form. I can see that they endanger the architectonics of the three cognitive interests. But I stick to the distinction I have made between rational reconstruction and self-reflection. So far as the latter goes, I cannot imagine any seriously critical social theory without an internal link to something like an emancipatory interest. That is such a big name! But what I mean is an attitude which is formed in the experience of suffering from something man-made, which can be abolished and should be abolished. This is not just a contingent value-postulate: that people want to get rid of certain sufferings. No, it is something so profoundly ingrained in the structure of human societies—the calling into question, and deep-seated wish to throw off, relations which repress you without necessity—so intimately built into the reproduction of human life that I don't think it can be regarded as just a subjective attitude which may or may not guide this or that piece of scientific research. It is more. So I would—and I think could—defend that part of the basic structure of the theory of cognitive interests too. Its formulation was perhaps too immediately fundamentalist for the present taste. No doubt I would present it differently today.

You have often emphasized the move from a philosophy of consciousness to a philosophy of communication in your own transformation of the Frankfurt heritage. How important do you feel this transition is in the general history of philosophy? Would you regard it as comparable in significance to the rise of the philosophy of consciousness itself at the beginning of the modern period?

Looking at it from a certain distance, it is obvious that in the Frankfurt tradition my work has represented a shift towards communication theory. But in other traditions there are equivalent moves. The whole history of analytical philosophy from Frege onwards was a sequence of such movements: first from consciousness to sentence, and then with the later Wittgenstein from sentence to utterance; and that means to context, and hence to life-forms, and ultimately to life-world. You have parallels in the Heideggerean tradition. When I was recently looking again at *Sein und Zeit*, I was surprised to see how monological its whole construction was. It was written in the wake of Husserl's cartesian ego, as a reply to it, but also still depending on it. The subsequent move into the area of a history of Being employs an appeal to language—yet there is no single analysis of language in the later Heidegger. The invocation of language is not really a serious one. On the other hand, Gadamer, while starting out from Heidegger, made a genuine move to hermeneutics proper—that is, to linguistically constituted contexts and life-forms. Maybe even structuralism can be taken as another legitimate parallel. If you look at it that way, as a threshold which has been crossed from very different angles more or less simultaneously, then I would expect—let me put this mildly—that this move might turn out to be a paradigm shift in a very strict sense. For prior to that we had only one paradigm in modern philosophy: that was, as Foucault nicely explains in *The Order of Things*, a subjectivity which is centred in the self-relation of the knowing subject.

But couldn't one reply that an argument has been going on between the two ever since Vico's critique of Descartes—that in fact theories of consciousness and communication are two traditions within modern philosophy, rather than a transition within twentieth-century philosophy?

My friend Apel has written a whole book on the Renaissance precursors of Vico's hermeneutic thinking, from Dante onwards. It does appear that just such a tradition did exist, but much more visibly in the Renaissance than later. After Newton, we find only figures like Vico on the other side. This tradition was an undercurrent which never became sufficiently explicit, clarified, if you like highbrow, to compete with the mainstream philosophical discussion. So we had Vico versus Newton, we had Hamann versus Kant, and then maybe within the German historical school we had Ranke, Droysen and Dilthey—to mention only its methodologists. There was a philosophy implicit in the historical school, as I learnt from my teacher Rothacker. But it presented itself only as the dualistic self-understanding of the humanities as against real science: it was not brought to the level of a philosophical shift in paradigm. You can check that this is true in, for instance, Dilthey. For thinkers like Dilthey, Simmel or Bergson—those from which *Lebensphilosophie* took off—were finally fixated in the categories of a subject which—as in the early Marx—externalized its own essential forces into cultural objectifications. Their whole cultural criticism sprang from that starting-point—attacking the estrangement of those objectifications from the living productivity of the subject. These people too, *philosophically* speaking, were captives of the dominant philosophical paradigm—even while they fought it on another level.

Why do you think Adorno resisted the move—which you were to make—from what you describe as the impasse of his own philosophy of consciousness to a theory of communication?

I never talked about that with him. In any case, the shift to communication wasn't so clear a move for me yet. When I knew him, Adorno was at the height of an intellectual career. He had reached his solutions if you like. What he did in Frankfurt—at least while I was there, after 1956—was to elaborate ever further his *Negative Dialectics* and his *Aesthetic Theory*. He wasn't reading much else. He was so much focused on his own work that it would never have occurred to me to ask: look, shouldn't you consider this? All our discussions were immanently on his own terrain.

You've argued, however, that 'Adorno cannot appeal to any structure heterogeneous to instrumental reason against which the force of totalized purposive rationality must collide', because he had no confidence in the 'rationality which is immanent in everyday communicative practice' as a bulwark against such totalized purposive rationality.[1] Your phrasing seems to claim that such confidence can always be given to everyday communication as a source of human resistance. But could someone who lived through the epoch of fascism, as Adorno did, possibly have the same faith in the saving rationality

1. 'A Philosophico-Political Profile', p. 155, above.

of everyday communication? Surely that must have been one funda-
mental reason why he would never come to the kind of conclusions
which you reached?

What I wanted to say is only that there has existed, as long as we can
remember, a mode of social reproduction which is linked to linguistic
communication. This does not mean that there cannot ever be
historical circumstances under which this whole infrastructure
might be eroded—even finally crushed. For the rest, if I understand
you correctly, you refer only—only!—to different life-experiences.
Of course, what you say is true—what can I add?

Isn't there a suggestion in your respectful criticism of the original
Frankfurt School that their work possessed a logic which then went
adrift at a crucial point: as if they took a wrong turning?

Maybe I did express it like that once. But no, they didn't really have
either biographical or philosophical access to the alternative which I
came to prefer. The categorial framework of their theory in the
thirties left no space between the alienating systems of capitalist
economy and state on the one hand, and subjective nature on the
other. There was no room for ideas of the life-world or of life-forms
(Dilthey or Wittgenstein). So they were not prompted to look into
the no-man's-land of everyday life, which for them was a mere
epiphenomenon either of the totalizing force of the administrative
world, or of suffering nature. Intersubjective relationships left no
philosophical trace. I've argued that there are some passages in
Negative Dialectics that show Adorno had intuitions which could be
and should be saved within a very different, communicative framework. But he himself was deaf to that alternative. You should realize
that biographically the last political experience to which Horkheimer
and Adorno spontaneously reacted was McCarthyism. That shaped
their outlook for the rest of their postwar German existence. I think
that for them the reconstitution of a more or less liberal, even
democratic state in West Germany acted only as a confirmation for
the intuition that the normative model for all that had been lost, and
all that was going to be lost, was the liberal era of early capitalism. In
that sense, the actual historical experience of the Federal Republic,
of post-war West Germany, was more or less impenetrable to them.
This does not mean, of course, that they were not in daily life, apart
from theory, aware of the redeeming features of a Western constitutional regime—particularly Horkheimer.

You have sometimes indicated a utopian dimension of communication, which could be seen as rendering more concrete certain of Adorno's intuitions. Wouldn't that require, however, putting more stress than you usually do upon the intertwining of identity and non-identity in communication? Do you think it would be valuable to balance your emphasis on explicit consensus with more attention to the oblique aspects of communication?

That is just. What happened is this. If you enter a certain universe of discourse, you are forced to deal in the first instance with ideal or standard cases. But that this in itself is not enough is clear. As far back as the early sixties—when I was at Heidelberg—I did not treat communication so much technically as paradigmatically. If you look, for example, at my review of Klaus Heinrich,[2] you will see that I stressed the broken nature of all intersubjective relationships. In other words, even if these are idealized, they must still be conceptualized in such a way that their tensions remain irreducible— otherwise that whole structure collapses: tensions, not just between subjects, but reflexively as well, between different perceptions and self-perceptions of what constitutes an individuality and which nevertheless is perpetually in flux, in charge, never identical with certain presuppositions which are nevertheless necessary and unavoidable. Today, having gone through more standard cases, I would say that you have to analyse idealizations in such a way that you stress *both* : the idealizations and their failures. For instance, there are no identical meanings in the terms in which we are now trying to communicate, from the third person's point of view there are *none* : it is easy for psychologists and for Derrida too (if he would analyse anything!) to show that there is only non-identity over the whole space of communication. On the other hand, we have simultaneously to realize that any human communication would break down the moment you could not presuppose that we exchange identical meanings. You have to show both. Only if you do so do you have the core of the idea. Of course this is easy enough to show for meaning-identity. It is less easy—but still not too hard—to show for pragmatic presuppositions in discourse. But it is much more difficult to show—and it's from there you started—when it comes to identity-formations of persons which are also always symbolic constructions. It was with that problem I actually set out in the early sixties. But it

2. 'Von der Schwierigkeit, Nein zu Sagen', in *Philosophisch-politische Profile*, 2nd enlarged edn, Frankfurt 1981, pp. 445–52.

still lies before me. Here Adorno's categories are much more appealing, since they are closer to the phenomena.

What do you mean when you say, 'Unlike Nietzsche and his disciples, Adorno has no illusions about the genuinely modern origins of aesthetic experience, in whose name modernity falls victim to a levelling, undialectical critique'?[3]

That is one of the theses of my new book, *Der Philosophische Diskurs der Moderne*. I think that from Nietzsche onwards—this is also true of Bataille and Derrida—the experiential basis for the Other of Reason, from whose standpoint they criticize reason as a narrowly objectifying, instrumentalizing force, is a field which was only opened up with modern avant-garde art, from Baudelaire to surrealism. In other words, the self-referential criticism of reason is nourished—that is the key to it—from an experience which is no older than avant-garde art. Yet this experience is projected—by Nietzsche and his successors—backwards into archaic origins, onto the Dionysian, the pre-Socratic, the exotic and primitive. This kind of *nachgeahmte Substantialität* was completely alien to Adorno and Benjamin. It never occurred to them to mystify peculiarly modern experiences in this fashion. For that is what this radical criticism of reason in effect amounts to, with its fabulation of pre-civilizational states. We have had all that, in Germany, so immediately at hand that you can smell it ever afterwards: the artificial mystification of something so close into something supposedly so primordial.

You've said that philosophical systems are no longer possible today and that every philosophical work must tacitly forego systematic thinking. Yet you certainly don't renounce in the same way systematic social theory. In fact, you pursue it quite freely. What explains the contrast?

It is in the strong notion of theory and of truth that the difference between metaphysics and post-metaphysical thought lies. The idea of theory since Plato was that of a thought capable of grasping the totality of entities, or the world as a whole; and the idea of truth implied a clearly non-fallibilistic element of fundamentalism. Yet these notions have been in a process of decomposition—as Marx

---

3. 'A Philosophico-Political Profile', p. 158 above.

said—since Hegel. In that sense, I think we are just contemporaries of the Young Hegelians still. Nothing has changed since then, basically. The decomposition has proceeded. But for some the farewell to philosophical systems was and is still so painful that they have to dramatize the whole question. This was true of Adorno and it remains true of Derrida. They made a drama of something which should be trivial by now: a fallibilist conception of truth and knowledge. Even I learnt this from Popper! But if systematic thinking in philosophy has this sense of strong theory- and truth-concepts, it does not in the field of science, where it is more or less innocent to speak of a systematic approach as opposed to, say, a historical one. History itself, of course, is also amenable to a systematic approach as opposed to, say, a hermeneutic one.

You make a very sharp distinction between the tasks that you will allow philosophy in the field of ethics, and substantive moral theories. But what difference does it actually make—other than one of a salutary pathos—to say that 'the philosopher ought to explain the moral point of view' and no more: 'anything further is a matter for moral discourse between participants', in which, if the philosopher happens to advocate any actual principles of justice, these can merely be an—unphilosophical—'proposal among citizens'?[4] Elsewhere, you go so far as to write: 'Everyday moral intuitions have no need of the clarification of the philosopher. In this area the therapeutic conception of philosophy, introduced by Wittgenstein, seems to me to hold without exception.'[5] In other words, philosophy leaves everyday morals as they are. Could you have written that in Germany in the late thirties?

Philosophers are not teachers of the nation. They can sometimes—if only rarely—be useful people. If they are, they may write books like that of Rawls, for instance. Rawls hasn't systematically cared when he speaks as a philosopher and when he speaks simply as a committed liberal in his society. This is what I think philosophers should also do: forget about their professional role and bring what they can do better than others into a common business. But the common business of political discourses among citizens nevertheless stays what it is. It is not a philosophical enterprise. It is the attempt of

---

4. See ibid., p. 160 above.
5. 'Diskursethik—Notizen zu einem Begründungsprogramm', in *Moralbewusstsein und Kommikatives Handeln*, Frankfurt 1983, p. 108.

participants to answer the question 'what now?'—in these circumstances, for us particular people, what are or would be the best institutions?

Why is that not also true of what you say is the task of the philosopher: clarification of the general grounds or rules under which moral claims can be justified? You could say that's also our common business.

No, that's different. Because there you can develop arguments—within a fallibilistic framework, of course—which are *binding*, not just for us here and now, being members of a particular community, but which claim to be true, simply true. That is what I mean by 'explaining the moral point of view'. By the way, it is not an easy thing to do — at least not in our times.

Are you implying that by contrast it's an easy thing to arrive at a theory of justice?

What philosophy should seek to do is to maintain its competence in those areas where it can defend universal statements. Therefore in morality it is only the universal core of the moral point of view which is a matter for philosophers. Here they can do what they are equipped to. On the other hand, if they want to design just institutions for a certain type of society under given historical conditions, philosophers can only join those who are involved in the democratic process as active citizens or serve as assistants with a certain expertise. There they move within the horizon of a shared tradition from the start.

Would you say then that Rawls's Theory of Justice *is not a philosophical work?*

Yes. When he tries to explain the moral point of view through the construct of the veil of ignorance, he is doing what the philosopher can do as a philosopher. It is a reasonable proposal. But as soon as he moves to his two principles, he is speaking as a citizen of the United States with a certain background, and it is easy to make—as has been done—an ideological critique of the concrete institutions and principles which he wants to defend. There is nothing universal about his particular design for a just society. I think one could argue methodologically that *particular* moral principles always need agreement within particular communities. I can't think of any non-procedural, substantive principles which could be applied to everything at every time. It makes no sense. Justifying particular principles is a different task. Whether we call it philosophy or not, I'm the last to mind.

So ultimately you regard the question as an issue more of presentation than of substance?

No—it's definitely a question of substance for me: a very important one.

How far then could one compare your positions with those of the Oxford philosophers of the fifties, who also put a strenuous emphasis on the non-prescriptive role of the analytic philosopher, in keeping with the same Wittgensteinian recommendations? In their case, the restriction of philosophy to the elucidation of ordinary language uses—including the language of morals—had a notoriously conservative cast. Austin, whom you often cite, after all maintained that existing everyday speech and its stock of distinctions contained all the practical wisdom that preceding generations had found necessary, and so everything we should need or want to know. The suggestion was always that matters were being perfectly well handled out there in the non-philosophical world, and philosophers had no reason to interfere with them. How do you distinguish your view—letting citizens get on with things among themselves—from this? What if things and the way they are being debated are not very satisfactory? Mightn't the philosopher have some role here, between the teacher of the nation and the semantic amanuensis?

But there is a world of political difference between my position and theirs! The Oxford position was non-cognitivist: you restrict your business to linguistic and semantic analysis and leave normative questions to whomever. I defend a cognitivist position. In fact, I am defending an outrageously strong claim in the present context of philosophical discussion: namely, that there is a universal core of moral intuition in all times and in all societies. I don't say that this intuition is spelt out the same way in all societies at all times. What I do say is that these intuitions have the same origin. In the last analysis, they stem from the conditions of symmetry and reciprocal recognition which are unavoidable presuppositions of communicative action. Theoretically, the difference is clear. Practically, it is—or should be—clear too. For any attempt—not only mine— to defend a cognitivist-universalist ethical theory involves the public assertion that in your own society and in others all practical and political questions have a moral core which is susceptible to argument. The logic of this position thus directly affects the self-understanding of the existing political culture, which can no longer be immunized against rational demands for legitimation. That it has this political impact I know from my own experience over the past ten or fifteen years in West Germany. If there is one thing that makes our neo-conservatives wild, it is this. So I don't think that it is an apolitical stance.

Let me give two further motivations for my view. The first is that my restrictive view levels down the old philosophical claims to normative theory, be it in politics or in ethics. For it means that you put the responsibility for decisions on the shoulders of those who anyhow will suffer their consequences, and that at the same time you stimulate the participants who have to make up their minds in practical discourse to look around for information and ideas that can shed light on their situation—which can clarify their understanding of themselves. The problem, by contrast, with classical normative theories is that they give people the illusion that they simply need to find the theory and then act on it. Which is nonsense. You cannot just read Rawls and say, 'Look, these are the two principles—let's now reconstruct our institutions in keeping with them.' That is not our situation. The normative part of the theory should be only procedural, while everything else that matters for practical purposes should be learnt from science, from social theory and not from moral philosophy. What I have in mind is a certain division of labour where the limited role of moral philosophy leaves a larger space for social theory. I am sorry that social theory is basically not in any shape to perform the role I say it should.

There is also however, on the moral side of the question, the Aristotelian argument, in the *Nicomachean Ethics*, that nobody can deal with ethical questions who has not been raised properly. I do not think that this is quite true. I feel inhibitions about saying that. But it is fair to ask: how could anyone focus on moral intuitions and reconstruct them, before having them—and how do we get them? Not from philosophy, and not by reading books. We acquire them just by growing up in a family. This is the experience of everyone, except perhaps the limit-cases of psychopaths with no moral sensibility whatsoever. There can't be anyone who ever grew up in any kind of family who did not acquire certain moral intuitions. The difference between these is then only in the degree of their universalization. The presuppositions concerned may not reach farther than your own kind, your own folk, your own nation. It is only modern developments which have brought a real push to universalize these intuitions. Thus, if I used the formulation that 'philosophy leaves everything as it is' here, that is partly true. For I don't believe that we can change moral intuitions except as educators—that is, not as theoreticians and not as writers.

Couldn't one make out a strong empirical case against this view? Think of Rousseau. It can be shown pretty clearly in cases like his that moral intuitions are not quite so naturwüchsig *as you make them out to be—that they are more susceptible to illustration and advocacy of change.*

That is important to add, for intuitions can become clarified, and that clarification may be very important. Just by entering the medium of words, something can change. Such transformations from 'know-how' to 'know-that' are sometimes only achieved through art or literature, or the work of artist-philosophers like Rousseau. I wouldn't deny that. But for me the problem is really a political one. What is the harm if I write something on civil disobedience as a political man, and not as a philosopher?

None at all. But one might reply—how many of your readers on civil disobedience forget that you are a philosopher? Your words have a different weight, because of your philosophy—as was true of Russell or Sartre.

Now you're talking about the sociology of reception . . .

You've said that you defend the outrageously strong position that there is a universal core to all moral judgements. On the other hand, you argue that 'forms of life' can only be judged by cultural standards internal to them, which then permit 'clinical intuitions' as to their value—but you doubt whether these have any universal core, as moral intuitions do. Can these positions be reconciled? Take the example of the United States in the 1850s. Two opposed societies coexisted within the frontiers of the same state—North and South. Their differences were such that war eventually broke out between them. The principal defence of the slave-owners, in that conflict, was that Southern civilization was an intergrated Lebensform—*a way of life as a whole—which was threatened by Northern abolitionism, based on a quite other way of life. Given your postulates, how could you arbitrate the conflict between the two?*

This is a very tricky question. I had to supervise a dissertation on the South, so I am a bit familiar with the arguments of its spokesmen, which I found at first sight rather persuasive. I think one needs to distinguish between two sets of questions. The first is the political and implicitly moral question whether the institution of slavery could be justified within the framework of a set of specific constitutional laws. The answer to that is not difficult. The Northern position was that slavery could and should be changed in accordance with the constitution, and also in accordance with moral intuitions, which were fortunately not just expressed in books, but were codified—as principles—in law. Few of the Southerners ever said that they would fight to the death on the ground of legal amendments, as such. But others could have objected on different grounds. They might have said, 'Look, in the end we will agree that slavery should be abolished. But in intentionally implementing this aim now, you will destroy a form of life in the South which has its own historical value, and whose treatment of its slaves is more or less preferable to the lot of your proletariat in the Northern cities.' Complicated questions are posed by this line of defence. To resolve them, it may be useful to look at another textbook example of these dilemmas. Would the English, on first entering India and encountering the ritual of burning widows, have been entitled to stop it? Hindus would have said that this institution—a burial rite—belonged to their whole form of life. In that case, I would argue that the English should have abstained, on the one condition that this life-form was really self-maintaining—that is, not yet in inevitable dissolution and assimilation to a a different way of life. There could be no analogy to this example today, because there are no such traditional cultures left after three hundred years of capitalism. But the Indian case illuminates the American one, by contrast. For Southern society never represented a form of life which was freely chosen—if we can use this term as a naive-philosophical, normative redescription of *naturwüchsig*. No unforced consensus could—counter-factually—have ever sustained it. For this was not a self-reproducing indigenous form of life, but an artificially produced one—an agrarian zone within a capitalist system of which the plantation South and the industrial North were equally part. If this common system could only flourish under a legal order that was more implemented in the North than in the South, then from a normative point of view there were no real grounds for maintaining the Southern form of life— even in the face of its own clinical intuitions.

Nevertheless, a problem still remains here. Southern society can be criticized once you just single out the dimension of justice. The question of freedom, of the violation of human dignity, is fairly straightforward. But this is not all there is to a form of life. If we say, for example, that a way of life is 'alienated', the judgement applies not to something which is generalizable, but to something concrete, to the totality of that life. All of us participate in different forms of life, and we have intuitions about more or less pathological cases— we sense whether people can grow upright in them or not. Now here I would make at least one general assumption: that there is no developmental logic to discover. For example, medieval societies, notwithstanding higher degrees of oppression than modern or primitive societies, could in certain circumstances be clinically healthier than either of them. It is possible that further research may refine our knowledge here, and eventually reveal certain universal conditions necessary for non-pathological ways of living together. I think that justice—historically conceived—may be one such condition. But if we do discover parameters for more, or less, repressed forms of life, they probably won't possess any directionality.

You've argued that 'even social theory would overstep its competence ... if it undertook to project desirable forms of life into the future, instead of criticizing existing forms of life'.[6] *This position seems to raise two sets of problems—one concerning 'forms of life', and the other concerning 'projection into the future'. Taking the first, isn't there an inherent ambiguity—hence danger of confusion—in the notion itself? The term has a strongly cultural overtone, and in that register is acceptable enough. Your emphasis on the incommensurability of life-forms makes sense if we are comparing, say, national cultures in the West today. If someone says, 'I prefer living in Germany to living in France or England', the choice is not amenable to common value-judgement or argument: it is a question, if you like, of existential taste. But the term also has a holistic connotation—it suggests a 'whole way of life' that then necessarily includes a social structure. That is the case, for example, in the contrast between North and South in the USA which we've just discussed. There*

---

6. 'A Philosophico-Political Profile', p. 171 above.

political comparison and differential evaluation are surely inevitable, and indispensable. So the question arises, how do you theoretically demarcate a 'life-form'?

I think I would do so by reintroducing the famous distinction between form and content. I'm not sure where this leads me. But I would retain Hegel's concept of totality for something de-Hegelianized: namely for a life-world which can be accounted for more or less only narratively and intuitively, in everyday language—not theoretically. Precisely because it has these holistic features, which are present to our daily self-understanding. We cannot but live in a total world. The world constitutes a totality—inevitably— in the background of our everyday activities. Now the problem is whether one can employ a theoretical language to analyse a concrete life-world, as a particular totality, or whether one refrains from that claim and restricts oneself to an analysis of the presumably universal infrastructure which all life-worlds share with each other. It is this infrastructure that I'm interested in. But social theory can, of course, also compare general features of a number of life-worlds— say plebeian subcultures in proto-industrial societies with those in pre-industrial or industrial societies, in terms of their optional structures in daily actions and transactions: how many options exist in different fields?—in order to pin down differences in the institutional core of these life-worlds. That you can do.

What about the second problem—your prohibition of projections into the future? Doesn't the way you put this rule out of court much too drastically any form of utopian thinking? Here too the ambiguities of the notion of a 'form of life' seem to be at work. For you say that Marxist theory cannot 'cash out the expression "socialism" in terms of a concrete form of life'.[7] *This seems precisely to abstract the idea of a life-form from any 'institutional core'—as if it were essentially a culture, rather than a social structure. For Marxism certainly does specify institutional features of socialism, above all defining it as a classless society. But even setting that objection aside, is it the case that 'concrete forms of life' cannot be constructively projected in social thought? After all, you have yourself just spoken appreciatively of Marcuse's* Eros and Civilization, *a utopian work which certainly*

---

7. Ibid., p. 171 above.

attempts this. A more recent case would be Gorz's work, which also seeks to depict a future form of life, quite concretely. Do you really want to debar these kinds of projection from social theory?

Look, I am convinced that we still live in the modern epoch—not in some post-modern sequel to it. That fact means, among other things, that everyday politics remains mediated by a *Zeitgeist* in which utopian and historical modes of thinking constantly intermingle. Utopian thought has been integrated into historical and everyday political thinking to such an extent that in the present period we manifestly suffer from an apparent retreat of utopian energies, from a closure of horizons. This is a typical indicator of the fact that utopian perspectives are constitutive of modern political thought. I think that social theories too live from their connection with these utopian contents—in spite of all denials from Fourier and Saint-Simon onwards. Nobody wanted to be utopian— it was not just Marx. However, the implicit connection of the theory of Marx with the utopia of self-activity—emancipation from heteronomous labour—suffered, I believe, from two mistakes. The first was the productivist bias which was built into this particular vision —as it was into all utopias from Thomas More onwards: namely, the idea that scientific control over external nature, and labour to transform it, is in itself liberating. The second error was more important, perhaps. It was not to realize that the only utopian perspectives in social theory which we can straightforwardly maintain are of a procedural nature. For the utopian lineaments of any future emancipated society can be no more than necessary general conditions of it. They cannot be in the nature of a design for a form of life. If Marcuse advocated a certain mode of socialization and concomitant changes in general structures in *Eros and Civilization*, or Gorz advocates a disconnection between employment and income, then I think these ideas can be formulated in a way that avoids the misunderstanding that social theory can project concrete or particular new forms of life. Gorz's scheme is essentially a demand for the abolition of the labour market and the reconstruction of the economy in such a way that certain imperatives of the occupational system can no longer invade everyday existence. But it is not a recommendation of one particular mode of life. It simply poses conditions under which people could then lead their lives—not individually, probably, so much as in their cultures. Similarly, I think that Marcuse's ideas could be reformulated as a principle that socialization processes should meet certain conditions such that the conflicts are not resolved by external discharge of aggression. The important thing—in the face of false, neo-conservative attributions —is to lay a clean conceptual cut between utopian perspectives in general and the projection of particular forms of life. The one refers to necessary conditions—and is what socialism is about. I don't say that socialists should abstain all the time from projecting concrete forms of life. But Marx was pretty hesitant about doing so. What he meant by socialism politically was just—we can say now after fifty years of Soviet history—*just* the abolition of the private ownership of the means of production. As the simple specification of a necessary condition, that was very cautious, I must say. But, we see today, not cautious enough.

You've often argued that the important shift to make in thinking about contemporary society is from a production to a communication paradigm. Critical social theory should no longer rest, you maintain, on the expressivist model of alienated labour and the re-appropriation of its essential forces. But is it really necessary for one model or paradigm completely to supersede the other? It is not clear from your reasoning why they couldn't complement each other. You started out by remarking that Marxist theory has traditionally been weak in the whole area of democracy. But it doesn't seem to follow from that negative deficiency that the positive concern of the theory with production has to fall by the same token.

We need to be clear about in which theoretical context, or at what level, the respective merits of the two paradigms are to be debated. At the very basic, quasi-anthropological level, I have proposed a conception of communicative rationality which does include the cognitive-instrumental elements of teleological action. In other words, the communication model is inclusive. When I introduce the idea of communicative action, I emphasize that all types of action display the same teleological infrastructure. So at that level I would maintain the inclusive character of one of the two paradigms, but not vice versa. On another level, we come to more specific assumptions about the evolutionary primacy of different sectors of our society. This is an empirical question. There, as you know, I have argued that the social-integrative core of the institutional framework of society undergoes developments which are at least as important as innovations in the forces of production and science. That is a second level. There is a third level, however, which is where I more usually compare the two paradigms: that posed by the question—where do social theories get their non-arbitrary, normative potentials from? Here, I have good reasons to maintain that the expressivist model is dependent on philosophical-anthropological assumptions, about how human beings are constituted, which acquire a methodologically dubious status. My procedure, by contrast, is to have recourse to a reconstruction of the intuitive knowledge we must inevitably possess, if we want to do something. That is a very different approach. Finally, and this is a fourth level, I think that the expressivist model inherited by Marx, which derived from the transference of certain aesthetic ideals into the sphere of industrial production, finds less and less empirical confirmation in the organization of contemporary labour processes. It becomes increasingly difficult to imagine how under current technical conditions, or even humanized versions of them with smaller-scale plant and equipment, work processes could ever be reintroduced that would bring with them the type of fulfilment originally derived from the exemplar of the artistic genius, who objectifies his most essential nature into his artefact and then contemplates and re-appropriates what he has externalized. I just don't think that our world affords a foothold for that any longer.

Isn't there some tension between these theoretical positions and the political judgements you yourself make about oppositional forces in West Germany today? For while you emphasize the positive potential of the Greens and the new social movements allied to them, as the basis for an 'anti-productivist alliance', you also say very positively that their weakness is that they 'occupy no vital functional domain of industrial society'.[6] Isn't that just because they are, indeed, marginal to production? You go on to remark that one of the most important effects the Greens might have would be to produce shifts inside the SPD — 'without which, if we are realistic about it, nothing can be moved' in the country. Doesn't all this amount to conceding that, while an alliance — or capacity for joint action — between the new social movements and the labour movement is an important objective, its centre of gravity must lie in the majority of the population that is actually involved in classical forms of production?

In assessing the Greens, what is significant in the first instance is whether the potentials they represent are structurally generated or just contingently thrown up. My view is that there are systematic reasons why these potentials are still expanding. Now it is true they

---

8. Ibid., p. 182 above.

occupy no central functions, more or less by definition. That circumscribes the kind of power they exercise, in the second instance. This is not to say they have none. They lack the kind of power which the labour movement possesses, embodied in the strike. But they have a measure of the old reformist resource of the vote. That has a certain impact. You can see the effect from the fact that they behave more or less insanely in Parliament, yet increase their share of the vote in one election after another, till they can now get eight or nine per cent. That's not nothing. Thirdly, of course, these movements have a certain veto-power of disorganization too. For all these reasons, co-operation between the Greens and the Social Democratic Party, and even some of the unions, would not be ineffective in any case. But there are very strong opponents of it on both sides—the fundamentalist wing of the Greens (Petra Kelly is one of them), and the traditional right-wing of the Social Democrats.

What is your view of the SPD itself, then? The West German labour movement is in many ways one of the most strongly organized in Europe. The limitations of the social-democratic and trade-union tradition in the Federal Republic are obvious enough, but doesn't this also contain, or preserve, certain important cultural and political values? British writers of the Left have often seen working-class culture as a significant 'form of life' in its own right, embodying specific kinds of solidarity and struggle and self-education essential to the hope of any future socialism. Would you concede any pertinence of this emphasis to German working-class culture or the SPD—which has, of course, shifted somewhat to the left in recent years?

It is very difficult to put much hope in the West German labour movement today. The Bad Godesburg Conference of the SPD in the late fifties marked a fundamental turn in the history of the party. Abendroth saw this very clearly. The SPD opening to the middle class at that time was accompanied by a real political mutation. Thereafter it did nothing to counteract the steady erosion of the socio-cultural bases of the older social-democratic tradition. German working-class culture had been largely destroyed in the epoch of fascism and the Second World War—there was much less left after 1945 than in England. The self-organization of leisure-time, for example, in the clubs and colonies of the classical labour movement had disappeared. There are only a few traces of this heritage left in the Ruhr today. The party is now threatened even in its bastions by adverse sociological trends, as the unions are weakened by mass unemployment and technological change. The printers, traditionally the backbone of the politically educated labour movement, are an obvious case in point. The party now has great difficulties in recruiting younger people, as well—there is a breakdown of older motivations in the 18–32 age group. In many ways, the underlying situation of the SPD is worse today than it has ever been since the end of the War.

After a brief period of progressive initiatives under Chancellor Brandt, in a quite exceptional constellation which soon passed away, things got bad in the final years of Schmidt's rule. On the other hand, it is true that the party has become more politically active since the *Wende*—the installation of the Kohl government. For people like me, it is good luck that the SPD is now in opposition again—we are not so marginalized any longer. I vote for the SPD, and have always done so. Naturally, I would like to see an alliance between the SPD and the Greens, what is left of the labour movement and the new social movements. But this is not a *natural* alliance. How can unity be achieved among such heterogeneous groups—anti-productivist, old-productivist, new-middle-class? Above all, what kind of political vision can be developed beyond the impasse of the welfare state?

Index